Advance Praise f

"*Easy Street* is a witty and charming n[...]
comedy. With thrilling and unflinchin[...] ...owe tackles the heavy stuff: mental illness, envy, and what the haves owe the have-nots. A laugh-out-loud book that makes you want to do better. I couldn't put it down."
—Maria Semple

"There is a magic in Maggie Rowe that is able to reveal the unsung beauty, art, grace, and humor of mental illness (along with the struggly, super shitty parts of mental illness). Read this book."
—Sarah Silverman

"*Easy Street* had me laughing out loud from the very first sentence. Maggie Rowe's captivating storytelling is not only a reflection on her personal life experiences, it is an enlightening exploration of the human mind. Shockingly honest, brilliantly funny, and imbued with deep wisdom and a touch of Buddhist philosophy, *Easy Street* is a masterful memoir."
—Annaka Harris, *New York Times*–bestselling author of *Conscious: A Brief Guide to the Fundamental Mystery of the Mind*

"Similar to Truman Capote, Maggie Rowe writes like the most fascinating person at a dinner party who captivates the table with a strange, twisty, funny tale about the human condition. It's incredibly difficult to describe losing your mind and Rowe does it masterfully and unflinchingly. Her tenderness and insight make you root for everyone, especially her. (Spoiler alert: kindness and love light the darkness.)"
—Nell Scovell, author of *Just the Funny Parts: And a Few Hard Truths About Sneaking into the Hollywood Boys' Club*

"A romp of profoundly funny self-revelation."
—Bill Maher

"*Easy Street* is like donning a VR helmet and finding yourself in the middle of this amazing, moving story in real time. Pride, guilt, kindness, anger and comedy happen in dizzying succession. *Easy Street* is not a cloying tale of virtue-signalling do-goodery. Rowe virtually waterboards herself to get at the uncomfortable truths beneath her acts of kindness, which are often hidden even from herself. Yet with every ruthless admission of masked resentment or malice, she exposes not just herself, but all of us; we're all presenting a curated self; we're all acting nice. But Maggie Rowe is one of the few people brave enough to go excavating so deeply. An amazing book."   —Peter Baynham

"Rowe's memoir is both moving and *hilarious*. It teems with truly indelible comic scenes—many of which jackknife into poignant moments of crushingly honest self-revelation. Which are also funny. It's a story you'll neither be able to stop reading nor easily forget. I love this book. I could blurb all day about it."

—Mitchell Hurwitz, creator of *Arrested Development*

"Rowe manages to make each phrase of *Easy Street* more dynamic and incisive than the next. Her unsparing display of what she considers her own weaknesses brings in and includes the reader like an intimate confidante."   —Joey Soloway, creator of *Transparent*

Praise for *Sin Bravely*

An NPR Best Book of the Year

"Everything about *Sin Bravely* is unexpected. It's a deeply personal examination of what can happen when you take religion to the extreme, but it's also hilarious. Maggie Rowe tells her own story of checking into an evangelical psychiatric facility after years of worrying she isn't devout enough. Her fear of eternal damnation is real and at times uncomfortable to read about. But what I found so refreshing about this book was the way Rowe balanced serious religious reflection and humor without an ounce of snark or cynicism."

—Natalie Friedman Winston, *Morning Edition*, NPR's Best Books

"A highly intriguing, personal and bravely written memoir about the author confronting her childhood terrors of eternal damnation and faith."

—*HuffPost*

"*Sin Bravely* is an unflinching examination of the dangers of literalism in the religion department. And while you might be distracted by the sound of your own laughter, it's a dead-serious message that won't soon be shaken off."

—*Chicago Tribune*

"Brimming with characters wacky and sincere."

—*Entertainment Weekly*

"A gripping exploration of the necessity of disobedience on the road to authenticity. A beautifully written, deeply funny memoir."

—Joey Soloway

"Rowe deftly juxtaposes dark humor with raw emotion without ever yanking the reader out of the story."

—*The Guardian*

"A powerful debut memoir that hits the unusual sweet spot of rigorous theology, candid sexuality, and laugh-out-loud humor. Who knew theological inquiry and obsessive questioning of one's eternal fate could be so damn funny?"

—Mishna Wolff, author of *I'm Down: A Memoir*

"Maggie Rowe suffered for our sins so we don't have to. There are many laugh-out-loud moments in Maggie's deeply moving account of her spiritual wrestling match with a god she both feared and worshiped. A book with an original voice that should definitely be on your reading list." —Annabelle Gurwitch, author of *You're Leaving When?*

"Anxiety, guilt, and a debilitating fear of going to hell don't feel like they'd make for a great vacation read, but *Sin Bravely*, Maggie Rowe's hilarious—and ultimately heartwarming—story of her time spent in an Evangelical Christian rehab, is . . . laugh-out-loud funny." —Goop

"This book is so honest, so chock full of struggle and philosophical profundity—and ultimately so heartbreakingly funny—that one is only left to conclude that if heaven is a place that won't let in the likes of Maggie Rowe, then why the hell would anyone even want to go there?" —Mitch Hurwitz

"A sharp, genuinely funny book about the dangers of literalism and fear of the afterlife. A must read for anyone on this side of eternity." —Bill Maher

"Rowe's fantastic book is a born-again version of *One Flew Over the Cuckoo's Nest* . . . Not for the faint of heart, this is a cutting examination of Rowe's spiritual evolution that plunges into the big questions with the fearlessness found in the most brilliant of comics." —*Publishers Weekly* (starred review)

"Readers who have wrestled with self-doubt over the strength of their convictions will find a funny, frank companion in this frantically compelling memoir . . . Rowe's book does not provide easy answers, but her capacity to eventually sin bravely signals a new beginning. This engaging and adventurous book is an excellent companion for fellow seekers." —*Booklist*

Easy Street

EASY STREET

A Story of Redemption from Myself

Maggie Rowe

Counterpoint
Berkeley, California

COUNTERPOINT
2560 Ninth Street, Suite 318
Berkeley, CA 94710
www.counterpointpress.com

Printed in the United States of America
1 3 5 7 9 10 8 6 4 2

For Joanna and Handsome Jim

Behold the gates of mercy in arbitrary space,
and none of us deserving the cruelty or the grace.
—"COME HEALING," LEONARD COHEN

Part One

2006-2016

1

A Bind

I am not a nice person. I am going to admit that right here and now. I mean, I look nice, I behave nicely, I do nice things all the time, and the people who know me mostly think I am one of the nicest people they know. But I'm not.

Oh, I do have a nice life, that's for sure, on my well-paved street, where famous Southern California sunshine filters down through sheltering sycamore and long-trunked palm trees, where jasmine and birds of paradise bloom all year round.

Wait, I will question myself on a walk into town, gazing up through tropical foliage, *am I on vacation?* It can take me a second to get my bearings. *Oh no*, I'll catch myself. *That's right. I live in Los Angeles now.*

Even twenty-five years removed from a midwestern family's modest midwestern roots, it takes me by surprise. I guess I'll always feel a bit of a fish out of water on these leafy, enchanted streets.

A nasty fish, as it happens, though, because despite these rather fortunate circumstances, I am not content. I am not grateful.

I am envious, in fact, and on my daily errands and afternoon musings on the patio by my pool, in the privacy of my mind, behind my mask of friendship and kindness, I cultivate my envy like an exotic plant.

Everybody, I am increasingly convinced—not just in Los Angeles, but everywhere in the world—is better off than me. I am missing out, I feel, on the good stuff, all the good stuff, the real juice of life, that single-malt elixir that makes the endless bullshit of being human worth it, and everybody else is slurping it up.

Right in front of me.

You might ask why.

How could I not be pleased with a lovely Los Angeles life on a lovely street with palm fronds and flowering jasmine swaying in the temperate breeze?

I ask myself the same question. A lot.

I'm married, by the way, and the guy I married is a good guy. Also, ten years ago, I lured my childhood best friend to town with the bait of a charming British writer and now they live five minutes away in a home where they've agreeably produced two appealing godchildren for me to enjoy.

Outside an average list of concerns for my age, I am physically healthy.

Nonetheless, I often feel fate has dealt the gloriously high and fantastically lucky cards to others.

If you meet me, none of this pettiness will be apparent. I will seem quite nice. You'll notice how I listen when you are speaking, how I nod, how I widen my eyes at key points and laugh generously at even your mildest of jokes. You'll observe how I sustain eye contact and keep my focus pinned no matter what happens over your shoulder. You will get the impression, which is probably correct, that even if Bradley Cooper were behind you, furiously gesturing that he needed a dance partner, my focus would not waver.

A nice lady, is what I predict you'll think upon making my acquaintance. *Maggie Rowe is nice.*

You will, I'm afraid, be mistaken.

Because here's the truth: that stuff is all just a cover, elaborately expressed and highly convincing, but a cover nonetheless. If you pick up the stone I live underneath, you will find a seething system of covetous rivalries and discontents.

To begin with, I am envious of mothers. This despite the fact that I have deliberately chosen—and not out of lack of support or opportunity—to not have a child. For twenty years, every year, my husband asks, "Do you want to have a baby?

"No," I always say.

Every time. Every year.

Twenty refusals of the call to motherhood.

But this does not stop me from being fiercely envious of all women who have procreated or otherwise are in a situation where somebody calls them Mom. Recently I saw a woman, tall like me with blondish hair like mine, in our town square walking with a little girl wearing a red ladybug helmet.

"Here," the mother said, casually pointing her daughter toward the local ice cream parlor. "This way."

And that "this way" just crushed me. That single uttered phrase.

This way.

I wanted to fall to my knees on the pavement and curse every choice I had ever made.

A preposterously strong reaction to have in the middle of the mild afternoon, standing under a flowering jacaranda. But what I saw before me was a woman with an undeniable purpose on this earth: a guide, a protector, a necessary, valuable creature who knows *which way* and has been tasked with sharing it.

I had encountered the mother and her ladybug on my way to our local bookseller to buy my goddaughter a gift. When I entered the store, I saw Maria, a writer friend turned literary superstar, checking with the cashier to see if her new book had been restocked.

A new book? I was struck to the core. How could Maria possibly have written a new book while raising those robust children clearly poised to change the world? How could she have been typing out yet

another manuscript while cultivating those adorable little social ac-
tivists who still enjoy donning zany Halloween costumes and being a
delight to all? Didn't Maria's last lauded book come out, like, *last week*?

The news of this second book, which had already landed on the
shelves, was not the sort of blow I was expecting on a breezy summer
day. Maria turned away from the cashier and saw me.

"Oh, hey, Maggie," she said with a soft, easy smile.

"Hey, Maria," I said, and then, taking a deep breath, rising up
against the mighty foe of my own envy, "So cool that you have a new
book out. Your last one really was wonderful." Smiling through a
wince, I added, "I guess I agree with all the critics."

"Thanks, Maggie," she said.

"Well, it's true. It's a marvelous book. I'd be pretty proud if I were
you, Maria." Bright on the outside, dismal within.

Why her? I fumed as we waved goodbye, chafed by the unexpected
confrontation of what felt like my lowly station in life. If it would not
have exposed my inner petty nature, I would have thrown my arms
into the air right there, shaken my fists at the sky, and bawled like a
thwarted toddler.

As I looked through the shelves, I thought about the mother and
daughter I had seen on the way to the ice cream parlor. The stab
I felt from *this way* was more than a simple longing for motherhood, I
realized. *This way*, in whatever situation, speaks to me of a calling: an
accumulated body of experience that leads to knowing the way, along
with a being who needs the way pointed out to them. That right there
is a calling, or, less mystically, a vocation.

What is *my* vocation? It has zigzagged through the fabric of my
life with no recognizable pattern whatsoever. It's not that I don't work
hard; I've been disciplined in all of my creative pursuits, but I've aimed
wide with little thought to how all the many jobs and projects might
add up to a career and now, well, it shows. My lack of trajectory makes
its awkward presence known every time someone asks me "what I do"

and I have to answer "Well . . ." and then try to come up with something comprehensible.

I've acted on the stage with true devotion, taught acting and theater history, done a bit of television and some film, but as happens to so many of us in the sun-bitten City of Angels, that path petered out somewhere in the woods a long time ago. And then I was writing. First, I was ghostwriting, which paid decently, then I was writing and performing personal essays, but my only payment was in free drinks after the show. Bought by my husband.

I've created productions satirizing elements of fundamentalist culture, but there's only so many of those you can do. I've sold several television pilots and screenplays, all of which now languish in the bottom right drawer of my desk, next to the trash bin, just in front of my dog's favorite spot to vomit after she's eaten too much grass.

Because of my dismay at the scattershot nature of my endeavors, I envy anyone whose life has focus, an unwavering dedication to a narrow discipline. Somebody like Caroll Spinney, for example, who dedicated his life to being Big Bird, delighting young and old alike all the world over since 1966 and defining the great *Sesame Street* brand.

My envy is not limited to people with significant careers, though. I envy one-offs as well. I envy a fellow writer for the acclaim she received for a television pilot about her personal experience growing up as a hearing child of deaf parents. I am pierced by the fact that I lack that sort of advantage in terms of personal biography. I bemoan being raised by a sighted able-bodied computer programmer and an infuriatingly ambulatory insurance man. I envy the producers of the famous long-running spoken word show *The Moth* because I produce a less famous, slightly less long-running spoken word show.

I envy all musicians. I envy Miles Davis and Miley Cyrus and bluegrass fiddle players with names like Pickin' Joe Carmichael who lose track of time and play old, familiar songs with lifelong friends deep into the night.

It really must be nice for all of them. Truly.

I envy surfers and skiers for their balance, and expatriate writers who drink at outdoor cafés and talk about literature, and Miss America contestants, vapidly beautiful, and Serena Williams, beautifully powerful, and all women in their twenties with trampoline-taut stomachs and curves that lilt instead of bulge; hydrated, resilient skin; peach fuzz instead of chin hairs.

I envy twins. I want their lifelong assurance of deep and individual recognition.

Triplets, I'm convinced, have won the jackpot. I saw a Swedish trio clogging together in perfect synchronicity on the NBC reality show *World of Dance* and a flame of longing streaked through me. Why do those three get to be born in Sweden with identical sisters and a gift for synching their feet and *not me*?

I envy belly dancers, when I'm out with my husband, though I try to hide it. We once met a dancer with a law degree at a place on Sunset Boulevard—I'll never forget it. Nobody should be able to move their body like that and pass the bar exam. It's bullshit.

I envy opera lovers. They seem to take so much pleasure in their arias de capos and arias parlante, tilting their brandy snifters, closing their eyes, awash in music that sustains their soul, music that would only make me wish the singer would stop being so overdramatic.

I envy those in the throes of mania, elated with lofty ideas, capturing everyone's attention with their glaring personal light, however brief, however ill-fated. I envy their moments of brightly felt life.

I envy rugged Americans who fight for their ribbons; here in L.A., we get them at parties and forget what purse we stashed them in.

I envy J. D. Salinger and Virginia Woolf. I envy Don DeLillo, David Foster Wallace, Walt Whitman, and Nikos Kazantzakis. I envy Anne Sexton. I envy Sylvia Plath, her "Daddy"—"you bastard"—and *The Bell Jar* and even her grand exit and all that sweet, sweet posthumous fame.

I envy independent bookstore owners in Napa Valley, with their handwritten "store favorites" tastefully presented on papyrus cardstock with deckled edges. I didn't even know what that was, deckled edges. I had to look it up.

I envy Greek fisherman who wake at dawn. They rub arthritis from their hands and throw coir nets over their sparkling, wine-dark sea, and then while away the afternoon drinking ouzo until the evening when they dance their Zorba-the-Greek dances and dine on fresh fish and olive leaves and collapse into bed lulled by the repetitive rhythm of their rippling waves.

I envy Krista Tippett, host of the NPR spirituality podcast *On Being*. Boy, did she play her cards right.

I envy wise old women on their deathbeds, whispering to their children and grandchildren gathered in close. "May your lives be as marvelous as mine," they murmur so kindly it grieves me. "Have wonderful adventures and think of me fondly. Good night."

I envy most people, really, for something they have that I lack. And what makes it worse is that I should really be able to appreciate my life and not be looking around, because I know what it's like to be in a situation where appreciation of even the smallest pleasure is impossible.

I suffer from a form of OCD called pure O. For the last fifteen years, the symptoms have been rather negligible, but I have had two flare-ups, which became raging conflagrations that tore through my life.

The spark of my OCD was itself fiery: a fear of hell.

I learned about hell in Sunday school, where I needed to assent to a series of propositions about a historic event, feel bad about my past behavior, and resolve to be better from then on out. If I did these three things sincerely and in good faith, all my sins would be forgiven. Except one: blaspheming the Holy Spirit.

What was blaspheming the Holy Spirit?

The answer: Nobody knows. Just don't do it.

With this confounding directive, fear of hell nestled itself right in there beside me as my shotgun companion through childhood. When

I was nineteen, after my increasingly unmanageable fear had erupted right before Christmas my sophomore year of college, I wound up at an Evangelical mental hospital called Grace Point, a last resort. You might think it would be problematic to seek treatment for the fear of hell from an Evangelical facility that holds as one of its prime doctrines the notion of an eternal hell. And you would be correct. But I did receive a type of help at Grace Point, what in the early days of Christianity might be called *succor*.

I was diagnosed with a type of obsessive-compulsive disorder marked by an excessive concern with moral and religious doctrine. This idea of "scrupulosity" has a long tradition of devoted religious sufferers, including Protestant reformer Martin Luther. With encouragement, the help of a doctor, and a cocktail of three psychotropic medications, I was able to complete college. Little by little, the punishing theology became less convincing and the notion of divine retribution troubled me less and less. For the next several years, I experienced relative mental stability until, at twenty-five, I was seized once again by terror.

This time around, oddly, there was the hell fear, but without the actual belief in hell, so I was experiencing terror over a doctrine in which I had ceased to believe. My body stubbornly refused to be convinced by my conscious mind's revision of reality. My frontal lobe was calmly articulating the equivalent of *the monster we thought was under the bed is not real*, and all my nerve endings were shrieking back, *The monster is too real! It's right underneath the bed!*

I had a reemergence of a obsessive childhood tic as well, a self-punishing mechanism that had first snatched hold of my mind when I was eight. I would find, when I was worrying about blaspheming the Holy Spirit, that a part of me would devilishly repeat the word *blasphemy* in spite of myself. In my eight-year-old mind, these mental outbursts were clear and apparent evidence of my ultimate damnation.

The prohibition once again created a self-referential feedback system, what writer Douglas Hofstadter refers to as "a strange loop." The more I tried to stop the word *blasphemy* from arising in my mind, the more I summoned it forth. My lack of control over my own thoughts scared me and then my fear itself frightened me until the terror bloomed into full-blown panic; an even stranger, more damning loop.

Now, at twenty-five, I began to wonder, what if I started doing the same thing? Started to repeat the word *blasphemy* like I had done all those years ago?

And I did, but this time with a strange twist: The word *blasphemy* morphed into the term *blastoff*. So *blastoff* was what I began repeating.

I recognize that everything about this phenomenon is lunacy, and really embarrassing lunacy at that. Even the word *blastoff* is preposterous. But more than embarrassing, I find this mystifying mechanism terrifying. It's a chill I can't shake because, since I've never been certain how I was able to stop the previous looping cyclones that tore through my mind, I'm aware they could return at any moment, if the conditions and pressures were just right. I would be left defenseless.

So I suppose I'd say that most of all, I envy people who do not feel that their sanity could be whipped away at any moment. Those with the great mental health privilege; those hearty, healthy souls who have not crashed through to the terrifying basement of their psyches, who tread easily on the floors of their minds, undisturbed by the acute awareness that the beams beneath could give way at any moment, without warning.

Their minds have always been something they can rely on.

Must. Be. Nice.

But for now, I'm relatively healthy. On solid mental footing. For the last fifteen years, in fact, I've suffered only mild manifestations of what I call "looping." So I should be grateful. What mercy! What grace! A relatively functional ordinary mind! Who cares about the other stuff?

Well, I do, unfortunately. Which is not very grateful and not very nice. And I know it.

I know I'm responsible for this dingy cramped ego space, full of resentments and jealousies I've crammed myself into. I am not proud of my pettiness and puniness. Who would be? Plus, here's the really shameful part: Do you know *why* I want to expand beyond my myopic self-focus? Because it sucks *for me*. That's why. Dedicated self-focus does not bode well for *my* future. I know I need to put my desires outside myself, onto another ship, so to speak, so that when the worst happens, there will be something still afloat. And since I don't have kids, which are natural other ships, I must figure another way to do it.

I understand that letting go of my own happiness to focus on the happiness of others so I can ultimately increase my own happiness is contradictory and bound to fail.

But that is where I find myself at the beginning of this Los Angeles tale. It's a simple time, really, this starting point: when minor struggles still seem major, when common unhappiness is confused with singular misery; a time before obsessive looping returns to snarl up my mind, before an act of casual generosity becomes a formal responsibility, and before a lunch at a charbroiled chicken franchise alters my life forever.

2

Larchmont Ladies

My husband Jim met Joanna ten years ago. I remember the morning clearly. Jim had returned from the barber and was not happy with his new haircut.

"Shit," he growled, walking up the three steps from our patio to the kitchen door, "he gave me a Ryan Seacrest cut. Now I've got 'young-guy hair, old-guy face.'"

"Young-guy hair, old-guy face" is a Hollywood fashion faux pas we like to keep track of. Robert Redford is the most notable offender.

Jim is close to sixty and his naturally blond hair had been feathered on the sides and tousled on top, a style fashioned perfectly for a member of the latest boy band. He pulled at his roots, as if he could yank his hair back to the way it had been that morning.

My husband is fifteen years older than I am, but I suspect most people don't pick up on the age difference.

"Your boyish charm saves you," I said.

There's something familiar about my husband. He reminds you of the casino host that gave you the free ticket to the buffet that time, or the stand-up you saw once, or the funny guy at RadioShack. New Jersey roots roughen the edges of what could be considered a Hollywood smoothness, just like many years of smoking cigarettes have graveled his voice and his laugh, perfected over many years on sitcom sets, that both invites and commands you to laugh along with him.

Jimmy can also be exuberant, approaching life like a rambunctious kid jumping up on a bridge railing and peeking over the edge, sometimes almost literally. Like when we approach a construction site walking to the store on our way to grab Hot Pockets (or Lean Pockets if we're on a health craze) and Jimmy spies a large, gaping hole in the ground where a building has been razed.

Pure celebration. I have never met anyone in my life who loves the sight of a sprawling, mighty hole quite like my husband.

There are certain people walking around in the world that, when they break into a smile, you are just . . . done. Movie stars can do that, of course, but so can my husband. The night we met at the bar in a comedy club with the delightfully braggadocious name of "The World Famous Hollywood Improv," he flashed me one of those smiles and I thought, *Well, isn't that like taking a little vacation?* I pulled over a bar stool and sat next to him.

For some reason, though, the moment that sticks with me from that first night was Jim's interaction with an elderly man who had been drinking alone beside us. At around 11:30 p.m., the man awkwardly jostled off his bar stool without losing his composure and made his way to the door with the assistance of a cane adorned with printed butterflies. It was a cane, I surmised, he would not have chosen had it not been on sale at Rite Aid.

The man said goodbye to nobody, and nobody said goodbye to him, but just before he reached the door, Jim called out to him in a sharp, clear voice, "Straight home!"

The man turned, surprised.

"Straight home, you hear me?"

Everyone in the bar laughed but no one more than the man himself.

"Got it. Will do," the man said, lifting his butterfly cane in a waggled farewell.

"No monkey business, alright?"

"No, no." The man shook his head, still laughing. "No monkey business tonight, I promise."

And I was, as they say, "in."

There is the typical Hollywood humor and then there is Jim Vallely's humor and I noted the difference right away. My husband's humor is generous. It includes rather than excludes; his humor is an invitation to participate in the joke.

Humor as an invitation. That is what is spectacular about his talent.

With the children in our life, he does a character I love named Tortilla Man, where he secures a flour tortilla to his face with a pair of dark glasses. Tortilla Man does not speak, but he waves, dances, and shakes his hips. As Tortilla Man becomes increasingly excited, the waving and hip shaking becomes more frenzied until finally Tortilla Man "eats his face," by using his hands to shove the entire tortilla into his mouth.

"No!" the kids yell, "Noooo, Tortilla Man! Don't eat your face!"

It's true my husband has a genuine charm, but with me—and I know this is a by-product of his ease with me after all these many years—this charm is not always forthcoming. With me, Jim will often be reduced to monosyllables by his phone or the television or whatever shiny thought he's rolling around in his head like some marble he won't let me play with. On this particular day when he returned from the barber, I had wanted some charm. I wanted to hear funny anecdotes. I wanted to be amused.

"So how was Gary?" I asked as soon as he walked in the door. Gary is Jim's barber.

"Oh, you know," Jim said, pouring a cup of coffee from the cold pot and putting the cup in the microwave.

"No, I don't know."

"Gary's great." Jim stared at the microwave intensely as if the heating process required his unaverted gaze.

"How so?"

"You know . . . you can tell Gary anything."

Jimmy's focus was laser-like. If anything went wrong with the microwave, he would be the first to know.

I was determined to get at least five sentences of conversation out of him. "What do you tell him?"

The microwave dinged and Jimmy removed the cup, checking the heat with his finger.

"Gary's, you know. He's a gay man with five biological children, so . . ." He trailed off as he walked over to the table.

I follow him. "So . . . what? What does that mean?"

"So he's pretty much seen it all."

It's an odd conclusion, but this is gossip and I like gossip. Even if it's about a barber I've never met. "Do you think Gary knew he was gay when he was having the children?"

Jimmy pulled his phone from his pocket. "I don't know. He's Gary."

Jim takes a picture of himself and looks at it.

"Shit."

"What does that mean? I don't know Gary. What's Gary like?"

"You know, you gotta love Gary."

"Why? Why do you gotta love him?"

Jim started texting.

I slapped the table to get his attention. "Just tell me one thing you told Gary and then I'll let you go."

Jim appeared to use all his strength to haul his gaze up from the screen to meet my eyes. "Okay," he heaved, displeased but willing to go along. He dropped his elbows onto his thighs and rubbed his forehead. This was not easy, he was letting me know, what I was putting him through here.

Finally he sat up, his expression easing. "I told Gary about this mother and daughter I met in front of Koo Koo Roo who knew my name from *The Golden Girls*," he said quickly. Then his gaze snapped back to the phone, his inner resources exhausted.

"Uh, what?" I knew he was holding out on me. "Come on, husband, I want to hear the story."

I finally got it out of him that on his way to the barber, he stumbled upon two women panhandling in front of the charbroiled chicken franchise Koo Koo Roo.

"I give them five dollars and I tell them not to spend it all in one place. The older one laughs for like a solid minute.

"She says I am very funny," he went on. "And she tells me I should write comedy for a living. 'Los Angeles is the perfect place for a comedy career,' she says. 'You have talent. You might have a shot.' She says her name is Sunny, and she introduces me to the younger woman, who hasn't said anything up to this point. 'This is my daughter,' she says. 'She knows I'm right. Right, Joanna?'

"Joanna agrees with her mother that comedy would indeed be a good line of work for me, and I talk to them for a while before finally admitting that, in fact, I do write comedy for a living in Los Angeles. They want to know how I got my start, so I tell them I got my first real job on *The Golden Girls*."

"Which they'd seen," I prompt, happy to have extracted the story.

"Yeah, the younger one, the daughter, Joanna, she shouts, '*The Golden Girls. The Golden Girls*! He wrote comedy for *The Golden Girls*! *The Golden Girls* is our favorite show!' Then Sunny asks me my name and when I say 'Jim Vallely,' Joanna starts jumping up and down. She goes crazy. 'I've seen that name! Vallely! Jim Vallely!' she shouts, grabbing at her mother's arms with both hands. She's squeezing so tight I think she's going to leave marks."

Jim explained how Sunny had calmly and expertly quieted her daughter's wild enthusiasm. Sunny then confided that she and Jim had a lot in common, for she herself was a kind of a comic.

"'I used to send jokes to *Reader's Digest*,' she says. 'And some of them even got published.'"

"Wow," Jim had said with, I'm sure, his usual forthright generosity toward strangers.

"Then she asks, would I like to hear one of her jokes? 'Sure,' I tell her. 'I'm always up for a joke.'"

"What was the joke?"

"'Why does Tiger Woods always carry an extra pair of pants?'"

"Why?"

"'In case he gets a hole in one.'"

"Ah," I said, "I bet you gave her a nice big laugh."

Jimmy shrugged.

And that's how it started.

For the next several months Jimmy gave me regular updates on his adventures with Sunny and Joanna. Every time he passed the two women in front of Koo Koo Roo, which turned out to be their regular spot, he would give them a few dollars, until one day he said, "C'mon, ladies, I'm buying you lunch," and marched into Koo Koo Roo with the women in tow. After that first meal, Koo Koo Roo lunches became a monthly thing, and the fifth time, as much out of curiosity as at Jim's insistence, I joined them.

Sunny, who Jim had depicted as about seventy and the well-mannered and relatively taken-care-of partner, had sunbaked skin that made her look like an outdoorsman at the end of a long life spent under the sun. Her hair was matted, dyed jet black by a product that stained her hairline as well as the tops of her ears. She clumped along in laceless men's athletic shoes several sizes too big for her feet, drawstring sweatpants, a stained T-shirt unassisted by a bra, and an 1980s suit jacket with shoulder pads broad enough to qualify as protective equipment.

Her daughter Joanna's presentation, however, suggested something

more awry. She seemed to be in a heightened state of alert, as if prepared for anything to come at her from anywhere at any time. Static
electricity had shocked her mop of frizzy hair into standing up from
her scalp as if in alarm. Her eyes managed to express vacancy and
hyper-focus at the same time. A yellowing paisley housedress hung
unevenly from her thick shoulders, Wicked Witch–striped socks puddled at her ankles, and a bulging macramé purse, whose soiled inner
lining protruded like a distended organ, seemed ready to split from the
pressure of her double-fisted squeeze.

"Maggie?"

Sunny was smiling broadly, ingenuously, as she pushed her hand
forward to shake mine.

I pulled my focus away from Joanna but felt hers remain on mine.

Sunny stood patiently, grinning. "We're so happy to finally meet
you."

"And I'm so happy to finally meet you two," I said in a tone I was
pleased to hear sounded light and cordial. I was concerned my discomfort would feel like an insult to the two women, but my voice and
manner, I felt assured, betrayed nothing.

Joanna was appraising me right back but without the bullshit cordial cover. She thrust her jaw forward like a bulldog and scanned me
from head to toe. Sunny interceded before the awkward moment could
develop into something worse.

"Say hello, Joanna."

"Hi," Joanna muttered while squeezing her purse into her chest
and staring down at the frayed sandals incompletely covering her wide,
flat feet. It did little to smooth the tension.

I glanced at Jimmy. He nodded, and in an attempt to assert normalcy, I repeated, "It's so nice to finally meet you."

Jim led the way into Koo Koo Roo, and when we reached the
cashier, Sunny asked if they could get the Supreme Original, which
came with three sides rather than one.

"Sure," Jimmy said, smiling. "Koo Koo Roo is all about the sides."

"Four Supreme Originals," he said to the cashier. "Give me the baked beans, mashed potatoes, and sautéed mushrooms. Maggie?"

I ordered black beans, yams, and a side salad, but Sunny and Joanna took a while deciding.

"We would both like garlic potatoes, green beans, and corn with our chicken," Sunny quite politely told Jimmy.

Then at the last minute, Sunny changed her mind and asked for mashed instead of garlic potatoes.

"Garlic lingers a little longer than I'd like," she explained.

Lingers longer than I'd like had a cadence to it that made me imagine Sunny in a different light. I repeated the phrase in my head as I pictured her with a teacup in hand, an extended pinkie, laughing lightly, her liquid wordplay alluding to the careful tutoring of a privileged child. *A parallel universe,* I thought, *an alternate environment.* A different Sunny.

When our orders were ready, the four of us squeezed into a small booth and spread our food out on the table. I sat next to Joanna, who ate in silence while Sunny entertained us with jokes she had submitted to *Reader's Digest.*

"What do you get when you cross a dinosaur with a pig?"

"What do you get?"

"Jurassic Pork."

Some were more sophisticated. "The problem with political jokes," she observed, for example, "is that more often than not they get elected." Sunny conversed easily, made eye contact, and had a knack for comedic delivery. How, I wondered, had this sharp, witty woman come to be panhandling in front of a casual chicken eatery?

I studied the two with curiosity as we talked and ate. Both Sunny's and Joanna's skin had a ruddiness that seemed to go many layers deep, making me think mother and daughter had spent many days out of doors. Sunny's hair, more than tousled or unkempt, was shiny and oily all the way from the inky-black roots to the tips; I imagined Joanna's electrified mop could not be tamed easily with a brush. Both women's clothing, as well as their teeth, appeared to be stained in way that a light cleaning wouldn't resolve.

I asked Sunny if she had any other children and was told she had a son named Jon who died in a board and care facility after being on dialysis for many years.

"And then," she said, "there was the Other One." At the mention of the Other One, Joanna's eyes hardened, and I felt I could detect a shiver go through her. I waited for Sunny to say more, but she did not.

I noticed in the silence that Joanna's nails were chewed to the nub while Sunny's were long and jagged with a thin black layer at the quick.

I continued to study Joanna as we ate, playing amateur shrink and attempting to diagnose what sort of disorder she might be grappling with. Somewhere on the high end of the autism scale seemed the strongest possibility: the lack of eye contact, the repetitive speech pattern, the nervous flapping of her hands, and the fact that, Sunny proudly told us, she had committed entire episodes of *The Golden Girls* to memory and could recite lines on command.

Where do they sleep at night? I wondered as I watched Joanna spoon her potatoes away from the encroaching juice of the baked beans. Maybe they slept in the tents by the Social Security office a few blocks north of Larchmont. Or in Pan Pacific Park by the Grove shopping mall? Yes, that made sense, I decided, Pan Pacific. On top of one of those grassy mounds always covered at lunchtime with blankets and school children. At night I imagined it must be a different scene with shadowy creatures, previously hidden, emerging from behind hedges and porta-potties.

Did Sunny, I wondered, have to negotiate a nightly spot among others for a tent she stashed during daylight? Or did she and her daughter have their own secret spot nestled in the bushes away from the path, hidden from probing eyes and searching flashlights; a canopy of trees shielding the two from the elements? Or perhaps they slept in their car. I tried to picture the arrangement. Both reclined from front seats? Or Joanna curled in the back with Sunny stretched across the console in the front?

During that first lunch, I learned that Sunny had gone to Hollywood High School, that Joanna's schooling had concluded with fifth grade, that Sunny liked big band music and wished she could play the French horn although she believed the instrument would not be fun to carry around on a bus, that Joanna thought the greatest song ever written was Abba's "Dancing Queen," that Sunny once won a vacation to Paris, France, which is in Europe, that Joanna once took a class at Barbizon modeling school where she learned to swing her arms in the opposite direction of her legs when walking (which isn't as easy as it sounds), that Sunny thought models should eat more sandwiches, and that neither could understand why Thai people put peanut butter on salads.

Walking home, Jim and I were both quiet. When we got to the house, he said simply, "So that's them."

"Yes." What else was there to say?

Over the following months and meals at Koo Koo Roo, I became more comfortable with the dynamic of our little quartet. I could keep Sunny happy just by listening to her jokes. Strained responses weren't required, and sometimes the punch lines were funny enough to give me a real laugh.

Then one day, looking up from his iPad at the breakfast table, Jimmy said to me, "You know, there's a *Golden Girls* marathon on Lifetime."

"Yeah, so?"

"How would you feel about inviting Sunny and Joanna over to watch it?"

The whole endeavor seemed like it could end up being wildly

uncomfortable and deeply awkward. But I couldn't say "no." I couldn't endure what that would say about me *to* me. So I was in a bind. Did I not have an afternoon to spare? What was I doing that was so important I didn't have a few hours to give to people who had been less successful than me at spinning the rigged roulette wheel of fate? Suddenly my discomfort seemed shamefully small, and I frowned.

"You hate the idea."

I considered my husband's lapis lazuli–blue eyes.

"No, no," I said. "That's not what I was thinking. I was thinking, husband, that I married a good man."

Sunny had a cell phone, and she had given Jim her number, so that evening we called to invite the two ladies over for the *Golden Girls* marathon. Sunny's recording greeted us: "Don't hang up. My friends tell me I have too many hang-ups already."

I get up before Jim does, most days, and the Saturday morning of their visit was no exception. I was drinking my coffee in the kitchen when Jim walked in.

"I'm afraid it's going to just be you and the ladies today," he said, picking up his car keys.

"What?"

"I have to go into work."

"You what?"

"You'll be fine, though, right?"

"What? Oh, sure, of course," I said. "No problem."

"Yeah?"

He knew this was probably too good to be true.

"How long did you tell them they could stay?" I emphasized the word *you* ever so slightly so there would be no mistaking who made the offer in the first place.

"I didn't say."

"Oh, okay," I said brightly but with a weariness I hoped suggested a great inconvenience was being overcome with magnanimity.

"You're the best," he said tentatively, gauging the level of my resentment.

"Yeah, well."

Jim would feel the knife of guilt, I knew, and that was my intention, but to a jury of marital conflict, nothing could be proven.

"Okay, sorry about this, but thanks," he said in way that assured me I had successfully made him feel he had done me wrong and at some point would need to make up for it.

When the doorbell rang at exactly 2:00 p.m., I was standing next to the front entrance, looking at my watch. Noticing my heart rate was a little rapid, I consciously slowed down my breathing, then composed a welcoming smile and opened the door.

"Here you are!" I declared, throwing out my arms too forcefully, as if the two women were beloved sisters I had been separated from for many years.

Sunny, inky-black hair shellacked more fiercely than usual to her nodding head, looked in from our porch with expectant eyes, while Joanna, apparently torn between curiosity to see the house and protest against the occasion, stood behind her, arms crossed over her chest, glowering.

"Please come in." I said, pulling back my enthusiasm and standing aside.

Sunny clomped over the hardwood floors of our living room, taking in her surroundings. I followed her gaze, watching her eyes transform my home from a modest Los Angeles two-bedroom into the palace of a queen. Her attention moved over the eggshell walls offset by teal trim, the ebony piano, the fireplace framed by ruddy bricks and topped by a simple stone fleur-de-lis, and paused at the pair of thickly framed Japanese prints. She took a step closer to the one on the right, an ink painting of a bridge over a mountain stream at nightfall. Then she looked over to the creamy couch and chaise lounge, made creamier by their dark burgundy occasional pillows and a crushed-velvet throw. She might have looked like a doting grandmother admiring her grand-daughter's newly appointed home—had she been wearing flats and a dress or tasteful pantsuit instead of men's athletic shoes and a stained T-shirt and trucker pants.

Joanna, on the other hand, stalked around the room, jaw loose, entire torso pitched forward. Occasionally she yanked her neck around to fix her eyes on me in a glare that seemed to mix envy with fright; greedy, as I imagined, for the material possessions on display, while at the same time expecting to be scolded at any moment for her unseemly desire.

"Where's Jim?" Joanna asked with her back to me.

"Oh," I said. "Unfortunately Jim had to work."

"Well," Sunny said brightly, "that's too bad, but we're happy to get to see you. What a treat."

Joanna's spine stiffened upon hearing the news, but she neither turned toward me nor said a word.

Maybe this wasn't the best idea after all, I thought, though I knew it hadn't been mine. It had been Jim's, who was not here. Jim who had made friends with these women and invited them to our house and then left me holding the bag. *Remind him when he gets home*, I made a mental note. *Remind him silently and with plausible deniability. Leave no fingerprints; deny him any counterclaim or defense.*

Joanna and Sunny followed me through the living room and into the dining area. Looking over the new room, they were drawn to a set of framed photographs displayed behind a pane of tinted glass in a large oak case along the wall. Sunny leaned forward—just about bumping her nose against her reflection in the glass—and scrutinized a glamorous eight-by-ten taken of me at my wedding.

"Oh, you look so beautiful!" she gasped. "What a pretty dress."

"Thank you," I said, suddenly embarrassed by the size of the photo and of Jimmy's absence in it. It was a wedding picture, for goodness' sake, not a modeling zed card. What had I been thinking?

"Are those roses in your hair?" Sunny asked, interrupting my train of thought while continuing to scrutinize the picture, which seemed to grow larger and more egregious by the second.

"Mm-hmm. They're called black roses. I really like that dark color. It's like red wine."

While Sunny looked over the rest of the photos, I tried smiling back at Joanna to relieve the tension, but her glare only intensified, as if I were her captor at whom she wished she could fling food, or worse.

"Joanna and I," Sunny said brightly, looking up at me, "think you look like Katherine Heigl."

"Oh, well—what a nice compliment."

"But not as pretty," Joanna interjected quietly but firmly, focusing intently on her feet.

"Joanna!" Sunny scolded. "Don't say that."

"'Like Katherine Heigl,' is what I said," Joanna growled under her breath, wrapping her arms around her torso, "but—not—as—*pretty.*"

Her unveiled hostility struck me harder than the insult. Joanna's growl, and the way she bit down on the adjective *pretty*, knocked me off center.

And you're not either I wanted to snap back but of course didn't, though my bunching jaw muscles probably gave away the restraint required. Instead, "That's true," I acknowledged. "Would you like to see the TV room?"

I led the way out of the dining area and into our TV room and gestured for the two ladies to take a seat on the sofa. Sunny immediately found her spot.

"Ooh," she cried, pressing the down-filled cushions with her hands and bouncing lightly on the seat. "This is so comfortable."

She looked up at Joanna.

"Sit. Sit!" she said. "You're going to love this."

Joanna, however, inspected the room with suspicion, still clutching her purse to her chest as if someone might leap out to snatch it at
any second.

I picked up the remote, turned on the television, and began flip-
ping through the channels.

Sunny was glowing. "Thanks for inviting us over," she said. "What
a treat!"

"Oh, I'm glad you could come, Sunny. It's so weird to have you
here."

Did I say that?

"I mean it's so *nice* to have you here."

And then, because I was nervous, I started talking fast. "Sunny,
you know I was thinking, is that your real name? Sunny?"

"Yes. When I was born, my mother said, I had hair the color of
sunflowers."

She was proud of this story, it seemed. She was beaming. "'Like
sunflowers on a summer day,' my mother used to say was what my
father said when he first laid eyes on me. 'Let's call her Sunny.' And
that's what they did."

My eyes drifted to her jet-black bob.

"I know," she said, picking up on my unspoken question. "I've
dyed it black since high school so I can look like Elizabeth Taylor."

"Right," I said, thinking, *as if all that separates Sunny from Elizabeth
Taylor is Clairol Nice 'n Easy charcoal rinse.* "Of course."

A familiar voice from the *Golden Girls* theme song crooned through
the speakers, Sunny clapped her hands, and Joanna did a dead-drop
butt-plop down next to her mother. Both women giggled, and I sighed
in relief.

"Well, then. I'll leave you to it," I chirped. "Have fun, guys." I
started to leave the room, but my ingrained hostess habits stopped me
at the door, turned me around, and worked my voice to ask, "Can I
get you . . . anything?" I chided myself for not asking sooner. I didn't

know what to offer them. Tea? Coffee? A glass of wine? Finally, I landed on my goddaughters' favorite snack.

"Cookies?"

"Oh, my. Cookies sound delightful," Sunny cooed.

"And milk," Joanna barked without looking away from the screen.

Her tone made me bristle but I shook it off, then turned to Sunny. "Would you like milk, too?"

"Oh, thank you. Yes, milk would be very nice."

It wasn't until I had pulled the door closed behind me that I noticed my expression locked in an absurd grin. I stopped in the hall and rubbed my hands lightly over my face, massaging my jaw to relax the muscles. What a ridiculous scene I found myself participating in. I felt my lips curl back into a smile, and a little laugh escaped my mouth as I walked into the kitchen.

Oreos? Chips Ahoy!? Fig Newtons? All three, I decided, lifting the bags down and placing them on the counter. As I plucked the cookies out and began arranging them on an eggshell-speckled ceramic plate, I imagined baby Sunny with her hair like sunflowers.

If I had a baby girl to name, what would I name her?

It's a little rut my mind gets to circling from time to time, maybe more often than I would like to admit.

Babette?

I like the way this name combines the sounds of both *baby* and *barrette*, conjuring for me the elegance of a French sophisticate but containing, as well, the familiarity of a nickname. I like the way it feels to say it aloud, two voiced presses of the lips, two short vowels and a light tap on the hard palette with the tip of the tongue.

"*Babette, Babette, Babette,*" I repeated softly, laying three cookies down on the place.

I like the name, too, for the character of Babette Gladney, a thick, earthy woman who appears in Don DeLillo's novel *White Noise,* where she teaches posture to senior citizens, perhaps the noblest occupation

I've ever heard of. I felt a bit noble myself, in that moment, as I admired the array of cookies I had arranged on the plate, and I gave myself a pat on the back for taking the time to do it nicely. *Good for you, Maggie.*

I immediately scolded myself for indulging in cheap pride over such a minor generosity. What had it cost me to let these two women sit in my rec room watching a—free, by the way—TV show? How much did it take to bring them some crappy cookies on a plate? Plus, my husband was the one who had thought of doing this kindness in the first place. I had just agreed, somewhat resentfully, so I could describe myself *to* myself as magnanimous, as a woman helping the less fortunate, even inviting them into her home. I liked the way that made me feel. Wasn't that true?

Maybe not entirely. Perhaps I was being a little too rough on myself. I did genuinely feel for the two ladies. Joanna offended me, that was true, but I thought about what it must be like to walk in her shoes, to look at the world through her eyes, sitting in front of Koo Koo Roo, a grown woman, hanging on to her mother's sleeve. The women tended to not be forthcoming about their daily lives or how they came up with their money, so I knew little of their world outside our Koo Koo Roo meals. But I recognized something in Joanna especially, the way she repeated phrases, hooked by an idea and unable to squirm free, and I sympathized with that. So self-regard hadn't been everything. Empathy had been at least a teeny part of my motivation. That was something. Then I wondered if nobility could be achieved by portions. Did one's motivations have to be pure? *Yes*, I thought, fairly surely. The pure-in-heart thing was central. I couldn't see a way around that.

I took the milk out of the refrigerator and poured it into two slender glasses. Another name for my imaginary baby might be *Josie Rose*.

I had thought about *Josie Rose* many times before, and I decided (once again) that the medial *s* in Josie would be pronounced voiced, as in *lazy*, instead of voiceless, as in *lace*.

That's a nice name, though, isn't it?

I like the repetition of the long *o* and the buzzing *z* sound, the tomboyish-ness of *Josie*, a girl who could pitch softballs hard and fast, her cap worn low to shade the sun, balanced against the womanly qualities of *Rose*, the fragrance and delicate petals of the quintessential feminine flower and the formality of its codified meanings, red for love, pink for romance, bright yellow for friendship, white for weddings and, oddly, also for death.

I had never wanted a child, and if you had asked me at that moment, I would have said I didn't want one then either.

And if you had noticed the dreamy expression on my face and asked what I was thinking about, I would have made up something else instead of telling you, "I'm deciding what to name my baby."

What percentage of women never give birth to a child? Infertility is more common than a lot of people know, so maybe more than you'd expect. What percentage of those who never bear a child also neither adopt nor marry into a situation with children? That was probably a lot smaller, I guessed. And of those women who never give birth to a child or adopt one or marry into a situation with children (Jim's daughter was a freshman in college when we met), what percentage stay that childless course despite the presence of a loving mate, financial security, and a cozy home? A small percentage, I bet. A very small slice of the pie of all the women in the world and their chances of entering motherhood, a tiny sliver, probably.

I was in that lonely sliver.

"That's me," I said with a sigh before putting the cookies and milk on a nice tray (that I had received as a wedding gift but never found an occasion to use) and walking back to the rec room. Balancing the tray, I imagined I was playing the role of Dutiful Mother in a theater company in which I was not just the only actor but also the sole member of an unusually intimate subscription audience.

As I approached the door, I heard Bea Arthur say, "My mother

survived a stroke which left her, if I can be frank, a complete burden."
I entered the room to peals of laughter and saw that the ladies were
indeed enjoying themselves. Joanna, though, immediately stopped
laughing when she saw me, then grabbed her purse from the sofa and
clutched it to her chest.

"Dorothy is hilarious," Sunny panted through continuing laughter. "She kills me."

"So true," I agreed. "Jimmy always says, 'If Bea Arthur couldn't get
a laugh with one of your lines, you knew you had written a bad joke.'"
I set down my wedding-gift tray, and Sunny admired the store-bought
cookies as if I had presented a selection of delicate French pastries.

"Oh, Chips Ahoy!" she exclaimed, her hands flying to her heart.

Joanna grabbed her lower lip with her upper teeth and begin
gnawing on the chapped flesh.

"Enjoy," I said, and then added, with far too much enthusiasm,
"It's really great to have you here!"

I went to the other room to write but couldn't concentrate because my mind was whirling around whether or not anyone would,
or should, ever read what I writing and thwarting the entire process
altogether. Eventually, I gave up on and returned check on the ladies.

"How's everything going in here?"

"Wonderful!" Sunny said.

She didn't look completely comfortable, though, so I asked again,
"Is there anything you need?"

"Um, yeah," she said, holding out the remote. "I don't know how
to work this. Do you think you could stop the show for a minute while
I go to the bathroom?"

"Oh, of course," I said, taking the remote and pointing Sunny
down the hallway. Then I turned to Joanna and said, "There are two
bathrooms. You're welcome to use the other."

Joanna shook her head and narrowed her eyes, marking my every
move as if I might suddenly take a swipe at her.

Her frank animosity felt like a challenge I should address. Without ever actually deciding to do so, I found myself sitting down next to Joanna on the sofa.

"Did you enjoy the cookies?"

"They were okay."

"You can't go wrong with Chips Ahoy!, right?"

"Yeah."

Joanna pulled her shoulder up to her ear and twisted more of her back to face me.

I continued, undeterred, "So *The Golden Girls* is your favorite show?"

"Yeah."

"When did you first start watching?"

That seemed to be the magic question. Joanna's reserve melted.

"It was 1992," she began, sputtering out words with a breathless urgency, talking more to herself than actually to me, "we didn't know Jim in 1992. Jim wrote lots of episodes of *The Golden Girls*. Jim wrote the second episode we watched today, we saw his name on TV, 'Jim Vallely.' The second episode is called 'Home Again Rose.' 'Home Again Rose' happens in the future when Dorothy has a heart attack and all of the women's heads are frozen sitting on plates. That's obviously a dream because in real life people's heads aren't frozen on plates. That's just logic."

Joanna's voiced monologue became more internal and turned into inexplicable grumbling as she seemed to drift into a world beyond the room.

"Good observation," I said, trying to retrieve her. "You're right. It's definitely a dream."

"Did Jim tell you that?"

"No, but he didn't have to. Like you said, it's just logic."

Joanna abruptly pressed her mouth shut. Her eyes narrowed again. She looked at me warily and I could sense her body stiffen.

"You're really lucky Jim lets you live here," she blurted.

"What?"

"You live here. In Hancock Park."

"Yes," I said. "I live here."

"Jim lets you live here."

My jaw muscles bunched up.

"He doesn't *let* me," I said. "Jim and I are married, so—"

"I know you're married." Joanna cut me off, sputtering half to me and half to herself. "I know that. Jim chose you, so you get to live in a big house on a nice street with big trees in Hancock Park. You don't have to worry about anything. You get to live on Easy Street with Handsome Jim with nothing to worry about, nothing to worry about . . ." Joanna's words degenerated and tumbled into a grumble.

My cheeks felt hot.

"I certainly do not live on Easy Street," I shot back, failing to keep the quaver entirely out of my voice. "I have problems, Joanna, just like everyone else—problems that maybe you don't know about."

I put a bit too much emphasis into the last four words, and I flinched inwardly at my tone. I knew better. Joanna's statement shouldn't have offended me. I *was* lucky. I thought that all the time, and this woman in front of me didn't deserve my irritation.

Joanna brought her hands to her mouth and began biting the skin around her fingernails, moving quickly from one finger to another.

Sunny—thank goodness—returned to the room before Joanna drew blood, and I immediately stood, un-paused the TV show, and dashed out of the room, yanking the door closed behind me.

It had been many years since I had to worry about how to pay the rent, and I've never had to worry about having enough food. Not even for one day. Sunny and Joanna, on the other hand, didn't have shelter at all, I assumed, and concern about hunger probably followed them wherever they went.

I stood at the kitchen window, silently scolding myself, looking out at the back neighbor's palm trees that reflected the light from their fingery leaves toward the end of the day. I didn't notice that the light had faded from the trees until Sunny and Joanna emerged from the rec room saying, "Thank you very much, Maggie. We're gonna go."

"Okay," I said weakly. "I'll see you out."

As the women walked down our steep front steps, a knot twisted my stomach. It was getting dark. Where would they go?

"Wait!" I called out, surprising myself.

They both turned and looked up at me.

"Where are you going to go now?"

"What?" Sunny asked, taking a step back toward me.

"Where will you sleep?"

"Our apartment," she said. "We'll sleep in our apartment, like we always do."

3

Dilettante

The two women turned left at the bottom of the steps and Sunny gave a little wave. "Night, Maggie."

An apartment? What? It never occurred to me that Sunny and Joanna lived in an apartment.

"Good night," I said, weakly lifting my hand. I watched until they turned the corner, then dropped my arm and scoffed at myself. My philanthropy had been pure foolery.

I walked to the bathroom and turned on the water to run a bath. *Ridiculous*, I thought. *I am simply ridiculous.* Why did I assume they did not have housing? Appearances, I suppose. Just like people assume I'm nice. Well, I suppose I *am* nice, but a surface kind of nice.

"Dilettante," I said out loud to my image reflected in the bathroom window, then sat on the edge of the tub and looked at my feet.

I remembered reading once that everyone has one secret word that, if leveled at them in the right moment by the right person, would have the power to obliterate the identity they'd spent their lifetime constructing.

Dilettante was my word.

"Dilettante toes." I said out loud to my feet. "Toes that dabble in an area of interest without commitment or knowledge." I knew the definition well. *Dilettante* comes to English by way of Italian from a

Latin verb that means doing something because you like it instead of because it's your job. My personal definition of dilettante is someone whose life lacks a clear trajectory, one whose varied pursuits add up to nothing, a bad steward of gifts, a surface person. A dilettante is like the lousy servant in Matthew's parable of the talents, someone who fritters away their talents rather than making a firm commitment to a singular endeavor; a person who is ultimately unworthy and, at least according to my initial reading of the Matthew passage (which apparently still holds sway in my mind), should be punished.

As I stared into the stream of hot water, I replayed Sunny's words and examined my sequence of emotions.

First, I felt tired and a bit numb as I led Sunny and Joanna to the front of the house. Next, when I opened the door and saw them leave, I felt relieved. After that, as they walked down the front steps, I felt that sudden knot of guilt in my stomach that made me shout, "Wait!" Then, I guessed, I must have pretty well decided I couldn't send the two wanderers into the night with nowhere to go, so I asked my question, "Where will you sleep?" And finally, instead of the essential act of human kindness I felt so proud of extending, Sunny's reply revealed my charity to be a kind of fraud, an unserious effort without real commitment or knowledge.

I undressed myself and eased my body into the steaming water. Memories of previous charity stints played through my mind.

Several years ago I volunteered to teach a creative writing class at a Hollywood nursing facility called Sunset Hall. I had seen a documentary called *Sunset Story* about the facility's extraordinarily vibrant residents. Those people might enjoy expressing themselves on the page, I thought. I could put my talents and education to work in the service of something important for a change.

My class consisted of ten or eleven eighty- and ninety-year-olds. It was gratifying to meet them, and our first couple of classes were engaging, but Sunset Hall's extraordinarily vibrant residents, it turned out, had no more interest in creative writing exercises than does your average college athlete in need of a humanities credit. Gossip was what interested them. They enjoyed gabbing endlessly about which staff members were bitchy and which were attractive and arguing whether the mashed potatoes served in the cafeteria were from a mix or came from actual potatoes. There might have been one or two participants in the group who would have eventually drawn value from self-exploration, but I hadn't stuck around long enough to find out.

Then I thought of Lynwood prison, a minimum-security women's facility in downtown Los Angeles where I taught yoga for several months in 2010. I had spent some time in an ashram delving into the Tantras and the minor Upanishads and the teachings of Patanjali. I earnestly instructed the women to find freedom in their spine before explaining that the Sanskrit word for freedom was *moksha* and that moksha was the goal of yoga, but the women were more concerned with figuring out who farted in dog pose and forcing the perpetrator to fess up to their crime than in quieting their minds.

So I quit. And why not? I had my experience. I had my funny stories. I could contemplate moksha on my own wrapped in a prayer shawl I purchased at YogaWorks.

Then I volunteered with an organization called Big Sunday. I would drive to a long warehouse in Atwater, next to the Los Angeles River, and sort donated clothes into sizes and fold them for shipment to Goodwill locations throughout California. The activity gave a satisfyingly textured sense of contributing to the general welfare. The warehouse was hot, and as I stood folding piles and piles of clothes, sweat would collect at the small of my back and my feet would begin to ache. These discomforts assuaged the guilt I felt at living beyond my means on the dime of a successful husband, and as new bins wheeled in and new piles of clothes heaped up on the tables, the opportunity to contribute seemed endless.

Then one day, after difficulty parking on the street outside the warehouse, it occurred to me that the clothes I folded weren't going directly to poor people, really. They were going to some Goodwill store where the whole bunch would sell for a pittance diminished by rental costs and further depleted by paying for staff, utilities, and maintenance. I wondered if donating $5 a week to the Salvation Army guy outside Rite Aid would do about as much good and told the volunteer coordinator in her booth by the entrance that I would be leaving early that day and not coming back.

I hadn't thought about Big Sunday in a long time, and the Salvation Army guy didn't show up till Christmas. As I pulled myself out of the bath and wrapped myself in a fluffy, oversized towel, it occurred to me that the *Golden Girls* marathon was the perfect icing for my dilettante cake. I imagined a headline: "Maggie Charity-Dilettante Rowe, Unserious, Humanitarian Dabbler, Exposed Again: Offers Helping Hand to Women NOT IN NEED, Extends Shelter to APARTMENT DWELLERS."

Enough! I thought. *It's time for a walk.*

Baths are nice and can often ease me out of a mood, but it's amazing how far a brief walk around the neighborhood can go toward making a fresh start. I walked over to our little Larchmont Boulevard. Larchmont is unlike the town squares of other more affluent Los Angeles enclaves like Beverly Hills or Malibu or the Pacific Palisades, whose main streets are sleek and shiny and golden and glittering and you worry about scuffing the sidewalks with your shoes. Their aesthetic could be called "Rich as fuck and pleased for you to know it."

Not Larchmont. Larchmont's wealth is hidden away in the distressed wooden floors of its shops, in the mismatched pottery of its homey restaurants, and the rickety wrought iron chairs that wobble on its sidewalks. Larchmont people don't want to be reminded they're rich while having the experience of being rich. That would ruin it.

Perhaps the most popular business on the two-block strip is Salt & Straw, the ice cream parlor where I saw the mother and daughter.

It calls itself an "old-fashioned scoop shop." Ye olde Salt & Straw sells $6 cones in a down-home atmosphere that might as well have sawdust on the floor and Ma and Pa themselves throwing open the door and welcoming you in.

Across the street is Bellacures, which offers manicures and pedicures with champagne presented to its guests, not in fancy Beverly Hills–style crystal flutes, but in teeny artisanal mason jars.

Burger Lounge serves "the original grass-fed beef burger" among black-and-white photos of rolling hills spotted with lounging cows, who by the expression of their faces, appear to have recently achieved enlightenment.

'Lette Macarons sells only macarons. That's it. You could purchase the entire supply of 'Lette Macarons, I'd say two hundred macarons total, and fit the whole load into a large picnic basket with room to spare. It would put you back a thousand bucks, but you could do it.

The only thing besides the price tag that immediately gives Larchmont away as more than just a cute little street in Middle America is the space between items in the stores, between blouses or belts or cupcakes or muffins or moisturizer or frozen yogurt toppings. The space confers dignity; it sanctifies the merchandise with its reverential expanse, turning food, clothing, and beauty creams into objets d'art worthy of its extraordinary purchaser.

I love Larchmont. Its brand of self-deception, wealth shame, and targeted flattery really works for me. And the burgers are fantastic.

My therapist, Lovely Lucy, has her office on Larchmont, right above the Burger Lounge. I would not have chosen Lucy as a therapist during either one of the two mental health crises of my life. Lucy practices narrative therapy, which is wonderful for developing a story of your life that is both true and helpful. I don't imagine it would be any match for some of my more severe struggles, but since I've been stable for so long now, since I've had the privilege of relative sanity for almost fifteen years, I have also had the privilege of talking to

Lucy about the everyday shabby business of life; of jealousy, envy, and regret.

I passed Koo Koo Roo, sans Sunny and Joanna, and came to Beverly Boulevard, where the homespun, overpriced, delicately curated, *true* Larchmont Boulevard begins. I walked past Lovely Lucy's office building and entered Larchmont Wine and Cheese. My eyes fell on a basket of plums whose color was a rather magnificent maroon, which I imagined would give way to deep burgundy if cut open. When was the last time I ate a plum?

Plums, I casually repeated in my head.

People who like fruit seem generally happier than me. Great writers always seem to like writing about fruit. I should like fruit. Maybe if I ate more fruit and started to appreciate fruit, I'd appreciate my life as well. I'd experience more gratitude for the simple moments. Like Cezanne with his pears. Cezanne didn't feel slighted, I bet. I should slice the plums up with cheese, I decided, and serve them to Jimmy whenever he gets home from work. I'll pour a glass of merlot, and we can sit outside by the pool.

Plums, I continued to repeat for no good reason. *Plums. Plums. Plums.*

I picked up three plums that looked particularly inviting but immediately thought, *Oh, this is silly. Jim won't want a little French snack when he gets home. He'll already have eaten at Craft Services. He'll be tired from writing all day and getting paid for it and having a career he can be proud of, and he'll just want to watch some TV.* Why, though, did he get to work in the industry and gain status and gratify his ego while I stayed home fiddling with our little faux charity and dabbling at dilettante pastimes?

The plums suddenly seemed unattractive, and I put them down.

But I didn't walk away. The plums were fresh, and even if Jimmy wouldn't want them, I'd enjoy a light French *repas* with a glass of wine for myself. Fruit appreciation, I'd become convinced, was going to open the taps of my joie de vivre.

I picked the plums back up, thinking about the fact that nobody had ever actually accused me of being a dilettante. It might not even have been something I'd been called behind my back. It was, however, a barb I'd hurled at myself quite often.

As I approached the front steps, a fierce determination came over me to follow through with Joanna and Sunny despite learning that their plight was not as desperate as we had thought.

I will not quit this time, I insisted.

My career path had been haphazard, and I didn't see how I could change that, but my personal life did not have to be. I was determined to be more focused. With Sunny and Joanna, I was not going to bail just because befriending them no longer flattered my self-image as much as it had before. The two women might not have been without some resources, but that didn't mean they couldn't use a little kindness.

The ladies began coming over on weekends to watch *The Golden Girls* and *Keeping Up with the Kardashians* and then we also began inviting them to use the pool on hot days.

Their first pool day was during one those late-August heat waves that can park over Southern California for weeks at a time. I gave Sunny and Joanna a few bathing suits to try on. They looked at the suits skeptically but then went valiantly into the bathroom and closed the door. After a period of haggling, involving what sounded like a combination of laughter and scolding, they emerged squeezed into my familiar suits, both covered appropriately as long as they didn't raise their arms.

Sunny and Joanna were both fair, so I gave them sunblock, which they slathered on until they looked like a pair of scantily clad mimes. They waded one slow step at a time into the pool, dog-paddled out to a giant pink swan raft my best friend Sascha brought us one Fourth of July, and made an entertaining show of struggling to mount it. Their torsos and legs batted the creature back and forth and pushed it across the pool until they managed to get on board, where they reclined together side by side and drifted in the afternoon sun.

I served them Oreo cookies on plain plastic plates and sodas in cans, no elegant wedding tray required. Jim and I, shielded from the piercing midday rays, looked out our kitchen window at the two white-faced women bobbing on the water and felt we were doing good.

One of the things I envy about the experience of motherhood is being able to say things like "Look at this!" "You want to see something cool?" "Isn't this pretty?" Or "See. The number 3 is like three blueberries. Count them. One. Two. Three. Three blueberries. " To share the little miracles that have long stopped seeming miraculous.

"Look, guys," I would say to Sunny and Joanna, bringing out a plate to the pool, "They're Oreo cookies. But *these* Oreo cookies have chocolate on the outside as well. And I put them in the freezer so they're *crunchy*."

Despite their age, both Sunny and Joanna were still open to amazement. Sunny displayed outward appreciation while Joanna expressed pleasure only through traces of a shy smile, but both were gratifyingly capable of being astounded. And it was not a burden. Jim and I did not feel financially responsible for the two, figuring that somehow they would manage to pay their rent and get by like they always had. I knew Joanna received some sort of disability benefit, that Sunny continued to get her husband's pension checks after he passed, and that they occasionally collected change from passersby on Larchmont. All Jim and I did was give the two money for movies or ice cream at Salt & Straw. Helping the women made me feel good. And it was easy.

Well, even during that time, sometimes not so easy.

A little complicating wrinkle with Joanna arose, which you may have already deduced. Joanna was in love with my husband. Plus, she gave the impression that she would have been thrilled to find out I was dead. I got this sense when Joanna said things like, "I know Jim married you, Maggie, but things could have been different. It could have been me with Handsome Jim on Easy Street. And anything can happen on Easy Street. Maggie." Once she added, "And it could happen tomorrow. It could happen any time."

Her desire for Jim poked through in ways other than open hostility toward me. For example, in her art. Joanna had boxes of crayons and a rainbow assortment of construction paper, and she liked to make colorful images of dogs and cats that looked longingly out at the viewer, as if begging to be adopted, or at least acknowledged.

She would show her affection for my husband by bringing one of these pictures over and thrusting it out to him with her gaze turned bashfully to the floor.

"I made this for you," she would say. "I hope you like it. I hope you like it, Jim. I made it for you."

The first time Jim looked at one of her drawings, it was hard for him to keep a straight face.

"Do you like it, Jim? Do you like it?" Joanna asked, bouncing up and down on her toes.

"Yes, I do," he said, his voice cracking. "Maggie, look at these."

The dogs and cats were at the level of artistry of Jim's eight-year-old granddaughter, whose drawings covered our refrigerator, but that wasn't why Jim had been feigning a cough to cover his laugh. In Joanna's world, apparently, dogs' and cats' paws and tails and noses were formed from something a little bit surprising.

"What do those shapes remind me of?" I asked, resisting the obvious.

It was undeniable. Penises were staring back at me. Not figures that looked like penises if you held the picture at a certain angle or under a certain light or if you let your vision kind of relax and your mind go blank until the image inside the image could emerge from the background. No. Neither an educated nor a biased gaze was needed to see penises, as plain as could be. The little kitten paws and the big dog noses were shafts and heads standing erect or lying down sweetly, as the postures of the animals required. Joanna's pictures would assuredly make Freud dance around on his toes, thumbing his nose at all his detractors and saying, "See, you guys! That dog's nose is a dick if I've ever seen a dick."

Joanna's feelings were clear. To Jim, she gave her amorous animal art. To me she gave looks that said, *I wish I could make you disappear by narrowing my eyes until you got smaller and smaller, and then you were completely fucking gone.*

We quickly developed several long-standing traditions with Sunny and Joanna. For Joanna, where Jim was involved, "long-standing tradition" described anything we did once. That was enough. After that, all parties were deemed to have entered into an inviolable contract. Strict adherence to detail was essential, and if a ritual were not observed the following year on the same calendar date as its establishment, Joanna felt a grave breech of etiquette.

I seldom told my friends about these rituals, or about the two ladies altogether, for fear of appearing to be making a sanctimonious display of virtue, which I tend to think is the worst of human weaknesses. But they would inevitably encounter the pair, from time to time, at parties at our home.

The first was our annual Christmas party.

Our musician friend Gary was playing the piano while various guests stepped up to sing pop songs and Christmas songs and Christmas-pop songs. Everyone joined in except for Joanna, who stood in a corner, pressed up into the right angle, arms crossed over her chest as if bracing for the moment when one of the guests might realize she was an outsider, cease their revelry, cry foul, and shove her out the door.

Recognizing better than she could have imagined the look of envy and insecurity on her face, I walked over to her. "Joanna," I asked, "would you like to sing something?"

Joanna did the classic *who-me?* double-take.

"Yes," I confirmed, nodding, "is there a song you'd like to sing?"

"A song?"

She looked at the room full of happy faces, backing further into the corner and gripping herself more tightly.

"What's your favorite?"

Joanna dug the heels of her hands into her eyes as if she could massage away her stressful mix of emotions.

"Come on," I said. "Gary knows everything."

Joanna stared, frozen.

"Hey, Gary," I called. "Joanna has one."

She didn't budge.

"Give it a try," I cajoled. "It'll be fun."

"Uh," Joanna managed, shuffling forward while looking down at her pigeon-toed feet. "Do you know 'Dancing Queen'? It's a song by Abba. 'Dancing Queen' is by Abba."

"I sure do," Gary said, launching into the opening changes without looking down.

It took a moment for Joanna to let her arms fall from her chest, but then she seemed to float toward the piano as if being carried by the familiar chords. When she reached Gary's side, she turned to look out at the gathered guests, her drawn expression relaxing into something that looked like elation, as if a radiant spotlight of stardust had fallen around her. She was so swept up in the heady moment that she beamed right through her cue.

Gary brought the vamp around again, slowed down the tempo, striking each note of the melody and mouthing the words to prompt her.

"Oooh," he mouthed. "You can jive . . ."

"Ha-VING the TIME OF your LA-AI-AI-AI-FE!" Joanna finally

jumped in, singing, for sure, but to an accompaniment only she could hear and in a key she had invented in the moment.

She sang exuberantly, carrying the song on enthusiasm despite reducing the two-octave melody to four or five notes and managing to somehow be both ahead and behind the beat at the same time.

I looked over to Sunny, wincing at the thought of the embarrassment I thought she must have been feeling, but she stood with a smile that seemed to erase all the worry lines from her face. At that moment, Sunny's face simply said "Proud mama," and "Look at my baby," and "See how happy she is."

Joanna waved her fists when the chorus came around. She jumped up and down to the rhythm, and her large breasts, unhindered by undergarments, bounced a wild backbeat one count behind.

That Christmas-party singing of "Dancing Queen" instantly became a carved-in-stone tradition, and Joanna has sung it again each Christmas since without ever losing the starlight glow of the first performance. She knew her audience would demand it. And why wouldn't they? After singing the song, there was always the roar of "Encore! Encore!" Of course it was led by Joanna herself, who screamed "Encore! Encore!" at the conclusion of her rendition. But everyone else always followed suit.

On our first Halloween together, which happened the following year, Joanna arrived as Jim and I sat on our front porch, enjoying the twilight and a cool autumn wind and giving out candy to neighborhood kids.

"And what have we here?" I called to the next trick-or-treater coming up the steps, who was substantially larger than the others.

"Is that an adult?" Jimmy asked, leaning over to me.

"I'm not sure."

"It's me, Joanna!" the large trick-or-treater shouted. "Do you know what I am?"

Joanna had put so much detail into her costume that we almost hadn't recognized her. To begin with, she had layered on more makeup than an Evangelical actress in a high school play, spreading ripe-tomato-colored lipstick wildly around her lips, smudging dark purple eye shadow over her eyes, and brightening her cheeks with rouge. She had jammed a silver crown down over her bramble of curly hair, which sprouted above her ears like Ronald McDonald's. She wore a pink satin bodice with Snow White sleeves (which, because the top was designed for a smaller frame, pulled Joanna's shoulders toward her ears) and a sequined aquamarine pencil skirt that tapered down to just above where a pair of clear "gummy" shoes jutted out like a fin.

"Hi, Joanna," Jimmy said. "You're supposed to say 'trick or treat.'"

Sunny's face appeared above Joanna's shoulder. "Happy Halloween!" she said brightly, and then plunked down on our front steps, reached into her gym shoes, and began massaging what I guessed were some painful bunions.

"Do you know what I am?" Joanna asked Jim.

"Well, um, you look great. You could be . . . uh . . ."

"A princess?" I guessed, though she hadn't asked for my opinion.

"No," she replied, her focus pinned on Jim. "What am I, Jim?"

"Uh . . ." He hesitated, looking down at Joanna's aquamarine skirt. "Are you a mermaid?"

"No." Her lips curled up into a smile.

"A mermaid princess!" I pronounced.

"No."

"A queen?" Jim guessed, eyeing the crown.

"No. I am not a queen," Joanna said, starting to giggle.

"A queen mermaid?" I tried.

"No!" She laughed outright.

"Miss America!" Jimmy said.

Joanna blushed and clasped her heart as if he had just crowned her winner of the national beauty pageant. But then, "No, no, I'm not. But I'm flattered, Jim. I'm very flattered you'd think I might be Miss America. Miss America is very beautiful. She's very beautiful."

"Okay," Jim said. "We give up. What are you?"

"You give up?"

"Yes, Joanna," I said, "We give up."

"I'm . . ." Joanna teased, looking into Jim's eyes. "I'm a . . ."

"*What?*" Jim said.

"A beautiful . . . princess . . . mermaid."

"But," I objected. "I said mermaid princess."

Joanna smiled, as pleased as I'd ever seen her. "I am a beautiful mermaid princess."

"Of course," Jim said. "I see it now. You're a *beautiful* princess mermaid."

"It's really a great costume," Sunny said proudly, still working on her feet. "Isn't it?"

Then I noticed a detail I somehow hadn't picked up on in all the Halloween excitement. Joanna was holding a knotted rope in her right hand that trailed behind her to a bright red, plastic wagon that held a group of small figures arranged.

"What are those?" I asked, peering through the darkness.

"My dolls."

I stood up from the stoop and stepped down to get a better view.

"Cabbage Patch dolls," I said to Jim, startled to be reminded of the 1980s craze.

"I have four," Joanna explained. "They're wearing Halloween costumes, too." And sure enough, they were.

"Do you want me to tell you what they are?"

"Sure," Jim said. "Tell me—"

"Okay. Okay. Okay. This is Frankenstein's Wife, and this is Zombie Prom Queen, and Pretty Witch, who is not a bad witch."

"Aren't there four?" I said.

"And this one," Joanna continued, ignoring me and pointing to the last doll, which was clearly dressed as a cat with felt ears secured in place. "Do you know what this one is, Jim?"

"Firefighter," Jim said immediately.

Joanna's attention snapped from the doll to Jim in surprise, and she scrutinized his face for a long moment. Then, "You're joking," she said, laughing. "Even I know that. Even I know you're joking, Jim. That's a joke. That's a very good joke. That's why you wrote for *The Golden Girls*."

Sunny agreed, wagging her finger, letting my husband know what a real rascal he was and what a perfect career choice he had made.

Then Joanna whipped toward me, pulled her elbows tight into her chest, and began flapping her hands up and down like a bird attempting to take flight. "Could you take, could you take a picture?" she blurted, breathlessly. "Could you take a picture of me and Jim? I brought a camera."

"Oh, this will be wonderful," Sunny cooed, bringing her hands to her mouth and tapping her fingers together in front of her lips. "Just wonderful."

Joanna turned all business. She reached into the wagon and swiftly produced a bright plastic Polaroid camera, which she extended toward me.

"Jim," she commanded, "stand over here. Stand over here with me."

"What about Maggie?" Jim asked, directing a raised eyebrow to me. He knew I would not be in the picture. I narrowed my eyes at him and shook my head.

"No," Joanna said. "Not Maggie. Not Maggie. Just you and me is good."

"Alright then," Jim said, "but it's dark out here. Let's go inside."

I followed him into the living room, leaving the bowl of candy on the front steps for the trick-or-treaters.

"You look in here, okay, Maggie?" Joanna said, pointing to the viewfinder. "This is where you look. This is where you look so you can see."

"Okay." I nodded.

"And then you push this." She pointed to the very obvious shutter button on top. "Do you see this? You have to push this to take the picture. You push this, okay?"

"It's the button on top," Sunny confirmed.

Joanna repeated the sequence for me and said to Jim, "Okay. Sit down there. Sit there on the sofa. Sit right there and look at Maggie who is holding the camera. She's the one holding the camera."

As Jim complied, Joanna pressed her palms into the sprouts of curls jutting out from under her crown and pulled them down over her ears. "Okay okay okay," she said. "Okay. I'll sit here. I'll sit here." She settled next to Jim on the couch and then slid over until she was smushed against his side, continuing to grab fistfuls of curls and press them flat.

I held up the camera and looked through the viewfinder. "Ready?"

"Yes," Joanna said while Jim put on his picture-perfect phony smile.

"One, two—"

"Wait!" Joanna shouted, jumping up. "I forgot the dolls. I forgot the dolls. *I forgot the dolls.*"

"Oh, of course, the dolls!" Sunny exclaimed. "You gotta have the dolls."

Like a mother just remembering she had left her quadruplets in a hot car, Joanna ran back outside in a guilt-ridden panic. She calmed, however, as she pulled the wagon in, picked up the four dolls one by one, and propped them up on the couch, positioning their faces toward the camera. They, too, were going to have their moment.

"Do I look okay, Jim?" Joanna asked, eyelids fluttering and lips parting like a silent movie star.

"You look great," Jim said, sliding over a bit on the couch, creating some distance between them. But Joanna would not be deterred. She pushed herself back toward him and gazed ever more deeply into his eyes before turning to me with a huge frozen grin. "Okay, Maggie. GO! NOW! GO!"

I looked through the viewfinder, aligned the outrageous tableau in the middle of the frame, and pressed the button.

"*¡Se ha tomado su foto!*" the camera declared in an assertive, masculine voice.

"Whaa?" I shouted.

"*¡Por favor, disfruten y sean bienvenidos!*" the camera shouted back.

I looked at the camera and then up to Jim, and then to Joanna, and then back to the camera, and started to laugh. "What was that?"

"Spanish," Joanna said.

"No, but why . . ." I said, laughing harder, "why . . .?"

"Spanish is another language, Maggie. Lots of people speak it."

"I know what Spanish is, Joanna. But since when do cameras talk?"

"Lots of cameras talk," Joanna informed me, as if explaining that bacon comes in strips.

"Yeah, Maggie. Lots of cameras talk," Jim said, smiling with an easygoing normalcy.

The Spanish-speaking camera vibrated with a buzz and when the developing picture slid out, Joanna held the picture under a lamp and examined the image with all the gravity of an oncologist scrutinizing an X-ray.

"Yes," she said at last, as if concluding that the dark area at the top of a lung was benign. "It's okay." Then she flew back to the couch, flung her arms around Jim's waist, and kissed him wetly on the cheek before he had time to object.

Afterward, Joanna directed me to take seven more Polaroids with Jim, her, and the dolls in different positions shot from different angles.

Perhaps it was Joanna's fantasy to send it out as a Christmas card: "Merry Christmas from Mr. and Mrs. Beautiful Mermaid Princess, Frankenstein's Wife, Zombie Prom Queen, Pretty Witch, and Cat who Handsome Jim calls a Firefighter—ha!"

"Happy Halloween," Jim said to me with a shrug, and another long-standing tradition was born.

"She loves animals, Jim?"

I was returning to the kitchen with a towel for Joanna, who had come in dripping wet from the pool, excited about something.

"Yes," Jim said. "Anna loves animals. Especially penguins."

"Penguins?"

"Here, Joanna," I interrupted. "A towel."

After several years of visits, she had become quite comfortable in our home.

"What?"

"Take the towel."

She took the towel I offered but held it by her side. "I don't have any penguins in my collection," Joanna said, agitated. "But what about other animals? Does Anna Michaela love animals besides penguins?"

"Sure. She's a big fan."

"A big fan of animals?"

"A big fan of animals, yes."

"She's not into penguins anymore, Jim," I said, "She's all about skunks."

"Skunks?"

"Yeah, she wants to move to Florida because it's the only state where you can legally own a skunk."

"Ugh, I hate Florida. Of course they let you keep skunks there, crazy bastards," he fumed, suddenly annoyed at the entire state.

"Well, no one's moving to Florida. I'm just saying Anna really likes skunks now."

"I have a skunk animal!" Joanna yelped. "I have a skunk. I'm not lying. I would never lie about something like that, Jim."

"Joanna," I interjected. "The towel is to dry off with."

"Are you talking about your animals?" Sunny asked, joining us post-swim and proceeding to contribute generously to the growing puddle on the floor.

"Um," I said, before heading to the hallway closet for another towel.

"I think I know what you're going to suggest, Joanna. And it's a great idea," I heard Sunny say as I pulled a striped beach towel from an upper shelf.

"Can we do it on Sunday, Jim?"

"Do what?" I asked, returning to hand the towel to Sunny, who politely thanked me before folding it up and holding it under her arm just like her daughter.

"Joanna does a wonderful animal show," Sunny said. "Just wait till you see it."

"Can we do it Sunday?" Joanna asked, bouncing up and down on her toes.

Joanna had been asking to meet Jimmy's eight-year-old granddaughter Anna for some time now, but we worried Anna might find Joanna's quirks disconcerting.

Jimmy looked over to me for counsel, and I nodded.

Truth be told, I was curious about the show. Were they stuffed animals? Beanbag? Plastic? I hoped they weren't taxidermied, imagining for one horrified second Joanna pressing her lips against the arsenic-preserved feathers of a crow and whispering, "Caw Caw Caw, nice to meet you, Anna."

That Sunday at 2:00 p.m. I opened the front door to Anna, who was dressed in a yellow princess dress and a skunk hat. She tore past me and shot toward the kitchen, beckoning our dog. "Holly! Holly!" Jim's daughter Tannis followed her whirlwind daughter inside, Sherpa-ing two brightly colored backpacks and an enormous mom-bag that appeared to have the capacity and number of distinct pockets necessary to organize the local Walgreens.

"Thanks for doing this," I said, relieving her of some of her burden, then kicking the door closed behind me. "Your dad's picking up the ladies and the mystery animals."

Tannis plopped down on the couch, appearing, as she often had since becoming a mother, to be *happily* weary, the kind of weary you get at summer camp where all your muscles ache and your mind is totally numb, but nonetheless you know that nothing will stop you from signing up for the following year. "So now," Tannis asked, "what's happening here? The Larchmont ladies are doing some kind of an animal show for Anna?"

"That is correct."

Through the front window, I spotted Jimmy climbing the front steps with two large black garbage bags slung over his shoulders. I opened the door and saw Joanna close behind, hugging a third bag to her chest, while Sunny kept pace, bending low to support her load from beneath. Jimmy staggered in and heaved his two bags to the floor in the middle of the rug, letting out a large "Whew!" Sunny and Joanna let theirs slide to the floor just inside the doorway and then pushed it the rest of the way.

Anna returned from the kitchen and watched the process with big eyes, especially fascinated by Joanna, who was kneeling on the floor and gazing at the three bags with reverence.

"Hi, Anna Michaela," Joanna said flatly without looking up. "I'm Joanna. I know that . . . that . . . that . . . you're Anna Michaela."

Anna watched warily while Joanna pulled out from the bags, one by one, her collection of what turned out to be at least sixty furry animatronic animals, ranging from one to two feet tall.

As Joanna lifted the figures from the bag, she paused to gaze deeply into each pair of eyes as if taking a moment to remember all the good times she had shared with that particular animal. Then, she ceremoniously stood each creature on the floor and pulled out another. The whole collection was arranged in assembly, in lines as evenly spaced as the Rockettes at their big Christmas show: cats, dogs, frogs, mice, a lion, a snake, a black bear, a polar bear, a koala bear, a lizard, a rat, a tiger, an owl, and on and on, down to a rhinoceros and one lanky giraffe.

"Jim told me you're a big fan of animals," Joanna said, less to Anna than to herself, as if giving voice to a fantasy—as if, it occurred to me, she were all alone in her room imagining what was actually happening right here, right now, in this moment. "I like animals, too. I've always liked animals a lot. The show has a lot of animals. I think you're going to be pleasantly surprised. I think you're going to be pleasantly surprised with the show."

Anna nodded, twirled the skunk tail of her hat with her hand, then walked over to the piano, keeping her eyes pinned on Joanna. When she reached the bench, she bent down and crawled beneath it.

"Okay!" Joanna declared, waving her hands in the air and walking a rapid circle around the animals. "The show is about to start. Everybody take your seats. *Take your seats, everybody.*"

Jimmy and Sunny joined Tannis on the couch. I sat down cross-legged in an armchair.

"Showtime!" Joanna cried, and one by one, she hit a switch on the undersides of the animals until all had been activated. Hopping and croaking, waddling and quacking, the animals filled the room with the sounds of an electric barnyard, savanna, and circus combined. Joanna, beaming, looked as proud as if she herself had pressed her lips against their nostrils and breathed the gift of life into their mechanical bodies. The racket was overwhelming to me, but it seemed to appeal to Anna, who emerged from beneath the bench to crouch in front of the action.

The animals lurched out of their evenly spaced rows in every direction and soon began running into each other. It started to feel like a junk-car demolition derby when the skunk ran into the back of the bear and then tottered sideways, bumping into the pig and knocking it over onto its front hoofs, where it could no longer ambulate.

The swine was stuck, with its snout jammed into the floor, as the skunk ran afoul of its hindquarters and got its pelvis jammed between the pig's gyrating legs, giving the distinct impression of an attempt at cross-species insemination. The large duck waddled over and poked its beak mechanism into the crotch of the chicken, which squawked and vibrated in what appeared to be paroxysms of arousal, and the whole show began to look like the kind of thing you'd feel pretty embarrassed about seeing with your father.

Tannis, entirely unembarrassed in front of *her* father, was giggling, tears streaming down her face. My chest was heaving with the kind of laughter that comes not from hearing a joke, but from the sheer delight of witnessing the oddity of a situation. Taking our laughter as evidence of success, Joanna grinned in triumph.

"I told you," Sunny said. "It's a wonderful show."

"You did tell us, Sunny," Jim said. "I've never seen anything like that."

I clapped effusively. "Wow!" I said. "Amazing. What a show!" I continued clapping as I got up. "I'm going to put on some tea."

Joanna followed me to the kitchen. "You and me are alike, Maggie."

"You think so?" I attempted a breezily congenial inflection as I pulled a chamomile tea bag from the cabinet. "In what way?"

Joanna stood right next to me as I turned on the burner under the kettle. "We don't have children."

As I looked straight ahead, my vision blurred, and I forgot for a second what we were talking about. "It's true." Joanna continued.

"You and me don't have children. Most women do. But we don't. We don't have children."

I steadied myself against the marble-topped kitchen island. One time when I was playing field hockey in junior high school, a girl kneed me in the solar plexus and I couldn't breathe for about five seconds. I waited now, in the same way, for my breath to return. Joanna's statement was factual, so why this extreme reaction? Why did it feel like a sock in the guts? Most women *did* have children. That's just the way it was. It was also just the way it was that both Joanna and I did not.

The word itself made me dizzy: *childless*. In the big kitchen window that looked out at the pool, I could see the two of us reflected, Joanna standing next to me, simple and erect, and me leaning forward, bracing my hands on the counter.

Childless.

I'd heard that the politically correct form of expression was child-*free*, but that had the ring of self-flattery. It was true, though, that I had more freedom than most of my parenting friends, so maybe "child unencumbered" could better describe me. That wasn't entirely true either, though. I had little Anna in my life, and Ava and Addie, my nieces, and my nephew Will, and two godchildren, Nerys and Ruby Fern.

As if intuiting my thoughts and knowing just how to target my vulnerability, Joanna said, "It's not like Anna Michaela is your child. She's Tannis's child. You can play with her, but she's not your child. Anna Michaela's not with you all the time."

"True," I said.

"You don't really take care of her."

"No."

What she didn't say, but what I heard, was that I was a dabbler, someone who never *really* did anything, a surface person, a bad steward of gifts. Having other people's children in my life hadn't required a deep commitment of time and energy. It was nice, sporadically, to play with the "little dudes and dudettes," as I called them, for limited intervals and then give them back to their parents. It was nice to buy Anna a skunk hat for her birthday and then move along to something else. It was nice to read a book with glossy pages to Nerys and then do Legos with Will and then watch Addie's horseback riding lessons and then go to parent-child yoga with Ruby Fern—just like a dilettante.

The kettle began whistling, but the sound didn't register as it got louder and louder until Joanna was pushing my shoulder and yelling, "Your tea, Maggie. Your tea!" Jolted back into the room, I yanked the burner knob to the right and the shriek subsided to a whistle and then to a breathy wheeze, not unlike my own.

4

Easy Street

Over the next couple of years, Sunny and Joanna remained a consistent although relatively minor presence for Jim and me. But one windy September night in 2015, that presence blew more fully into our lives.

I had come home and fallen asleep waiting for Jim to return from work. The phone rang and I picked it up, still half-awake.

"She broke her hip! She broke her hip!"

"What?" I said. "Who is this?"

"She broke her hip, Maggie. She broke her hip!"

"Joanna?"

"I have to talk to Jim."

"Jim's at work. Who broke their—?"

"I need to talk to Jim. My mother fell in the apartment and she broke her hip and she's at Kaiser Permanente hospital."

"Oh God. Okay, Joanna," I said, sitting up and putting on my glasses. "Is that Kaiser on Sunset?"

"Yes. Kaiser Permanente, Kaiser Permanente."

"Okay. And where are you, Joanna?"

"I'm here, too."

"At the hospital?"

"Yes. Kaiser is the hospital."

"Are you in the ER?"

"What?"

"In the Emergency Room?"

"What?"

"Did you go in an ambulance?"

"Yes."

"Alright, Joanna. Just stay there. Jim is at work, but I can come over."

"Jim can't come?"

"No, Joanna, but I can. I'm going to hang up the phone, alright? You sit tight."

Sunny had surgery the following day, and after a week at Kaiser was moved to a nursing facility called Pure Hearts Care, a small, private facility in North Hollywood run by a petite Filipino woman in her seventies named Reyna. Had women been allowed to command soldiers when she was young, I have no doubt Reyna would have risen to the rank of colonel or general in the Philippine Armed Forces. When she snapped commands to her staff, I could faintly hear platoons of boot heels clicking together seven thousand miles away.

Jim was in the middle of a particularly demanding period with a new show, so it fell on me to stop in on Sunny on a regular basis and take Joanna to visit her. We developed a routine. I would pick up Joanna on Saturday mornings, and on our way we would stop by Larchmont to buy a box of mango cupcakes from a store whose gimmick is offering super-small cupcakes for the same price as full-size.

On our drives to visit Sunny, Joanna and I would listen to songs from my iTunes library, a playlist that includes everything from lyrical folk music of the 1960s to lyrical folk music of the 1970s. On one of our trips, the thud of Joanna's half-sleeping head bouncing off the passenger window made me think that maybe I should play something *Joanna* liked. So I found a link to "Dancing Queen" and Bluetoothed it to the car's audio system. Leonard Cohen stopped crooning/

keening one of the dirge-poems I find so uplifting, and "Dancing Queen" began.

Joanna's lips parted. Her eyes lifted, as if she were seeing an apparition. Then her hands rose and touched her ears, because *there*, she seemed to realize, was where the miracle was taking place.

"I can barely believe my ears, Maggie," she said, hushed and reverent. "I can barely believe my ears." Joanna had seen my smartphone and knew the word "internet" and some of what the Wide World Web, as she called it, was capable of. But what was happening here in this car on the corner of Wilshire and Santa Monica was like nothing she had ever conceived. She held on to her ears like the boy with hearing impairment, whom I had once seen in an old photo, upon first hearing Beethoven: awed, thunderstruck, and a tad frightened.

I was a witch and now she knew it. "How . . . how did you . . . ?"

"Magic," I said, crinkling my nose like Samantha from *Bewitched*. Joanna stared at me.

"No, I'm just kidding." I said, breaking the spell. "I found it on my phone. On the internet. There's a way you can make it play in the car."

Joanna breathed a sigh of relief but continued to regard me with a new wariness and respect for the potential powers I might possess. That afternoon I played "Dancing Queen" seven times, thinking she would eventually tire of the song. But that was naïve. This was a woman who had demonstrated no ability to tire of "Dancing Queen," or anything else for that matter, and I knew that. I knew quite a bit about Joanna, actually.

Sometimes when I'd tell people the story of Jim's and my relationship with Joanna, they would conclude, "Ah, so she's like your family," and I'd think, *Weelll, I'm not sure I would exactly say* that . . . A biological connection isn't a requirement for someone to be part of your family, of course, but family *does* seem to involve some kind of shared roots or common cause or a feeling of being simpatico. Joanna and I had none of those things.

What we did have was familiarity. We were familiar with each other's little ways of being in the world. We were, you could say, *familiars*. Joanna often told me that there were things about her that only her mother knew, like what happened at her birth and what food would be too spicy for her, but there were things I'd come to know about her as well.

One Sunday, when we were driving up to see Sunny, I snapped off the volume, unwilling to be thrust once again into the chorus of "young and sweet, only seventeen, digging the Dancing Queen."

"Hey," I said, "Let's listen to something else. What's something else you like?"

"'Dancing Queen' is good."

"Oh c'mon, Joanna. Name something else. What's another song you like?"

"I like 'Dancing Queen' fine."

Undeterred, I pressed until finally she came up with a song from the *Golden Girls* episode "Journey to the Center of Attention."

"Dorothy sings it at the bar called the Rusty Anchor," Joanna told me. "Blanche is mad that Dorothy is a better singer. Blanche is the one who is supposed to be the good singer." Then Joanna sang the opening line of the song, zipping through like a conductor marking beats. "*Gone is the romance that was so divine. Tis broken and cannot be mended.*"

I typed the lyric and episode name into my phone, found a recording of Bea Arthur singing the jazz standard "What'll I Do?" and then clicked play, sending the song through the Bluetooth system. It took Joanna a moment to realize what she was hearing, that the song playing now was the very song she had just been speaking of. When she understood, she erupted in laughter, as if the absurdity of it all was just too much. She appeared to be whisked into pure glee. "I can barely believe my ears, Maggie."

I looked at Joanna, pleased. Joanna looked back at me, her laughter trickling away, now purely mystified. "How . . . how did you do it?"

"Like I said before. Magic."

I smile, trying to produce a twinkle in my eye.

"I know you're joking, Maggie. I know you're joking."

"Am I?" I purred, as I twitched my nose, "Because I can also read your mind. I know what you're thinking."

"You do?"

"Yeah, you're thinking, *When this song is over, can we play 'Dancing Queen'?*"

Joanna turned saucer-eyed. "Yes! That's exactly what I was thinking!"

At Pure Hearts, Sunny's face would light up when she saw us. "Oh, you're here! And you brought the teeny cakes! Mango. My favorite."

Reyna was reliably stern. She was busy and had no time for pleasantries or the charm of overpriced, undersized cupcakes. "Cupcakes no good," she said. "Too much sugar. Many patient diabetes. Diabetes no good. No cupcakes."

After a couple of these warnings, I told Sunny to hide the cupcakes so I wouldn't get in trouble. I didn't want to be on Reyna's bad side.

When we drove home from Pure Hearts Care, Joanna and I would often fall into silence, both thinking our thoughts, content to watch the scenery pass. When we passed the Hollywood Bowl I would invariably think, *I should go to the Hollywood Bowl sometime. I should start liking classical music. People who like classical music seem generally to be happier than me.*

To be in the presence of another human being while listening to music and not feel the need to talk was not something I was used to. I was surprised to find it felt like a small luxury, to be freed from the obligation of small talk and maintaining another's impression of me.

Joanna's favorite song after "Dancing Queen" was Bob Marley's "Three Little Birds." Once while we were listening to the reggae standard, I noticed Joanna snap for a couple of beats and was struck by the power of her snap. It was a strong snap, clear and sharp. Like a bandleader who had perfected the art of being heard above the night-club din.

"Joanna," I said with sincere enthusiasm. "That's a great snap you have there."

Joanna stopped, her right hand frozen, thumb pad to middle finger pad. Then she looked up at me. "I do?"

"Yes. Yes, you do," I said, pleased to see how this small compliment had moved her. "It's a really loud snap. I bet you could hear your snap from across the street."

Joanna laughed, shook her head, and repeated to herself, "Across the street." Then, in one swift motion, she slammed her middle finger down against her ring finger and . . . SNAP. Joanna seemed to assess her skill from an onlooker's perspective and concluded with pleasure, "I guess it *is* a pretty good snap."

That day began Joanna's and my "driving and snapping" tradition. I would initiate the activity with the phrase "Wanna snap?" because voicing this sentence always amused me. Really, the whole activity in general amused me. We would snap in the car on the way to and from visiting Sunny for the entirety of "Three Little Birds," despite the fact that neither of us was blessed with even the most basic sense of rhythm and could rarely get our snaps to consistently sync with either the beat or each other.

Yet we snapped on.

Joanna and I.

It's not an easy thing to do: snap for a whole song. Snapping tends to be an in-and-out "do it when you feel it" sort of thing. It's not an undertaking typically pursued with commitment and focus from the beginning to the end of a song. The way Joanna and I snap is not for the faint of heart, weak of spirit, or infirm of knuckle. I always hope someone in a car beside us at a stoplight will glance over and catch sight of us: two middle-aged women staring straight ahead and snapping. Badly, but dutifully, with rigor and dedication. If I were on the outside looking in, I would find it a glorious sight to witness.

Once, when I turned down the music after snapping through several songs, Joanna said, "I still get my period, you know."

"Oh," I faltered, "that's . . ."

The lift of her chin and the brightness of her eyes told me she was hoping for some sort of congratulations.

"That's *cool,* Joanna," I said, trying to deliver on the expectation.

Joanna's smile suggested I elaborate.

"*Very* cool," I obliged.

Joanna's announcement was actually a little surprising to me because, without having given it any thought, I assumed that a woman in her mid-fifties would have at least started menopause. My mother started at fifty. I'm forty-four.

"I get it every month," Joanna declared. "I bleed every month. That's the truth. And I bleed *hard,* Maggie. I bleed *hard.*"

"Oh, okay." I said neutrally, hoping to provide a blank canvas on which Joanna could compose her desired response.

Joanna studied me, then nodded before dropping her head. "I wish Jim could drive me to Pure Hearts Care."

"Well, yeah, Joanna," I sighed. "He's working, so you're stuck with me."

"I guess because you don't work."

Like an instinctive child, she knew just where to needle me.

"I most certainly do," I spat, sudden rage kicking in my chest. "I most certainly do work. I work hard."

Joanna's eyes remained focused on the road in front of us.

"Just because I don't talk to you about my work and just because I spend a shitload of hours driving you around and buying cupcakes for your mother and goodness knows what doesn't mean I don't work."

Joanna began rocking back and forth, but I hadn't finished.

"If you want to know, Joanna, I do a lot of work. I am working on a screenplay, for one thing. I am working right now to try to get a job on a television show. I'm writing a book. I'm doing a lot of other things all the time."

Joanna smirked, then she said, "I mean work you get paid for, Maggie. Like a job in an office. Work like a job in an office like Jim has."

Nobody had ever called me a dilettante, but Joanna was coming close. She would have taken the word and flung it squarely at my carefully constructed identity if she had known it. There was no need for that, though. What she was saying was enough.

My cheeks felt hot, and I was breathing in short, fast spurts.

"That's not true, Joanna. I *do* make money. I make money for writing jobs, sometimes."

"Not as much as Jim."

"Yeah? Well, a lot more than you!"

I am not proud of having said that. Offering to drive a woman to visit her injured mother at a private nursing facility and then yelling at her in the car that her income was smaller than mine wasn't a shining moment, and I knew it.

"Sorry, Joanna."

I felt embarrassed and crummy and just wanted to go to bed.

"For what?"

Joanna trafficked in truth. She felt no guilt at having provoked me with her insistent rivalry, and she felt no resentment that I lashed out. What she said was true, and what I said was true, and there was no problem to it. We drove along, Joanna seemingly without any emotional residue from the conflict, until I dropped her off.

The question I'm guessing you might be asking at this point is *why?* Why help this woman who could somehow pinpoint my most private, guarded insecurities and jab in a perfectly suited sword before twisting it until I doubled over? Why give my time and money to someone who had overt designs on my husband and would be happy to find out my life had been untimely snuffed out so that she could replace me and take over my life? Why would I choose to undertake such an aggravating and demoralizing enterprise?

You might think I would be well poised to answer this question. The motives I am probing are, after all, my own. But there are plenty of things I do that I find totally baffling. Here's an example: When my husband and I are talking, about whatever we might be talking about, at home, or riding in the car, or waiting in line for a movie, and he pauses for what I feel is an excessive amount of time, I will make a little joke.

I will say "Maggie," as if he had forgotten my name and needed to be reminded.

Although that little—and dizzyingly lame—witticism has not made Jim laugh or express even the slightest hint of amusement since sometime in the late twentieth century, I have continued to use it about twice a week, every week, over all the years since, which means that I've repeated it more than two thousand separate times. And I honestly can't tell you why. Why continue to do something that no longer amuses either of us? I don't know. And I couldn't tell you exactly why I helped Sunny and Joanna, although I am working on a list of possible motivations:

1. *Genuine Human Empathy.* Simple empathy must contribute something to my motivation, but I suspect in a pie chart of reasons it would represent a rather measly wedge of pie, a portion perhaps suited for an elderly diabetic lady on her birthday.

2. *Gratitude.* The pleasure of receiving thanks could be part of what drives me, and with Sunny, this pleasure could account for a sizeable slice. I enjoyed her robust appreciation of little gestures like a plate of Oreo cookies or the lending of a swimming suit. It was gratifying to hear

her say that I was her guardian angel and mean it whole-heartedly. With Joanna, on the other hand, desire for appreciation couldn't be counted among my rewards. I'm not a masochist—at least I don't think so, though in the complications of my inner life, anything seems possible.

3. *Image Maintenance.* The greatest slice of motivation pie, of course, belongs to bolstering my very own ever-wavering self-regard. It's a slice for a plump, pie-happy couple. The actions of caring sculpt my self-image in a way I find pleasing, upgrading my personal avatar, my existential bitmoji, up to something brighter and cuter than her natural anguished and shadowy shape. When I helped Sunny and Joanna, she grew wide, compassionate eyes, and her hands reached out like a dedicated NICU nurse or Bono to a fan.

4. *Comfort.* Comfort makes up a bigger slice than I would have expected. I go through life in a state of almost constant disquiet, and something about spending time around Joanna comforted me. Joanna more than Sunny, actually. It may be that spending time around Joanna felt comforting because, unlike me, she doesn't cover her private self with a public face. With her, there was no artifice to contend with. A cigar is just a cigar, or a rose a rose, or the nose of a dog or cat a penis, I suppose.

There's an interesting wrinkle in the comfort Joanna's naked honesty provided; it often came at an uncomfortable price, such as when I had to tell Joanna that Jim and I weren't going to be in Los Angeles one Halloween. It was the fifth fall after we established our family/Cabbage-Patch-doll Polaroid portrait tradition, and Jimmy and I planned to go to New Jersey to see his father. When I gave Joanna the news, she was heartbroken and cried like an infant. Tears and mucus ran unimpeded from her nose down to her mouth and puddled on her lips, mixing with saliva. When I leaned forward to console her, she wailed, "But it's Halloween!" and the salted concoction sprayed with the force of her breath into my own, very private mouth.

I did not recoil in disgust. Instead, engaged with Joanna's distress, I simply wiped my mouth and put my hands on her shoulders and said, "I know how sad you feel, Joanna. I'm so sorry to disappoint you."

A part of me observed that if Joanna had been an infant, and I her mother, I might not have been grossed out at all. An innate biological drive to care for my adorable, small, helpless being would have kicked in and rendered the transfer of bodily fluids tolerable. I was not Joanna's mother, yet there I was, full of acceptance and offering care. At this thought, a cartoonish image of a woman accepting the assault of alien bodily fluids despite the absence of a compensatory maternal drive formed in my mind, and my bitmoji threw up her arms and cheered to no one in particular, *How do you like me now?*

That episode was nice but certainly not comfortable, and neither was the time Joanna unleashed on me in a furious stream: "You're very lucky. Just like Tiger Woods is lucky. He wouldn't be a famous golfer if somebody hadn't given him a golf club when he was two years old. You wouldn't be able to get a job if you didn't get to go to school—"

I protested, but she wouldn't stop or even slow down.

"No, Maggie," she roared. "No, Maggie. You wouldn't have gotten those television acting parts that I saw you in on TV, either. Jim wouldn't have even married you, Jim wouldn't have even let you live at his house if you didn't look like Katherine Heigl. Like Katherine Heigl but not as pretty, not as pretty. Ask anyone, Maggie. You're lucky you get to live on Easy Street."

As uncomfortable as Joanna's compulsive honesty could be, on some level, I appreciated it. It was always good to know what she was thinking. There was no subtext. No hidden but deeply felt truth. No lurking, sublimated resentments like the ones I harbored so stealthily toward so many people in my life.

Instead of a backhanded "must be nice," Joanna offered a frank "You have it easier than me and it's not because you deserve it. You lucked out."

And Joanna was right.

I *was* lucky. I would never have gotten a writing job without an education. Without my marriage to Jim, I might not have gotten that first television acting job. It was also true that if I were less pretty, Jim might not have married me or "let" me live in his house. Joanna was just saying that I was the product of a variety of forces over which I had no control and for which I could claim no credit. That was the truth even if I didn't like it. Like most people in our culture, I privilege a narrative of agency over the reality of chance. I think that such privileging creates a lot of unnecessary pressure, a pressure the ancient Greeks didn't have, for example.

The Greeks saw themselves as subject to the whims of powerful and capricious gods, not as beings capable of manufacturing our own fates. Oedipus was really upset about how things came down, sure, but he didn't think, *I totally fucked everything up. I hate myself.* He believed himself to be at the mercy of powers beyond his control. Those who used to be called "unfortunates" are now referred to as losers, who must bear not only the burden of their tragedies but also the responsibility. We live in a world where we are even required to *make our own luck.*

Make our own luck? I know the cleverness of the phrase rests in the subversion of the idea of luck, and that the subverted concept has a valuable directive in terms of using all of one's resources and energy to create the circumstances where so-called luck can occur. I get the subversion and subsequent reorientation. I get that the phrase "make your own luck" is cool and catchy. I get that it's only four syllables and that four syllables makes for a fun slogan.

But . . . *fuck that.*

Fuck each of those four syllables.

I believe "make your own luck" constitutes full-scale cultural gas-lighting, as I will tell you after I've had a glass or two of merlot. I like to imagine the Greeks would have sympathy for my plight. *How does Maggie bear it?* I picture them crying to the sky, dropping to their knees, clasping their breasts. *How can she bear to think she creates her own fortune in light of the punishing, overwhelming evidence to the contrary? Why can't she lay down her burden?*

The song lyrics from the traditional hymn repeat in my head, but not unpleasantly.

Lay down your burden. Down by the riverside. Down by the riverside.

A loop maybe, but not a strange loop, not a punishing loop.

An assurance.

I hear the choir kick in from a long-lost memory.

Down by the riverside. Down by the riverside.

Hands are clapping and the tambourine rings out.

The Greeks are right, I think.

What a relief it would be to lay down my burden down by the riverside, to give up my preoccupation with how well I'm doing and assign responsibility to someone else, to anyone or anything else, or everything else other than my own infuriatingly inadequate personal power. I want to stop blaming this all-consuming, recalcitrant nub inside me called *self* who is always disobeying my wishes and messing everything up.

I have slavishly devoted myself to almost constant self-evaluation. Nobody but me is pondering the question, *How does Maggie Rowe stack up against others as an overall human being? How does she compare to other fortysomething, tall, thin, and artificially blond women in the arts and enter-tainment industry?*

How is Maggie Rowe compensating for her decision to not have a child? no one wonders.

They never ask me at Starbucks, when I'm ordering my double-tall nonfat cappuccino, "Is what you're doing today instead of raising children enough to justify that decision?" They don't say, and I'm sure don't think, "What *are* you doing instead and why can't you be better at it?" And none of the truck drivers dropping off produce at Larchmont Wine and Cheese are tweeting to each other from their vehicles, "What's keeping *that* one from getting a better overall existence score in comparison to an arbitrary sampling of other human beings? #what-I-can't-stop-thinking-about." "I mean, does anyone know when she's going to catch up to her chief competitor, KATHERINE HEIGL? #really-important-questions."

No. It's just me—or the *me* in me—or the *me* in me in me.

This joyless psychic activity has sucked up more of my energy than perhaps any other life endeavor, yet it is of no interest to any point of consciousness outside of my own head and it makes me feel . . . bad. It's like I'm starring in a shitty movie only I can get on VOD and then streaming it in a loop over and over and over.

And I wonder if that energy might be better spent. No, I don't wonder. I know.

I want to make an addition to my envy list. I want to add a category for those who do not suffer from envy. I envy those who are blessed with ease and gratitude, and I do mean "blessed" because no matter how hard I will myself to be grateful for all I have received—and I have received a *lot*—being a fundamentally grateful person seems as elusive to me as becoming a motion-picture star or writing like F. Scott Fitzgerald or singing like Lady Gaga or rocking in my boat like a fisherman on Mykonos who falls asleep contentedly to the slapping rhythms of the sea.

Gratitude shimmers perpetually in the distance, for me, as I wither in the glare of self-judgment. And gratitude was about to become even more out of reach than before. My cushy, easy situation, with my warm, witty husband on our leafy, tree-lined street, plagued only by a longing for the life not lived, was about to be slashed.

In only one month, I would find myself yearning for the miseries of anybody but me, even Joanna, Joanna Hergert, whom I had pitied so grandly and helped with such self-conscious kindness for the last eight years; whom I had flattered myself into believing I could rescue; whose own personal tragedy also waited; would shortly seem to me, despite everything, compared to my own ravaged existence, to be a breezy, uncomplicated rambler, taking a relaxing, post-siesta promenade down the wide sidewalks of Easy Street.

5

A Hard Birth

I f you were a dilettante who dreamed of being an accomplished professional able to use the phrase "my body of work" and not be referring to a desk drawer crammed with unproduced scripts, if your career ambitions were both focused and promising yet also frustrated at every turn, if you had one way and another wound up in Hollywood, California, and set your sights on a writing career in television or film, if you had worked diligently for a decade and a half and finally been offered a respectably paying job in the writer's room on a critically acclaimed, Emmy Award–winning comedy series, how would you feel?

Would you feel nervous that you wouldn't be able to do the job once you got there? Check. Would you wonder on the first day if you should put on a cozy mid-thigh suede skirt with your favorite shiny boots or, since that might make you look like a former go-go dancer foolishly clinging to her youth, opt instead for the more standard female writer uniform of old-concert T-shirt and fashionably ripped jeans? Check. Would you argue with yourself about whether you should keep quiet in the beginning and listen before venturing an opinion or speak up right away to show everyone what you had to offer? Check. Would you chastise yourself not only for being silent at the beginning like some "retreating daffodil" (before remembering that the phrase was "shrinking violet") but also for that pretentious suggestion that the character who felt like a monster should hide in a church, like Quasimodo in *The Hunchback of Notre Dame*, a pitch you for some reason felt compelled to clarify with "Quasimodo from the book, not the cartoon"? Check. And would you still feel, finally, that you had accomplished something tangible and be proud of yourself in your new job?

Maybe not. Let me explain.

Fifteen years into my Hollywood journey, I got staffed on a Netflix show. I was happy about it, but there was a catch. It was the same show my husband had been working on for four seasons. Classic nepotism, right? Another by-product of Easy Street? Except I had worked for the showrunner previously on several different projects, and Jimmy did not suggest me for the job. Also, showrunners don't just go around Frisbee-ing jobs out to writers' wives willy-nilly.

Yet, sitting at the table and chipping in my two cents, I still couldn't help flushing with the embarrassed conviction that everyone saw me not as a peer who, like them, earned her position through years of hard work and demonstrated excellence, but as Jimmy's wife.

I was afraid they all saw me as the Mafioso's girlfriend in a comedy-drama set in Little Italy, who has a seat on the cement-plant oversight committee or gets a role in a big film or is dealt into the exclusive poker game just because she's Johnny Bag-o-Donuts' special lady. Everyone rolls their eyes at each other when she asks things like, "Can the camera still see me even when I'm not looking at it?" or "Do I need to tell everyone if I'm bluffing?"

When I confessed to a friend that I was worried I was hired only as a favor to Jim, she assured me in her most comforting voice that nobody would say that to my face. Still, I was grateful for the job. It was great to be working even if the circumstances of my employment did as much to undermine as bolster my self-image.

One little-mentioned benefit of having a regular job is that it gives you a reason to dress properly and try to look reasonably nice on a daily basis. One morning before work, I was blow-drying my hair, hoping to move its texture toward bolt-of-silk luscious and away from its natural ratty-basement-carpet-after-a-flood stringy when I noticed that the phone was ringing.

I crossed into the bedroom to pick it up, bracing for yet another call from Tre the Tree Listener, who tirelessly marketed himself as "L.A.'s most intuitive tree trimmer" and seemed unable to accept that I was really just not interested in tree services at this time, even though I might not realize how much my trees cried out for trimming because I, unlike Tre or the Lorax, could not hear their innermost tree-hearts' desires. But when I picked up the handset, the caller ID read not TREE-LISTENER TRE, but my New York–based literary agency. I sucked in my breath.

She told me that we had just sold my first book.

It was a present I wanted to keep unwrapping to discover it anew. My book was going to be published. It would have an actual cover and actual pages, and real-life people, not just those who populated my imagination, would read it.

Oh, what a fine and mighty morning it was.

I sailed down the road in my Camry, windows down, cool wind whipping, feeling as if I were on the high seas. Amazingly, I hit no stoplights on my way to Beverly Hills and no cars got in my way. The light was at its Los Angeles best, warm and rosy, and the air felt the way it always did the first day of summer break, fresh and free. It was as if the town and Nature herself had conspired to honor this hallowed day.

But I started to feel uneasy. And then, there it was. I felt the awful twinge, sharp and familiar.

The hell twinge. The same feeling I used to have as a child when I worried about eternal damnation.

Even after I lost the theological concerns in my twenties, the bind did not fully resolve and I continued to feel the "hell" twinge every now and then. And here it was, hard and sharp. I reminded myself that it would pass, as it almost always did. I just needed to shift my focus. I drew a deep breath and let my mind be consumed by the glorious fact that I was about to have *my very own book published.*

That night, brushing my teeth before bed, I looked at my reflection in the mirror. A soon-to-be published author and working television writer looked back at me, without apology or excuse. *Dilettante* did not fit as well as it had before.

I spat toothpaste into my vessel sink with a powerful, victorious flourish. I plucked my bottle of Paxil from the medicine cabinet, unscrewed the top, and shook my regular forty-milligram dose out into my palm, just I had been doing every night before bed since I was nineteen. I paused.

Do these pills even do anything for me anymore? I wondered.

I was first prescribed Paxil at Grace Point. With the help of a doctor and a heavy dosage of Paxil along with two other medications, I was able to complete college. Years later, when my looping led to a second breakdown, I turned to secular therapist Dr. Rosen and Klonopin. Over time, the inexplicable "hell" fear and corresponding word looping began to subside. I would still have rash-like flare-ups, but over time they became less severe and less frequent until eventually I found I no longer needed either the therapist or the Klonopin. I continued to take my daily dose of Paxil, but from time to time I would skip a day, or occasionally two, and I'd never really notice any difference. *I'd really been fine for so long,* I thought. Maybe I was more normal than I gave myself credit for. I was now gainfully employed. I was a functional member of society.

I looked at the pale green, lozenge-shaped pill in my hand. How much efficacy could all its little Paxil molecules really have in my system after over two decades of daily exposure? Maybe it was just functioning at this point as a placebo, and maybe I could live perfectly well without placebos, and maybe I was just perfectly fine, and maybe I had been just perfectly fine for a good long while. I thought about calling Dr. Rosen, but his office was all the way over in Santa Monica, and he was expensive. Plus, I was fine. I felt fine. I would be fine.

As I turned on the faucet to clean the basin, I made a decision that may or may not have been wise.

Eighty-three degrees Fahrenheit and 87 percent humidity.

Los Angeles is famous for its comfortable climate. It can be hot in the summer, but everyone says, "It's a dry heat." And they're right, on average. But occasionally the air can be surprisingly humid, and giant thunderclouds can build up over the mountains. You can get flash-flood warnings for the desert washes and sometimes even a spate of hail in town that sends children running into their front yards with palms cupped for the exotic ice particles, their faces turned upward to the surprising sky.

That Saturday had been warmer and more humid than most. The thick air reminded me of the sultry summer nights I loved so much growing up in Chicagoland, and I left my office door open to the velvet breeze. Working with my dog, Holly, on my lap, I was attempting to reach a verdict in the case of "right before falling asleep" versus "right before falling to sleep" and going over and over it in my mind when I heard a wrenching wail from somewhere outside the house.

The dog's ears stood up, but she didn't move.

"What was that, Holly?" I asked.

She burrowed her snout into the crook of my elbow and sighed.

The wail came again.

An injured dog, I thought, imagining a stray caught in the ribs by the fender of a car and a horrified driver looking through his windshield at a moaning beast in the middle of the road. I petted Holly, safe and sound, then picked her up, placed her on the ground, and stood to investigate.

The wail rose again and deepened into an unbound howl.

Could it be a coyote?

I stepped through the open office door out into the damp, heavy night, blocking Holly from following and closing the door behind me.

I'd only ever heard an actual coyote howl in movies or as recorded sound cues in Sam Shepard plays, so it was hard to know. A coyote seemed unlikely, but someone had tacked up flyers around the neighborhood reporting sightings on the nearby golf course. COYOTES ARE LIVING ON THE GOLF COURSE AND COME OUT TO PROWL THE NEIGHBORHOOD AT NIGHT, the flyers warned. THEY ARE BOLD, HUNGRY, AND CRAFTY. "Crafty" I figured was probably based less on actual reported behavior and more on the flyer-maker's remembrances of Warner Bros.' cunning Wile E. Coyote, who, while no match for the Roadrunner, could probably outsmart the run-of-the-mill, average-witted dogs of Hancock Park.

I walked down our front steps and looked from one end of the street to the other. I saw no dogs, no coyotes, nothing out of the ordinary. The street was quiet but charged somehow, its damp air electrified by something not quite right. Inside, Holly was whining with an unusual plaintiveness, as if sensing something was amiss. I turned to walk back up the steps to comfort her when the sound came again, fierce and desperate.

The cry seemed farther away than when I had been in the house. Could it be coming from the *back* yard?

I opened the door and went back into my office, bending down to rub Holly on the soft folds of her chin as I made my way to the hallway. As I walked toward the TV room, the sound got louder and became more distinct. It seemed almost human now, almost like speech.

"Myrrrhah!" it seemed be calling on a long descending howl. "Myrrrrrhaah!"

When I got to the kitchen, I hesitated. The room was dark, but the lights were on by the pool in the backyard, and through the picture-glass window behind our breakfast table I could see the wounded creature. Joanna stood on the brick patio, head thrown back, mouth gaping wide, grabbing her hair by the roots and howling into the sky. The primal scene reminded me of Greek tragedy, Medea standing over her murdered children, Agave holding the head of her son in her hands, Hecuba wailing for her slaughtered daughter.

I flung open the door and ran down the steps.

"Joanna!"

"Myrrrhaaaah!" she bellowed.

"Joanna! What happened?"

"Myrrrrrrrhaaaaah!" she roared into my face, her eyelids peeled back.

"What are you saying? I can't understand you, Joanna. What is it?"

Joanna clutched her belly as if she'd been shot and needed to hold in her guts. "It's MUR-DER," she spat out clearly.

"Who?" I asked, feeling as if I'd stepped into a scene from an unknown play.

"When you're at that age . . . when you're that age," she bleated in broken sentences. "You're old, you're too old, when you're old in a place like that . . . nobody . . . nobody . . ." Her eyes were darting to the left and to the right, to the ground, to the trees, to the house. Her hands yanked at her shirt and then at her pants, pulling the fabric away from her flesh as if she could rip herself out of her own skin. Then, suddenly, she became still and spoke quietly with a lucidity that shot a chill down my spine. "They don't check. Nobody checks what happens in a place like that. Anyone can get away with murder."

"*Who* are you talking about, Joanna? WHO?" But as Joanna's eyes snagged desperately onto mine, I knew.

"Oh, no," I said. My heart knocked in my chest. "What happened? Tell me what happened."

"When you're old in a place like that, nobody checks. Nobody checks. The police don't check. 'Accidents happen,' she said. And then she laughed. *She laughed!*"

"Who did? Who laughed?"

"'Accidents happen,' she said."

I guided Joanna toward a patio chair, as if I were following stage directions. I was obeying a script in my head, but the scene wasn't right. I had never seen a play like this one and didn't know what character I was supposed to be playing. Nonetheless, I made a choice. I pulled a chair up next to hers and took her hands in mine. "Now, Joanna," I said in my steadiest and firmest voice, "please tell me what happened."

Joanna yanked her hands away and drove the heels of her palms into her cheekbones, curling her fingers over her eyes.

"I saw her yesterday. I was with her."

"You were with Sunny?"

"A taxi at the stoplight took me because I knew the address of Pure Hearts Home Care. I knew the address because I had it written down on a card in my purse." Her fingers pulled together to create blinders on the outside of her eyes. "I went to Pure Hearts Home Care, and Reyna said my mother wasn't paying enough."

"Wasn't paying enough *rent*?"

"Reyna said that all the other people at Pure Hearts Home Care were paying fifteen hundred dollars a month in rent, but my mother was only paying twelve hundred dollars a month, twelve hundred dollars a month."

"Okay, so then what?"

"'Your mother,' Reyna said. 'Your mother has to start paying fifteen hundred dollars a month like everybody else.' But I said we couldn't pay fifteen hundred a month like everybody else. We could only pay twelve hundred. We could only pay twelve hundred, so Reyna killed her."

"But Joanna—"

"*That's what happened!*"

"Alright."

"*It's NOT alright!*"

"No," I said, pulling back, "it's not. Nothing about this is alright, but Joanna, I'm sure Reyna didn't kill Sunny. I can promise you that."

"She did!" Joanna cried, dropping her hands from her face, baring her teeth, and slamming her hands onto her thighs. "She killed her! She killed her because we didn't pay. Because we *didn't pay*. She said 'accidents happen' and she laughed. 'Your mother died last night,' she said. 'Accidents happen.' And then she laughed. *She laughed!*"

I inhaled and released an extended exhalation before nodding with a controlled calm. "Alright, can you tell me about Sunny? How did she seem yesterday? How was she when you left her?"

"She had a chipped a tooth." Joanna ran her tongue along her front teeth, stopping at a right incisor. "This one." She tapped the tooth with her tongue. "This one."

"Okay, so she had a chipped tooth." I said, stacking up the facts.

"She chipped it because Reyna took my mother's walker away. She took my mother's walker away because she said she didn't want my mother walking around in the middle of the night and falling and then making a lawsuit. My mother needs the walker to go pee, but Reyna wants my mother to go pee in her diaper, but my mother doesn't want that. She wants to go in the toilet. She wants to go in the toilet, so she went to the bathroom in the middle of the night without her walker, and she fell and she chipped her tooth."

"Okay, so . . . but when you left her yesterday, was Sunny okay? Besides having a chipped tooth, how did she seem?"

"She's always had her mind, Maggie. You know that. She's got her mind as much as you do, Maggie, as much as you. Wouldn't you agree she's got her mind?"

"Yes. I would. Nothing wrong with her mind."

"No. She can figure out how to ride a bus to anywhere in the city, and someone who doesn't have their mind wouldn't be able to figure out how to ride a bus to anywhere in the city. They wouldn't be able to figure that out. You've got to agree with me on that. Even I know that much."

"You're absolutely right. But, Joanna . . . you're saying that when you left Pure Hearts Care yesterday, your mother was okay, right? She had a chipped tooth, but she was okay?"

"She was okay and then . . . today . . ." Her voice trailed off and she became almost eerily still.

I reached again for her hands. "What happened *today*?"

Joanna didn't pull away this time. Instead, her hands became soft in mine and her shoulders slackened. "What happened today . . . I was in the apartment and Reyna called me. Reyna called me and she said, 'I'm sorry to tell you your mother is dead.' And . . . and . . . and . . . 'You can come pick up her belongings any time you want,' she said. And so I went to Pure Hearts Home Care in the taxi because I had the address on the card and Reyna gave me a big plastic garbage bag of belongings of my mother's and she said, 'Accidents happen.' And she laughed."

"What kind of accident? Did your mother fall again?"

"Reyna said it must have been her heart. 'She must have had an arrest.'"

"An arrest? Did she say *coronary* arrest? Did Sunny have a heart attack?"

"That's what Reyna said, but she's lying."

Joanna curled her hands into fists and rubbed her knuckles against her eyes so violently I feared she would damage them. An awful image of fluid bursting from bloody sockets and pouring down her cheeks flashed through my mind.

"Careful!" I said, pulling her fists away. But her hands broke from my grip, flew to her scalp, and grasped her hair by the roots, pulling as if to yank the thick curls from her head.

How do you comfort Medea or Electra or Clytemnestra? I had no idea.

"Oh, Joanna," I said. "This is so so *so* sad. So terribly, *terribly* sad. But you're going to be fine. It's going to be alright, Joanna." The lie in my voice was blatant. Everything was *not* going to be all right. Joanna was not going to be fine, possibly ever again. The only person in the world who knew her, besides Jim and me, had been her mother, Sunny, with hair like sunflowers but dyed black to look like Elizabeth Taylor. Sunny, who loved tiny mango cupcakes and French horns and seeing her only daughter belt out "Dancing Queen." Sunny, who was Joanna's only living relation. And now she was dead, and Joanna was alone.

Joanna had clearly been thinking the same thing. "My mother," she said, her eyes now locked with mine, "is the only person in the world that loves me. I know Jim likes me, but I'm not family. My mother is my only family."

I looked away from the red-rimmed, pleading eyes to which I could offer no comfort. Next to me on the patio table were some empty beer bottles, one lying on its side, and a bowl of opened pistachio shells.

This poor woman, I was thinking when the crunch of Jim's tires pulling up the driveway and the familiar whir of his car engine prompted me to jump to my feet.

"Stay here," I instructed Joanna. "I'll be right back." I felt compelled to tell Jim myself. I wanted him to hear the news from me, though as I walked quickly toward the gate, I wondered why. Did I think I could control his reaction? Did I want to prepare him? For his sake? For hers? I opened the back gate and stepped into the driveway, assembling the bits of information in my mind. Joanna was here. She showed up in the backyard howling like an animal, in shock. Sunny was dead.

I waited for Jim to get out of his car, wondering if Reyna could *possibly* have actually murdered Sunny. The idea was preposterous, of course, but I could follow Joanna's logic. It *did* seem like an awfully big coincidence that Sunny died the day after she refused to pay more money. But no, the idea was crazy. Life wasn't a nineteenth-century melodrama featuring a villain twisting his black mustache between spindly fingers updated to a seventy-year-old pint-size Filipino nurse greedy for an extra $300 a month.

Although, why would Reyna say a heart attack was an accident? A heart attack isn't an accident.

When Jim saw me frozen in the driveway, my thumbs locked beneath my chin, palms cupping my mouth and nose, he knew something was wrong. He parked the car, unfastened his seat belt, then got out and stood with a wide stance, bracing for my news. The door sensor beeped its warning.

"What?"

What could I say?

"Sunny is dead."

"*What?*"

"Joanna's here. She's in the back."

Jim dropped his head and the tension left his body with a ragged sigh. "Damn it," he said. "Shit."

"I know."

"Shit."

"I know."

He looked up at me. "What happened?"

"J-i-i-i-m?" Joanna wailed from behind the gate.

"Shit," Jim said again, retrieving his keys and closing the car door.

I followed Jim through the gate. As soon as Joanna saw him, she shot to her feet. "You're here, Jim. *You're here.*" For a moment the shock and fear and distress fell away from Joanna's expression, and she looked up at my husband with the face of a young child, soft and pliable, a child still believing in the absolute powers of an infallible parent. Jim, she seemed to feel, might somehow be able to fix everything, to set it all right. But the moment couldn't hold and she started wailing again.

"I'm going to get you some water," I said, taking the opportunity to escape into the kitchen and thinking of the first time I met Sunny, of her looking up at me, bright, expectant, eager to make a new friend. She was a woman, I decided now, ready to go where the day took her and meet the people it brought her way. Sunny, indeed; how aptly she had been named.

Yet how strange that even after all the time we had spent together, I had never learned her full story. Sunny didn't like "going back into the past," so the mystery (to me) of how she came to be in her circumstances was unsolved and now assuredly would remain so.

No more Sunny.

I thought of a Warren Zevon lyric about how people you've lost remain tied to you like the buttons on your blouse and the instruction to keep them in your heart for a while. *Yes*, I thought. *I will keep Sunny in my heart. Perhaps for more than a while.*

Apart from the devastating emotional toll this would obviously take on Joanna, I knew there would also be practical concerns. What was going to happen now? Joanna wouldn't be able to afford the apartment anymore without Sunny's pension check. She did receive a disability check each month, but that was small. It certainly wouldn't come close to covering rent. Jim and I helped out some and could help more, I figured, but we couldn't take on the care of an entire human being.

Joanna had never been without Sunny. Even though they were separated now, with Sunny living at Pure Hearts Care and Joanna still at the apartment, I knew the two spoke—and sparred—on the phone every day, Sunny instructing Joanna on the minutiae of living a life in her absence. I knew that they watched the same television programs together, with their phones on speaker so they could point out and share significant moments, none more significant than when Jim's name appeared at the beginning of *The Golden Girls*.

I thought of Sunny looking up at me, bright and sunny that first day, and wondered if she hoped even then that I might be able to help her daughter. Did Sunny harbor a much deeper wish than for a Supreme Original meal when we walked through the doors into Koo Koo Roo? I shook the thought from my mind, focusing on the task at hand—water. The glass I grabbed from the cupboard was smudged, so I wiped it with a dish towel before taking several ice cubes from the freezer and letting them clink on the bottom. *Poor, poor Joanna*, I thought. *The world has not been kind to you, and it's about to become even less kind.* I held the glass under the faucet and behind the rush of water over ice cubes, I heard the sound of Joanna weeping. The sounds blended together and I began to feel dizzy, disoriented. But I focused on my task: fill the glass.

I walked outside with my offering of water to hear Joanna saying, ". . . only my mother knew that and how the nurse in the delivery room, in the delivery room when I was born. The nurse in the delivery room was Lorenzo Lamas's cousin. Lorenzo Lamas was on *Falcon Crest*. And it was a hard birth, Jim. A hard birth. More than a whole day it took for me to be born. Only my mother knows about that, in the whole world, and only my mother knows my dad used to call me Cloddy."

"Why 'Cloddy'?" I asked far too pertly, as if my crackerjack small talk skills were going to save the day here.

"I don't know," Joanna said, taking the glass from me without averting her eyes from Jim's. "Just 'Cloddy.' And my brother Jon, my brother Jon who died in board and care where they take your whole paycheck, was 'Froot Loops,' but that was because he had curly hair. My hair was curly too, like Jon's, but my dad didn't call me 'Froot Loops.' He called me 'Cloddy.' Only my mother knew that."

Well, now Jim and I know, I thought. *Maybe that's worth something. Isn't it worth something? No,* I answered myself, *probably not.* What's worth anything, to a child, at the loss of a mother? And Joanna was fifty-five years old, but in some ways more of a child than most children.

"There are lots of things only my mother knows. Like when she took me to the Natural History Museum when I was nine, and I said, 'Look! That mummy's sleeping in his sleeping bag!' and she laughed because the mummy wasn't sleeping in a sleeping bag, silly. It's a sarcophagus!"

The word *sarcophagus* jumped out at me. That one word opened a window for me into the possibilities of Joanna's developing nine-year-old mind. What might have been different for her if they hadn't been closed? I imagined avenues of light slamming shut on her like an iron gate.

"The mummy isn't sleeping. The mummy's dead." Joanna rubbed the heels of hands over her eyes. "I thought the sarcophagus was a sleeping bag. I thought the mummy was asleep. But mummies don't sleep. Everyone knows that, silly. Mummies are dead."

The word *dead* appeared to yank Joanna back from memory. The word itself made a thud like a body hitting the ground.

She looked at Jim, eyes welling again with tears. "Only my mother knows that."

Thud.

Joanna explained to Jim that her mother's body had been taken away before she got there, and the police don't question deaths in nursing homes when the person is old. It was, she assured him, a case of murder.

Who was I to question her understanding of events? Maybe thinking her mother died from a homicide was easier than facing a random, inexplicable coronary arrest striking out of the blue. Maybe her outrage was a kind of protection, some sort of emotional cellophane sealing her off from the chaotic truth.

"I'm so, so sorry, Joanna," I said softly. "I know how much you must be hurting."

Jimmy spoke after me, his voice stronger, more resolute.

"You're going to be alright, Joanna," he said. "You *will* be alright.

Do you hear me? You *will* be alright." I was impressed with his assurance. The way he emphasized "will" almost made me believe him myself. Where had he learned that?

Without thinking about it or consulting Jim, I surprised both of us by asking, "Do you want to stay here tonight?"

I looked to Jim, anxious about his response, but he nodded.

We both looked turned to Joanna, who was silent for the first time since her arrival.

"Yes." She nodded.

The three of us sat without speaking for several moments.

I stared at the empty pistachio shells, sun-bleached and dew-soaked and now slightly rotted. After a long while, I looked up to make eye contact with Jim, silently asking, *What should we do now?*

Jim pressed his hands into the patio chair seat, leaned toward Joanna, looked intently into her eyes, and asked, "So . . . do you want to watch some Kardashians?"

Jim didn't want to continue sitting there with Joanna and her grief. My husband is warm and wonderful, but his tolerance for sitting with uncomfortable emotions and problems he can't solve is low.

I shot him a look of reprimand.

"Or we could keep talking," he added quickly, shrugging at me.

Joanna's eyes darted from corner to corner of the yard, searching the trees and the shadows, as if she might find something out there to release her from this terrible moment. Eventually, she brought her forearms up and covered her mottled face.

"Okay," she said into her elbows, in a tone as ordinary as her posture was dramatic. "I guess some Kardashians would be okay."

"Good, then," Jim said, standing but turning back toward his studio instead of the house.

"Wait a minute!" I snapped. "Where are you going?"

"I have to go over some notes on the script," he said. "It's just a couple of pages. I'll be quick."

"Great," I said, not hiding my displeasure. Then I stood up and shrugged dramatically. "Well, I'll be here. Here with Joanna."

I led Joanna into the TV room, and while I searched On-Demand for *Keeping Up with the Kardashians*, she sat first in one spot, and then another, and finally a third, where she crossed her arms and gripped her torso and started rocking back and forth.

"Jim likes me," she said, to herself as much as to me. "He likes me, but he doesn't love me. I'm not family. Only my mother is family. My mother was born on the same day as Angie Dickinson. Angie Dickinson played Sergeant 'Pepper' Anderson in *Police Woman*."

"Oh, wow," I said, distracted, while managing to start the most recent episode of the Kardashians. "The same birthday."

I looked over at Joanna, sitting on the edge of the couch. She had stopped rocking and was now motionless, her body limp, her arms slack, her gaze focused somewhere in the space between the couch and the TV screen. Her eyelids were still peeled wide, and her jaw dangled as if stuck in that first moment after hearing the horrible news.

"Are you hungry?" I asked.

"Okay."

Her tears had formed a wet spot on her pale blouse. *As if her heart were leaking*, I thought.

"How 'bout . . . do you want me to make you a sandwich?"

"Okay."

"Peanut butter and jelly?"

"Okay."

"Okay, then. Peanut butter and jelly it is!"

I set a plate on the counter, opened a bag of whole-wheat bread, lay two slices on the plate, and thought about how many times in her lifetime a mother will make a peanut butter and jelly sandwich. Thousands, I figured. Thousands of peanut butter and jelly sandwiches. I remembered all the loaves of Wonder Bread my family went through when I was growing up, red and blue circles on cellophane packaging and the sweet airiness of white bread that melted almost as soon as it touched your tongue.

I took a jar of peanut butter from the cabinet and removed the lid. Mothers do a lot of things on a daily basis that I never do. All the snaps and buttons. The zippers and Velcro. The teeth brushings and hair brushings, and ponytails, and pigtails, and braids. All the bedtime stories. The building blocks. The beanbags. The beads. The Lincoln Logs and Legos. The laces. The pulling of socks over little feet and trimmings of nails. The hats. The cold hands, and the mittens. The carrying of small, warm, sleeping bodies upstairs.

Bodies made me think of Sunny. And then of a zipper closing over her face. I spooned a dollop of peanut butter out onto the bread. As I spread the thick substance out to the edge of crust, I pictured Joanna arriving at Pure Hearts Care.

Getting out of the cab.

"Here is the bag. Your mother's belongings. Accidents happen."

Could it possibly be true that Reyna had laughed? Could anyone be so callous? Maybe it was a nervous laugh. But how could she not have stifled the impulse? Everyone knows what it means to lose a mother. Even if it hasn't happened yet, they have envisioned that moment in dread and feared it instinctively from the moment they drew their first breath.

I heard Joanna stomping down the hall from the rec room to the bathroom and the phrase *pitter-patter of little feet* pitter-pattered through my head.

It made me think of empty-nesters missing their stocking-footed children, resonating as it did with absence more than presence, as if pitter-patter came more clearly in memory than ever in life.

As I screwed down the tin lid and put the jar away, I listened to the sounds.

"Pitter-patter," I said aloud. "Pitter-patter, pitter-patter."

I thought about little Babette, my imaginary child—"Pitter-patter,

patter"—and her imaginary sister Josie Rose, following in the hall. "Pitter, pitter, Patter, patter."

"Pitter-patter, *peanut butter*," I added, and the phrase caused an echo in my head. *Pitter-patter, peanut butter. Pitter-patter, peanut butter.*

I imagined the children laughing as they finished the peanut butter sandwiches I made for them, just like I had a thousand times before. I imagined them barreling through the living room to meet me in the kitchen, where I would catch them up into my arms. I saw myself kissing the tops of their warm heads, pressing my cheek into the sweet yeasty scent of their scalps, knowing that one day all my rooms would be quiet again.

I took a jar of strawberry jelly out from the refrigerator, listening to Joanna's heavy steps returning from the bathroom.

As I began spreading the jelly on the second piece of bread, I made a promise that Jimmy and I would make sure Joanna was taken care of. *She must not be hungry. She must not be alone in the world. And she must always have a TV, with many channels, chock-full of pseudo-celebrity, reality-show programming.*

I pressed the two pieces of bread together and tried to picture all the peanut butter and jelly sandwiches my mother had made when I was a child, and the Ziploc bags she had carefully placed them in: *thousands* of sandwiches carefully placed in *thousands* of Ziploc bags.

How intimately acquainted mothers are with Ziploc bags. I looked at the sandwich I made and paused, deciding whether to slice it in half vertically or diagonally. Diagonally. Like my mom always did, I concluded. As I sliced, I thought of my mother's hands. Small and delicate with clean unpolished nails. Smaller than mine by the time I was a teenager. Like she was my child instead of me being hers.

The sandwich on the plate struck me as insufficient. It looked lonely there on the white porcelain circle. I didn't want to hand Joanna an insufficient plate with a lonely sandwich. That would be just too unkind on a day like this. On a day like this, a day when one's mother dies unexpectedly and leaves one orphaned and bereft, a person should at least have something next to their sandwich. I looked in the cabinet and saw a bag of Fritos.

I grabbed a handful of the fragrant corn chips and placed them next to the sandwich. *What else?* I looked in the refrigerator, located a forgotten jar of cornichons behind the bottle of diet 7 Up, and placed several of the little pickles next to the chips.

There, then. That's better.

I took out a Coke, poured it in a cup, and took it along with the plate to Joanna, whom I found sitting in the exact same spot on the couch and in the exact same posture as I had left her. Everything was the same except her blouse. The leak from her heart had wetted it from the center of her chest down to her belly.

I held out the plate.

"Okay," she said, taking it and examining the snack. "Are these Fritos?"

"Yup, they're Fritos."

"Oh."

"Do you like Fritos?"

"They're okay."

"May I join you?"

"Okay."

What I've been calling the couch was actually more of a love-seat. Joanna was sitting in the middle. As I slid in on her right side, I expected Joanna to scoot over to give us both space. But she stayed planted, and we remained that way, pressed next to each other, stiff and unfamiliar, like teenagers on a date.

We watched TV. While Joanna nibbled at her sandwich, I wondered . . . were Jim and I the plan? Like a spider mother laying her eggs in an unsuspecting host—or in this case, a host and hostess. I thought back to that first time Sunny and Joanna came to our home and I had carried their snacks to them on that silver tray.

During the end credits of our fifth episode, I saw Joanna's eyelids drooping over her bloodshot eyes and felt the fatigue of my own long night.

"Joanna," I said softly. "I'm going to bed."

Joanna nodded solemnly, her eyes hooded, all internal resources clearly exhausted. She hoisted herself heavily from the couch and dragged down the hallway toward the bathroom.

"I'll get you a pillow and some blankets."

I retrieved a pillow, sheets, and two throws from the linen closet and returned to make some semblance of a bed, laying out the sheets, tucking the ends under the cushions, unfolding a white thermal blanket, and spreading my favorite pink velour bedspread over the top. The corners of the ancient bedspread were frayed and ragged from where I had clasped them to my mouth as a child, and there was a hole burned near the middle from when I nearly set myself on fire smoking in bed when I was in college.

I laid the pillow for Joanna at the end of the couch nearest the door, noticed that the stuffing had spread out into little lumps at the corners, and then realized I'd never actually fluffed a pillow before. How could that be? I'd seen my mother do it many times when I was child, and I'd watched my sister fluff her children's pillows while they were brushing their teeth or washing their faces, but I had no one's pillow to fluff. Jimmy had his three pillows that he arranged to his own liking, and one didn't fluff one's own pillow, it seemed, at least if one were me.

I decided Joanna should have a fluffed pillow tonight, so I placed my hands on the sides of the pillow and pressed, pushing the downy insides into a billowing rise in the middle. I repeated the gesture, then inspected my work. Nice, I decided. It really did seem more inviting than it had before.

Joanna climbed onto the couch, pulled the covers over, and laid her head on the pillow. Sleep, as she would say, took her right away.

I watched her there on the couch, her breathing steady and settled, its rhythm slowly smoothing her face until it was soft as a baby's. As if nothing at all had happened tonight. As if this were just another day.

I thought how if Joanna were a baby, a recently orphaned baby, her head cradled by a fluffed pillow, wrapped in a pink blanket, the world would rush to her, arms wide, hearts full. Babies draw you to them, their skin, their exquisite tininess, but maybe most of all their promise.

As I watched her sleep, I remembered a lyric from a vacation Bible school song. "I am a promise. I am a possibility. I am a great big bundle of potentiality." Joanna was not the future. She was not full of promise. Her appearance did not drive you to pull her to your breast, like a newborn or a puppy or a lover. Her skin was wet, pink, and raw from many hours of tears, chapped as if it had been assaulted by bitter winds. Her hands were not adorably miniature with teeny fingers that could clasp around your thumb and make your heart quicken. They were thick and crepey and mottled, *like those of an old woman*, I mused as I glanced at my own. And she would never grow up to be a doctor or a lawyer or Matisse, for she was not being launched into the world, but rather, facing descent.

How terribly, terribly unfair.

I knew Joanna would wake up in the morning alone in a strange room and a stranger world, and that from now on, no one would know how Daddy used to call her Cloddy or how she thought the mummy was sleeping in a sleeping bag and made her mother laugh or about the hard birth that brought her into the world, the hard birth that lasted more than a whole day.

Tomorrow, I guessed, would feel as slow and agonizing to Joanna as that long day must have felt to her mother.

Part Two

2016

6

A Movie

It is heartbreaking to see Joanna without Sunny. It feels like Chip without Dale or Lady without the Tramp; impossible to imagine even when seeing it in front of you.

With some help shopping for groceries and using the machines at the laundry and other day-to-day tasks, Joanna is able to manage on her own. When I ask how she is paying for the apartment or about her landlord, she begins talking about other topics. Somehow, I figure, Joanna's disability checks must be going directly into some account or the apartment was part of a deal worked out long ago. Joanna did not seem worried about it and so I did not worry about it.

I focus on my career, finally harvesting all the seeds I have planted. I am hired on another television show, and a film I had written and produced receives distribution.

One evening, as I sit outside with a glass of wine, the light from the setting sun reflects off a bank of high clouds and gives our garden of desert plants an enchanted glow. It seems as if fairies might emerge at any moment from behind the agave and California sagebrush and run splashing into the mauve-tinged pool. *What is the word for what I'm feeling?* I ask myself. And then I find it: *delight*. This is delight, and this day, this night, this instant of my life is overflowing with the stuff. It's all simply *delightful*.

I feel as if I am a child again, and my father is lifting me high in the air and spinning me around, and I am sailing in circles over his head and shouting "Again, again, again!" before he can even begin to slow down.

Again, I repeat in my head. *Again, again, again.*

Everything in the world feels designed to give me joy. The fuzzy spa socks my mother gave me for my birthday suddenly feel so *soft*, like little blankets made of warm clouds. The glass of merlot I sip tastes of sweet berries and is smoothing out all my jagged edges when Holly bounds up to me. And, oh, what a dog! Has anyone ever seen such a dog? Black and sleek like a seal, with silky fur and deep, dark eyes, strange and familiar at the same time.

Holly jumps into my lap and looks at me intently, then curls into a soft, doggy donut in my lap, closes her eyes, and exhales a contented dog sigh.

Yes, I think, sighing as well. *All is well in our little world, and don't we both know it.*

This feels easy. Soothing and warm and easy. Joanna is right: I do in fact live on Easy Street. I smile and shake my head and let the deep ease wash through me. Then, as the light outside turns toward lilac, with one hand on Holly's warm neck and the other gently holding the stem of my glass, I take stock—the beginnings of a television writing career and my first book on the way. I roll the accomplishments over in my mind like a squirrel, back at its den at last, alone and undisturbed, examining all the nuts stashed in its cheeks from a long day's forage.

All my demons are at least temporarily vanquished and feel far, far away, as if they had been a dream all along, specters from another land.

Ah, I exhale, releasing and then *squeezing all the air out of the bellows of my lungs,* as I used to instruct in yoga classes, and feel my body easing into the chair's cushion. This will be the first time in I can't remember how long that I don't need to feel guilty about not furthering my career or laboring toward making a mark or matching any external metric of any kind. I am free to do anything.

How should I spend my reward of anxiety-free hours? How should I celebrate?

Nothing fancy, I decide. No dinner. No champagne. No manicure. No pedicure. Not even a $500 macaron.

No, I know what I'll do. I'll finally watch that documentary about J. D. Salinger I've been wanting to see. I have been rereading *Franny and Zooey* for the first time since high school. Though I'd enjoyed the novel then, the world of the Glass family had seemed far off from my own. But now as I reread, I feel an uncanny kinship with Franny, as if Salinger had been privy to a very deep part of myself and my history.

Franny just seems so much like me.

Franny and her strange compulsion to recite the "Jesus Prayer" over and over.

Franny at nineteen, in her sheared-raccoon jacket at the train station, waving, not knowing her mind is about to unravel.

Franny who can't stop despising herself for being a phony, a sham, a dilettante.

Well, tonight, I do not feel like a dilettante. No. I. Do. Not.

"Hey, husband," I say to Jim, who is coming down the steps from his studio, "would you want to watch the Salinger documentary with me tonight?"

"Sure," he answers in a most agreeable tone, sitting down next to me at the table. "Whatever you want."

"It's nice to have a 'Jim,'" I say, indulging in one of Jim's favorite compliments. "I'm lucky to have a 'Jim.'"

He smiles, and I smile to see him smile. "I'm going to have another glass of wine. Do you want something?"

"Always up for a cup of coffee," he says.

I brew a pot of coffee, marveling at my husband's ability to drink caffeine right up till the moment he falls asleep, and pour myself another glass of merlot. On my way back to the bedroom, I take several sips of the berry-tinged liquid that leads me even further into a spacious mood of warmth and easy contentment. Jim cues up the film and I cuddle next to him in bed. I call Holly, who comes barreling into the bedroom, rises in a flying leap onto the bed, and scooches between us, craning her neck to look toward the television as if she had been anticipating the documentary just as much as I had.

The film explores J. D. Salinger's life from the premise that his stories sprang from a psyche warped and wounded by war, and it contained many details I knew nothing about. I had not known, for example, that Salinger served in World War II or written his great novel, *Catcher in the Rye*, by flashlight at night following days spent under a hard sun, freeing prisoners from Nazi death camps.

The film features footage of bodies stacked in heaps, some dead, others alive, some still, others barely moving, some with open, vacant eyes, others with eyes squeezed shut as if against the pain of having witnessed incomprehensible evil. The images are deeply disturbing. The awful disregard of individual life they memorialize horrifies me with an electrifying sensation of dread.

Live bodies are not distinguished from those of the dead. Corpses are tossed from one heap to another, like bags of garbage onto a pile at the dump, discarded appallingly, abominably, unspeakably.

I haven't seen anything quite as gruesome or graphic as this footage, but I've seen similar images before.

What if, I suppose to myself with horror, *I begin repeating the name of that place, just the word,* Auschwitz, *over and over in my head?*

I don't wonder what will happen if I can't get the vile documentary footage out of my mind.

I don't think, *I'll never be able to forget these images.*

I don't abruptly realize that I would never be the same, knowing in this new way the depth of cruelty we humans are capable of inflicting on our brothers and sisters.

I just ask myself, in a voice that sounds like a hiss from my own terrorist, *How horrible would* that *be? If I do* that? Nothing else. Just the word itself, *Auschwitz*. Just the word. How horrible would it be to repeat *Auschwitz* over and over? Just like I had done with *blasphemy*?

Auschwitz, Auschwitz, Auschwitz.

With Jimmy next to me on our happy little magic carpet of a bed, with our happy little companion snuggled between us, I do just that.

Auschwitz, I silently say to myself, *Auschwitz, Auschwitz*, methodically enacting my hideous proposition, *Auschwitz, Auschwitz, Auschwitz*, and finding that it is every bit as horrible as I had thought . . . because then I can't make it stop.

Auschwitz, Auschwitz, Auschwitz.

As the repeating voice gains confidence and asserts itself more boldly—*Auschwitz, Auschwitz, Auschwitz*—the panic that creeps through my skin does not compare itself to any other.

It says *Auschwitz, Auschwitz, Auschwitz*, as calm and uninflected and opinion-free as any blank-faced hired assassin.

A wave of nausea rolls through me. Another crests as I think, *I can't let Jimmy know.*

I hate my weird, embarrassing affliction, which has always been unrelatable to anyone I've ever tried to describe it to. Including Jimmy. Discussing my condition with my husband always makes me acutely aware of the fact that he got a bum deal for a wife, that he was conned into an irreparably damaged model of a mate with an old-school bait-n-switch.

Once in our early days, driving back from a date, Jimmy had said, "You know what I like about you?"

"What?" I had asked, awaiting something along the lines of "you're so easy to hang out with" or "I can be myself around you" or "you really make me laugh."

"You're just so, so . . ."

He made a smooth gesture with his hand.

"You know?"

I furrowed my eyebrows. "Not really."

"You're just so *sane*."

Oh dear God, I had thought, *well, this isn't good*. It was false advertising, and I knew it. It was no different than if I'd lured him into marriage with my famous homemade beef bourguignon and chicken cacciatore when all along I'd been ordering in from Wolfgang Puck's.

Now, with tightly clenched fists hidden beneath the comforter, I toss my attempt at an easy smile over to my husband.

"Merry Christmas," I say.

It's a little joke I began making early in our relationship, saying "Merry Christmas" during nice moments in seasons other than Christmas.

Jim pats my leg through the comforter and replies with a warm, habitual "Merry Christmas, Mags."

Meanwhile, my heart bangs in my chest, my scalp tingles with terror, and just like it had when I was nineteen in that student union movie theater in Ithaca, New York, my lungs begin squeezing shut. I try to figure out whether I need to inhale or exhale, but soon find I can barely do either.

My mind focuses on that little bottle of pale green tablets in my medicine cabinet. Why had I stopped taking them last month? How could I be so stupid? Why would I take the risk when there was nothing to gain except the alleviation of a fifteen-second element of a bedtime ritual? Was it pride that led to my recklessness? A reaction to the shame of needing assistance in order to function in the world? Or is it covetousness? Do I covet mental health without enslavement to pharmaceuticals? Envy? Do I envy the lot of the normal?

Which deadly sin has felled me?

The pills are green. *The green of envy*, I think.

With both hands, I begin to wipe the sweat from my face but pause and let my fingers rest over my eyebrows and the heels of my palms to press into my chin. I rock back and forth slightly; an ancient, barely remembered self-soothing technique. Back and forth. Back and forth.

"What's going on, Mags?" Jim asks, pausing the documentary. "What's going on? Are you okay?"

I notice my hands are shaking and quickly steady them on my thighs. "Oh, yeah, totally. You know," I manage to say, "*Franny and Zooey* has one my favorite lines ever. 'I'm sick of not having the courage to be an absolute nobody.'"

"Something's going on."

"No, no," I say with forced cheer. "I want to keep watching. I love this. Hopefully they'll talk about Franny's breakdown and how Salinger thought of that."

Jimmy leans back and resumes the film, unconvinced. "Okay," he says.

I wipe the sweat from my head with the corner of the comforter and breathe out slowly through pursed lips.

Why this word? Why *Auschwitz*? I ask myself.

Auschwitz, Auschwitz, Auschwitz.

What has Auschwitz to do with me, or I with Auschwitz?

Auschwitz, Auschwitz, Auschwitz.

I'm not thinking about the camp in Germany. Or the documentary. Just the word itself. It's not like I am caught in some sort of aftershock from witnessing an abominable trauma firsthand. It is simply a word, a word that came into my mind from watching a documentary while cuddled in bed with my husband on an unseasonably warm October night in Los Angeles, a word that certainly was imbued with some sort of tone; a note, a chord, like the Hitchcock *Psycho* chord, the minor major seventh chord, the terror chord, *my* terror chord, but still, *it is just a word.*

I've heard Joanna repeat words many times, but for her the word repetitions seem to provide a form of comfort, like rocking in a chair, or rubbing the worn corner of a blanket to one's cheek.

Not me.

Auschwitz, Auschwitz, Auschwitz invades my thoughts without asking permission and without providing any benefit whatsoever. It is an unwelcome guest I attempt repeatedly to thrust out the door. It is a violation I perpetrate on myself, as if were saying "Stop hitting yourself!" while slugging my own face.

Why would someone do this? Why would someone repeat a word like this, when it was the exact thing they didn't want to do? My guess would be the Pink Elephant Phenomenon: if you tell yourself not to think of pink elephants on the wall, a herd of them will stampede through your mind.

The prohibition provokes the violation.

Don't eat that apple. That one is forbidden.

Don't play with that toy. That's your sister's.

Eve reaches for the apple.

The child grabs the toy.

But with thoughts, it's slightly different because the prohibition *contains* the violation. The prohibition and the violation arise mutually. "Don't think about pink elephants" contains the idea of pink elephants.

It's a double bind. It can't be resolved. Indeed, a strange loop.

But so what? Who cares about thinking about pink elephants on the wall? Certainly not the most exciting thing to contemplate, or the best wallpaper, but who cares? I don't, and I'm guessing you wouldn't. And when we don't care, the whole system just peters out. We just stop thinking about it and focus on something else. Not caring is the secret. Not caring is what prevents the double bind.

It's the way out of the Chinese finger trap. A way to settle the imp. I know this.

I'm doing it to myself, that's clear, but the generating impulse is not subject to my will.

The only entity I can blame is me, whoever that is.

Because if "I" can't stop what "I'm" doing, then who am "I?"

What "I" keeps defying the "I" who keeps clearly and vehemently commanding "I" to stop?

Is it me?

I can't answer these questions because I no longer know who I am . . . or is . . . or are. Did J. D. Salinger suffer from something similar? Is that why he wrote about Franny repeating that prayer, the Jesus prayer, over and over and over and over? Envy riddles my mind, even now. Why can't my wounds enable me to write a generation-defining novel about a disturbed young man in a red hunting hat who hates phonies or insightful stories about a family called Glass? That would at least be some sort of compensation. Why can't I invent a character like Franny, who has a breakdown in college and begins obsessively repeating a prayer she discovers in an obscure Russian text?

My mind spins faster in familiar little cyclones. Blood drains from my arms and legs. I can feel it.

Joanna says I live on Easy Street, and I know what she means, but we're both suffering. Joanna's life shattered on July sixteenth, mine splintered into pieces on the seventh of October.

Joanna's damage is overt, apparent to anyone, while mine lies within me, hidden from all. I am functional in society, while she is obviously broken. I am cared for, while she has been abandoned. I am a phony, while she offers defenseless honesty.

I can drive a car, file taxes, make small talk, chew with my mouth closed, inquire with my eyebrows raised, and smile when I feel like scowling. I can give compliments when I feel like insulting, laugh when I feel like jeering, offer warmth when I feel withholding, and say "Glad to help" to friends from college when I'm thinking *I hope you fail in a spectacularly public fashion.*

Joanna can do none of these things.

But we live together on the same street nonetheless, despite what she thinks, and it isn't *easy*, for either of us.

We enact our patterns and repeat our words, hers flying out of her mouth, mine imprisoned in my head.

Auschwitz, Auschwitz, Auschwitz.

"She killed her."

Blastoff, blastoff, blastoff.

"That's exactly the opposite of taking care."

Stop hitting myself, stop hitting myself!

"And it was a hard birth, a hard birth, more than a whole day."

Blasphemy, blasphemy, blasphemy.

"More than a whole day!"

Auschwitz, Auschwitz, Auschwitz.

7

It Is Back

My pillow has slipped away during the night and the side of my face is lying flat on the mattress. I do not yet recall the panic of the previous night, so for the time being my greatest concern is whether or not there are eggs in the refrigerator that I can microwave in my recently purchased as-seen-on-TV Egg-Tastic Ceramic Microwave Egg Cooker for Fast, Flavorful & Fluffy Eggs.

The Egg-Tastic Ceramic Microwave Egg Cooker cost me only $7.99 and turns out to be a truly *eggtastic* product. Not so much because it allows me to poach eggs. *Poach* isn't really the right word. Not like at fancy brunch spots with names like Oeff and Töst where morning-sun yolks and cumulus-cloud-on-a-summer-day whites smile up from crab Benedicts. The Egg-Tastic Microwave Ceramic Egg Cooker does not poach eggs like that, but it does cook them. There is no denying that.

Before my purchase, I never managed to poach eggs at home. Carefully cracking open the shells without breaking the yolks, gently dropping the fragile orbs into barely boiling water and swirling them just so, and the inevitable mishaps of splashed egg matter, overcooked centers, and the cursing such semi-accidents lead to—and on top of all of that, the cleanup—always just seemed like too much work, especially given how fast two eggs are consumed. You get maybe ten bites of eggs and then that's it, you're done. Time to wash the pot.

I like to microwave-poach two eggs in the morning for breakfast and sometimes I zap two more in the evening for a late snack. Since I've been going at the eggs so feverishly recently, I'm afraid I'm going to find that I've blown through the two dozen I purchased on Friday.

In this state of slight suspense, I motivate myself off the bed, pad sock-footed into the kitchen, and open the refrigerator. When I see two AA light brown eggs perched happily in their compartment, I breathe a sigh of relief. "Hey, you two," I say with a smile in my voice.

But then I remember.

Auschwitz.

It all comes back to me. Salinger. The bodies. *Auschwitz. Auschwitz. Auschwitz.*

Immediately I tumble in the foaming undertow of icy panic. *Auschwitz. Auschwitz. Auschwitz.* I grasp at the solid marble of the kitchen island and gather my bearings. *Auschwitz. Auschwitz. Auschwitz.* The skin on my arms prickles, my scalp freeze-burns, and I feel a cold draft chilling me from behind.

The refrigerator is standing open.

With one hand anchored on the countertop, I reach back to nudge the door closed with my foot. But I keep shivering, and I know why.

"It" is back. "It" is the name I have for my mental illness, an umbrella term for a variety of symptoms: anxiety about the afterlife, unexplained anxiety, obsessive word repetition, and a sense of destabilization that revolves around the question *what is I?* It's a big umbrella, but the symptoms are all connected, I'm convinced.

Focus on the normal, I think, turning to open the refrigerator again and pluck out the two eggs. *Look at the ordinary morning. La, la, la.*

"Everything is normal," I hear myself say, bracing against the flood. "Normal, normal, normal."

I tap the eggs against the porcelain cooker one at a time, cracking their shells and dropping the contents into the round containers. "Normal, normal," I murmur as I work. "Look outside. It's normal.

Look at the coffee maker. Look at the butter dish. Look at the sink. Normal, normal, normal."

I delicately poke a hole in each yolk, ladle a teaspoon of tap water into each container, and hit the timer button on the microwave.

Just like I did yesterday. Normal.

It is possible, I tell myself, that this time the brain dysfunction can be resisted, the chaos warded off. But can it? What will be different this time? How had it happened before? I need to remember. I need to inspect the previous malfunctions in order to prove to myself that this time could be different.

My first breakdown hit me during sophomore year in college. Cornell, the film trigger of Kurosawa's *Dreams*, fear of not being saved, and hell rush to my mind. The cause of that crisis was clear enough: theological poison that I worked hard to get rid of. And I had, to a great degree. First I began, within the framework of Christianity, to believe in a truly loving God, one that wouldn't revoke His love if you picked the wrong answer on the Great Test. I stopped listening to what Christian mystic Thomas Merton called the "magicians who turn the Cross to their own purposes and commit the awful blasphemy of making the Cross contradict mercy."

Then I read Joseph Campbell and for the first time thought, *Oh my goodness, the Bible doesn't just contain* metaphors. *The whole dang thing is a metaphor.* I began to see how it's not just that "Father" is a metaphor for God, but that "God" itself is a metaphor for something that transcends language or imagery, something we don't know how to explain, something not our ego. And that somehow, if we die to the ego, we'd rise to something else. And somehow, that something else has something to do with God.

And that is true resurrection.

Fear of hell still nagged at me, but intellectually the concept began to seem increasingly ludicrous. Sure, it was still a possibility. But it was also a possibility that I would wake up when I died and find that I'd been reborn as a hippo in my favorite childhood game, Hungry Hungry Hippos. That would be horrible too, an eternal realm of a hungry, hungry me, competing with hungry peers, but what were the odds? So the fear of hell started to seem as silly as the fear of hippos, and both started slowly, slowly slipping away until locating them was both hard and unnecessary.

So now, standing here in my kitchen, using the island here as ballast, I'm no longer dealing with the theological component of my obsession, so in that sense, I'm not as vulnerable as I was.

I try to remember how my second breakdown started.

That one's murkier, I think as the microwave timer blinks 1:03, then ticks through 1:02 and 1:01.

Time pushes the descending clock past 1:00, :59 and :58, and I feel my panic rising.

Focus.

:57, :56, :55.

I try to catch a memory from my soup of swirling thoughts. When, exactly, did the threads start snapping in my brain? Where was I? What I was doing? An image comes into view and I quickly stab it like a beetle through the thorax and peer intently at the mounted specimen.

I see myself in school in the spring of 1997, walking through a campus sculpture garden next to the theater buildings at UCLA. It's breezy and pleasant, like most all days in Los Angeles. Two undergraduates huddle together on the grass, reading from a script in low voices; three workers from the scene shop break for lunch on the long benches under the coral trees in front of the performance hall, saying nothing but passing a bag of potato chips back and forth; and somewhere, someone I can't see smokes a clove cigarette.

I am holding my Samuel French copy of William Gibson's play *The Miracle Worker* as I walk and think about the character I will be portraying, Helen Keller's mother, Kate. I am trying to imagine what it would be like to be a mother with a daughter so damaged, so disconnected and estranged from the world. I am as serious as a wartime surgeon about these internal imaginings, otherwise known in our graduate acting program as *the work*, which feels so important, so necessary for the world, that if the performance were called off, I would still think, *Well, at least I did* the work.

As I walk by the statue of a leaping boy peeing into a basin of water and listen to the delicate splashing sound, I imagine my daughter will never have this small consolation. I pass the bronze of a woman squatting on her haunches and looking out into the distance. *My baby girl will never see a horizon*, I think, digging around in my psyche, trying to locate a feeling of profound heartache and maybe even produce a tear.

Walking toward the giant, headless Auguste Rodin's *Walking Man*, I attempt to let "me" slip away and become Kate with her worries and fears for Helen, Kate with her disappointment at how motherhood has turned out, Kate with her feeling of being taken hostage the day her daughter was born.

But then, *Who is "me" really?* I start wondering. What do I really mean when I think of that object pronoun? It's the most basic and ordinary of inquiries for a young acting student walking through a campus garden doing *the work*, but at this particular moment, as my eyes move up the headless walker's muscular left leg, I suddenly feel as if something inside me has given way and I don't have anything solid to hang on to.

The ding of the microwave pulls my attention back to the kitchen.

I open the door and see that the two yolks are still covered in a white film. Too soon. I click the door shut and add thirty seconds, reaching for my interrupted train of thought. I remember I had a class coming up. I must have headed back to the theater building. I must have left the big Rodin, returned past the female bronze, approached the leaping boy. I must have walked across the bricks and pushed through the glass door to the lobby where we had our mailboxes, but what then?

An image comes into focus of the women's restroom, off the lobby. I'm standing in front of a sink.

I've heard people say you should never look in a mirror if you've taken acid. Maybe the same advice applies if you're disoriented, have a history of mental illness, feel a catastrophic panic coming on, and have wandered into the women's restroom before an afternoon acting class.

"How is that face my face?" I had asked. "I see it there on that shiny, two-dimensional surface over the sink, but what does it really have to do with me?"

I leaned closer, focusing in on a small brown birthmark that had always dotted my cheek just below my right eye. I remembered thinking when I was a toddler that this tiny splotch was a bit of dirt and rubbing and rubbing to get it off until my skin was red. I remembered covering the mark with pale-beige concealer when I was in junior high. And I remembered dabbing the dark pigment with a darker eyeliner when in I was in college, in celebration of imperfection and also in emulation of Cindy Crawford, whose beauty and supermodel lifestyle (and marriage to the Dalai Lama's bestie Richard Gere) had more influence on my personal aspirations in the early 1990s than I would like to admit.

That little speck beneath my right eye had always just been there, a constant part of my experience of reflected self. In some genuine way, it *was* me, *to* me. And yet at this moment, under the fluorescent lighting of the women's bathroom, as I focused on that small "Maggie mark" that had always been with me, I started to wonder, *Why do I think of it as my* Maggie *mark? Where did that come from? And who is Maggie, anyway? What if the mark has nothing whatsoever to do with Maggie, for one thing, and for another, what if she has nothing whatsoever to do with me? And what if the physical entity I perceive reflected in front of me is nothing more than a meaningless shell that houses my . . .*

I tried to dodge the end of that phrase, but soon enough "soul" provoked "eternal soul," and "unrepentant soul," and "lukewarm soul," and finally "soul damned to hell." Memories of watching Billy Graham on television after spaghetti and meatloaf dinners filled my head, and I was watching again with my family, the river of people on the screen flowing down to his pulpit to repent and save their souls, souls caught in frightful jeopardy. I was sitting next to my infant sister on the sofa with my eyes peeled and my scalp burning, furiously repeating to myself, "Jesus, I accept you into my heart; please be my personal savior. Jesus, I accept you into my heart; please be my personal savior. Please be my personal savior. Please."

Standing in the Theater Department bathroom, I knew I was no longer that child, pinioned helplessly in the loving bosom of her family, but my scalp is still burning, burning and freezing in a terrifyingly familiar way in which the two sensations become the same.

The hell fear was back. The word *blasphemy* seemed to shoot up my spine like an angry serpent into my skull.

And then—its strange linguistic corollary—the word *blastoff* began coiling into cyclones that whipped through my head, tearing up the terrain.

Blastoff. Blastoff. Blastoff.

I haven't noticed the microwave's ding this time, but when it beeps three times to remind me there's something in the oven, I release the exhale I have been holding and let air flood my lungs. I open the microwave and look into the cooker. The two white ceramic cups, with egg-yellow circles drawn around their rims, shine prettily in the interior oven light, but the egg yolks within appear to be two pus-bloated blisters. My stomach bucks up toward my throat.

This is not normal.

I swallow hard, carry my as-seen-on-TV, Egg-Tastic Ceramic Microwave Egg Cooker for Fast, Flavorful & Fluffy Eggs over to the garbage, and dump the contents.

My therapist Lucy's waiting room is more a cubbyhole than a room. The walls are not much further apart than the length of my arms, but I love this little room with its one narrow side table supporting an only slightly outdated selection of magazines, its one soft waiting chair, wide enough for me to sit cross-legged and gaze at the painting on the narrow width of the opposite wall, and nothing more.

I want this to be like any other Tuesday at 10:00 a.m., me sitting here awaiting comforting and thought-provoking conversation, but as soon as I sit down and cross my legs, I feel prickles tearing up my elbows to my neck while *Auschwitz Auschwitz Auschwitz* runs through my head. Stop it. Stop it. *Stop it.* I push back.

The woman in the painting in front of me keeps calm while everything around her seems to melt. The three forms in the composition—the woman, the bed on which she sits, and a dresser—appear loosed from the laws of matter. They slip down toward the horizontal line formed by the rough wooden frame bounding the canvas, the proportions warping strangely. The woman's legs extend absurdly compared to her average-sized torso, the bed bends and snakes out in the middle as if she were lazing on the back of a fat python, and the dresser splats outward at the bottom like a wide Christmas tree.

You would think a melting world might be disturbing to the woman sitting on the bed, but the artist has portrayed her face in conventional proportions and her expression remains serene. Despite the woman's solid world becoming slippery, as if the air around her has been greased, she doesn't show distress. She doesn't grasp at the mattress; she doesn't brace an arm against the headboard; she doesn't try to prevent her legs or the rest of her body from oozing past the wooden border of the painting to the unknowable space beneath.

The door to the office opens.

Lovely Lucy's eyes always appear heartbreakingly sad to me until she smiles. When I first met her, I felt instinctively worried about the difficult life she must have lived. Then she smiled, and the little wrinkles gathered at her temples, and the light collected in her gray-green irises expressed such a friendly serenity I wondered why I had ever

been concerned for her in the first place. I also find Lucy to be aston-
ishingly beautiful. Few people probably watch this particular sixty-
year-old woman walk down the sidewalk on Larchmont Boulevard
on her way to work with admiration, but that's just because there are
so few poets.

Since my first session with Lucy two years ago, I have loved coming to this little office perched here above the boulevard's magnolia
trees. Since I have not been suffering from "it" during that time, I
have had the luxury of talking with Lucy about simple, everyday dis-
appointments and anxieties. I've shared my fear of being a dilettante
and never finding an honorable calling. I've discussed the indignities of
aging. I've investigated the envy I feel when my peers succeed, and I've
confessed my growing regret over not having had children.

I don't want to talk about my distressing mental cyclones today.
I'm clinging to the hope that an ordinary Maggie-feels-rueful therapy
session with Lucy might snap everything back to normal so I can enjoy
my eggs Benedict at Eggslut this Sunday, just like before. This is also
why I haven't and don't want to tell Jim about the threat looming in
the shadows of my psyche. As if by naming it, I might call it forth.

Lucy stands aside and lets me lead the way into her office, as she
does every week. Then, as always, she asks how I'm feeling about the
temperature in the room with such grave consideration that it would
seem that a degree too high or too low might cause a person to either
develop hypothermia or spontaneously combust and flash out of existence. The room at the moment is entirely comfortable, but Lucy
nevertheless shoots me a concerned squint, glances over to her small,
window-mounted air conditioning unit, then looks back at me.

"Too cold?"

"No. Fine," I say like I do every time, settling into her slender
green couch.

"Too warm?"

"Nope. Just right."

"You sure?"

"Totally."

I've always appreciated the attention Lucy gives to such a seemingly irrelevant detail. She feels like a mother tucking in the corners of a blanket and fluffing a pillow, because if she can fix nothing else for me, at least she can fix this.

Lucy consults her notes. "Last week you were talking about pangs you feel when you see mothers walking with their children on Larchmont, and then you edited yourself and changed the word 'pangs' to 'contractions.'"

"Right," I say with a laugh. "I was being a tad dramatic. I was thinking about birth pangs to begin with, but then upped the metaphor to contractions."

"You're allowed to be dramatic."

I flash to being on stage as Kate Keller and my dramatic wail when I discover, by waving a fake oil lamp over a naked, plastic-faced doll in a bassinet (which constantly threatened to roll down the entrance ramp unless I jammed my left foot under its back wheels), that my daughter had been struck deaf, dumb, and blind. Since I was regularly having panic attacks by the time *The Miracle Worker* opened, I had easy access to feelings of terror and consider the guttural animal wail I let loose every night in that black box theater to be the best acting work I've done to date.

I tell Lucy about the woman and her ladybug daughter on their way to Salt & Straw and explain how I imagined their backstory, how the mother had given the daughter the helmet for her birthday and how the little girl was so happy and asked, "How did you know I liked ladybugs so much?"

Lucy's smile brings out the dark green in her eyes.

"Even though of course the little girl had mentioned ladybugs constantly and had drawn pictures of ladybugs everywhere and dressed as a ladybug for Halloween, but still it was baffling and wonderful to her that her mother knew her so deeply."

"Ah," said Lucy, instantly perceiving the moment's significance to me.

"Also," I continue, pushing the deeper concern down, "ice cream without a child misses the point of ice cream altogether. I mean, I certainly like ice cream. Who doesn't? It's cold and it's sweet and it tastes good. But then it's over and I immediately regret the calories I just took in and there's the lactose thing and I'll feel my stomach rumbling and think I should probably take one of those Lactaid pills which I may or may not have in the medicine cabinet back home, and then on top of everything, I have to find a trash can to throw away the empty ice cream cup I'm holding and the stupid pink spoon.

"But for a little girl in a ladybug helmet? You take her for ice cream? Whew. Oh, man. Magic in a cone. I haven't had ice cream in a cone in years. Why would I? A cup makes much more sense. Why would I use my tongue like a dog? I don't lick hummus off of pita bread and then eat the pita."

As I talk, I find myself wishing these ordinary, everyday bouts of unhappiness could be my real problem. Unhappiness is different from illness. You can write into *Reader's Digest* about unhappiness and someone named Pam or Amanda from Pittsburgh might have an answer for you with a link to a helpful website. Illness is repeating *Auschwitz* over and over and carrying the fear that my mind is not my own and my identity is under siege and that some infection lies in wait inside me to riddle my whole self with disease.

Lucy notices something about my manner or my expression and her face changes subtly. "Maggie," she says, studying the bunched muscles of my jaw, perhaps, or the protective hunch of my shoulders, or an absence in my eyes, "I see that you're thinking about something. Do you want to tell me about it?"

No, I think. *Don't talk about it here.*

I want to, though, especially here. I want Lucy, specifically, to tuck the blanket of her warmth and understanding around my shoulders and fluff a pillow for my tormented head. She will ask me if the temperature is good, and I will say, "No, it isn't," and she will adjust the thermostat just as much as is needed and not more, and everything will be all right.

No. Don't tell her what's going on, don't make it solid. Don't name it.

"Oh, I was just thinking about this, this other mother, not ladybug mother, another mother I saw on Larchmont, this one with a teenage daughter. The teenage daughter was wearing a school uniform, white shirt, plaid skirt and had these long legs—crazy long legs—that she clearly hadn't learned how to manage yet. The mom and the girl walked with Frappuccinos in their hands, and I figured the mother had recently decided her daughter was old enough to have caffeine and that this had probably made the long-legged girl feel all grown up, and I pictured the daughter ordering her mocha Frappuccino from a barista not much older than herself, proudly, like a woman, and adding, 'with extra whipped cream,' because she was still a little girl."

Lucy doesn't say anything. She waits, listening.

". . . I guess it just seemed so wonderful to have a daughter and also, well, we've talked about this, this woman had another ship, besides her own, to set her hopes upon. I'm not saying the only ships out there are children or even people. But having a kid definitely gives you a ship. From day one, you get a ship."

Lucy nods for me to continue.

"So then I noticed the teen, she was walking quite closely alongside her mother, I saw her see a chalkboard propped on the sidewalk outside Bellacures advertising a 'Pumpkin Spice Pedicure' in burnt-orange cursive letters."

"Oh, I saw that chalkboard."

"I'd noticed it, too! I'd thought 'Wow, pumpkin spice pedicure! That sounds amazing!'"

Lucy nods with a wisp of smile.

"But then, because I'm forty-four years old, I know that a pumpkin spice pedicure will only give me a whiff of something vaguely sweet that will soon be slightly nauseating and will be no different than any other pedicure I've ever had, and so I just go about my errands."

Lucy smiles ruefully as I continue, "But the long-limbed girl was all enchanted by the magic of the pumpkin spice pedicure and she pleaded with this look that was like, 'Can we, Mommy? *Can* we?' And the mother smiled. 'Why not?' And the two of them walked into Bellacures along with a perfect little ring-a-ling of ye olde fashioned doorbell."

I can tell Lucy feels how such a thing could prick me and, appreciating feeling known, I keep talking, puzzling it out for myself. "Then it occurred to me that this woman had had many daughters already before this particular incarnation of this particular teenage daughter, this almost grown-ish girl proudly sucking her caffeinated, whipped-cream coffee drink and picking out a color for her toenails. That woman might have had a daughter, same name of course, she dressed in tiny socks and carried in her arms, and another who learned to feed the dog all by herself, and one who ran in circles around and around the fountain in the courtyard of the medical plaza, and many others before this nail-salon daughter, who in a previous incarnation might have worn a ladybug helmet and ridden one of those scooter things and licked ice cream on a cone from Salt & Straw, and now was so happy to be getting maybe even her first pedicure with her person, this same person who witnessed all those other selves and knew their secrets and miraculously bought that ladybug helmet for the girl she used to be, all those years ago."

Lucy frowns in sympathy, a frown I know does not make her face traditionally beautiful, a frown that emphasizes the heaviness and in-elasticity of her skin, but a frown that seems poignantly graceful to me.

"What do you feel when you see this mother with her girl?" she asks.

"Loss, I guess."

"Loss?"

"Yes, loss and, I guess, frustration, or maybe anger at myself, be-cause why did I not do this thing women since the dawn of time have known they needed to do?"

"Mm-hmm."

"And barren. That word *barren* has been haunting me. It's such an ugly word. I've never identified with that word, but now it keeps coming to mind."

"But you've told me you are not barren, as far as you know. You have said that you made a choice."

"No, that's right, but the fact remains that—my fields, so to speak, are barren—you know?—unproductive, infertile. The choice part is somewhat irrelevant."

"Is it?"

"Well, I've not borne a child. Regardless of choice, that's still in-fertile, right?"

"Is that what you feel you're being told?"

I know what Lucy is doing. Lucy, as a narrative therapist, is sug-gesting it's my culture that tells me taking a girl on a scooter for an ice cream or a teenager in her school uniform for an autumn pedicure is what I need to be happy. She's inviting me to think about how our society instructs females on all sides that we are not women if we never become mothers. Narrative therapy, I've come to learn, is about recognizing the stories your culture has told you about who you are or should be and asking if they work for you or if you can discard them and get on with living out your life.

"I bet you had good reasons for not having children." Lucy prompts.

"I don't know about that. I mean, in my late twenties I didn't want to worry about a child of mine going to hell. I didn't believe in hell anymore, but it still haunted me. How could I bring a child into the world if there was a possibility, however remote, that it is run by that kind of God? People say they don't want to bring children into the world with this or that politician . . . but a politician, who cares? What about God with eternal vindictiveness?"

Lucy's eyes narrow slightly. I've talked about a lot in the auspices of Lucy's office, but not about these old hauntings that have not troubled me for many years. These are the concerns of a Maggie she has not yet met.

"Whenever I hear Christians say, 'Well, we just don't focus on God's wrath,' I think, *Really?* I want to say, 'You don't get any points for ignoring the atrocities of your leaders.' We can all spend our time focusing on how much Hitler loved his dog. And he did, by all accounts; Hitler loved his dog, Blondi, but that doesn't mean we can shift our focus from the six million Jews killed in the Holocaust to how loyal Hitler was to his dog or how many dog treats or runs around the bunker beloved Blondi got."

"Hitler's dog's name was really . . ."

"Yep, Blondi."

Lucy laughs with a grimace.

"Anyway, so the hell thing and then later, I was just trying to get my career going in Hollywood and doing that with a baby just seemed impossible and I was afraid of the anxiety a baby would bring. I remember thinking of the phrase 'hostage to fortune' and how a child immediately gives you something for fate, for the wheel of fortune to spin away, and I didn't want to be a hostage to anything, and then *time* happened, little by little so I didn't notice . . ."

I think it must be the end of our session by now, but Lucy doesn't say anything, so I keep going. "I mean, Jimmy asked me at least once every year for fifteen years, 'Do you want to have a baby, Maggie?' And '*God, no!*' was my answer every year, and now I feel like, I don't know, I've messed everything up."

Truthfully, though, I know I can deal with this kind of mess-up.

I promise, Dispenser of Demons, I bargain in my head, *if you let me be an ordinary disappointed career woman whose womb has dried up without bearing fruit, not to complain. I'll come to therapy every week. I'll talk about my sadness and confess my envy. I'll read articles in* The New York Times *about perimenopausal journeys of discovery. I'll write spoken-word essays that find wry laughter in my loss. I'll take my lashes and call it kindness. Just don't let me be crazy. Don't let me be ill.*

Lucy's steady gaze flinches. What has she noticed?

Ah. My arms have stolen across my chest again, like a shield. They're wrapped tightly. I find myself rocking.

I drop my arms, become still.

Lovely Lucy understands, and asks nothing.

"We're going to have to stop for now," she says kindly. "Let's pick this up next week."

Walking home I notice, beneath the sounds of traffic on Larchmont Boulevard, the opening and closing of car doors at the parking meters, people talking across the tables at the bistros along the sidewalk, and the sound of my sandals falling on the pavement, *thwack, thwack, thwack, thwack.*

Strange, I think. *I wonder why I noticed that.*

Then I become aware of my purse strap pulling against my shoulder, and the feeling of my heart thumping in my throat, and a prickling sensation gathering at the nape of my neck and spreading over my scalp.

I need to get back on Paxil right away, I think. In fact, that's really the first thing I should have done.

With a dash of hope, I think maybe if I can just get back on the medication, it'll be okay. Maybe that's all it is. I reason it through. Without a therapeutic serum level of the drug, my defenses have been down, and that's the only reason "it" was able to slip through. If I get back on the medication, all could be well.

I need to make an appointment with Dr. Rosen as soon as I get home. I quicken my pace as I remember David Foster Wallace's terrifying story, my object lesson for the pitfalls of going on and off psychotropic medications. He found a drug that worked for him; he started to feel okay, so he decided to go off that drug; he went back to feeling horrible again, so he went back on the drug; but the second time, because something really, really complicated in his brain had changed, instead of feeling okay, he killed himself.

I think of my parents and my sister, of poor Jimmy, of Sascha and her kids, of Anna and the legacy of Troubled Aunt Maggie.

"How much did anyone know about the trouble?" they will ask each other. "What was the trouble? It was such a weird trouble."

"It was something about repetition," they'll say.

"No. It was about anxiety."

"Or hell."

"That's right. It was about hell."

"It was something she couldn't let go of."

"She couldn't not think about it."

The abominable notion that suicides go to hell rushes into my head and floods through long-ago carved rivulets. How horrible that those who suffer most should be most deserving of punishment.

Unspeakable.

Waiting for the light at Larchmont and Beverly, I try to defuse my fear.

Sow peace with every step, I think, like Thich Nhat Hanh says, *even if you don't feel peaceful yet.* The light changes, and the green walking man and the low beeping sound for the visually impaired invite me to step, breathe, step, breathe, and find my calm. The problem is that my sandals do not support my collapsing arches and as I step, each foot sags inward, stressing my ankles and producing a sharp pain along the insides of my kneecaps, along with the chilling recognition, *I am old.*

Too old to be losing my mind like an adolescent girl. Franny in *Franny and Zooey* was nineteen. Sylvia Plath was twenty. I was nineteen the first time. That's a reasonable age.

But now I am forty-four.

How old, I tried to remember, was my grandmother when she had her psychological break? Fifty-two maybe?

I look up from the sidewalk and notice an explosion of pink bougainvillea blossoms blazing over a brick storybook house on the corner. The flowers are a kind of pink I particularly like: not princess, not "we're having a girl!", not like a scratch-n-sniff sticker in the Strawberry Shortcake book I purchased for my goddaughter Nerys, but a richer pink, like coral, like roses, like lips, like the palm of a baby's hand.

I think of a tree I loved, an Australian melaleuca Jimmy and I used to have in our backyard. It was like the Lorax's Truffula trees from Dr. Seuss, with whirling cotton candy tufts of lavender and lilac and violet, the trees from which the Once-ler wove his colored threads, the trees for whom the Lorax spoke. I felt lucky to look out at that whimsical tree each morning. The melaleuca's bursts of color reminded me of my fortune every day. But then we found out the tree's roots threatened the foundation of our home, and it had to be cut down. I think about how easily foundations can be penetrated, by trees, by disorders, by the passage of time and age. I think of loss. I can take some loss. I know how to lose a tree. I can lose a friend. I can lose the child I never had. I just can't go back to—

Klonopin, I think. *I need to ask Dr. Rosen for Paxil* and *Klonopin.*

I began taking Klonopin when my panic attacks began in acting school.

The first dose hit my quaking system like a purring wave of dry-ice mist on Halloween, and my anxiety began to disperse. From then on, whenever panic arose and began to escalate, I would take two little orange pills, and the solid-seeming panic would loosen into faint, floating wisps. Eventually, simply knowing the pills were available calmed my nerves. Carrying the orange prescription bottle in my purse was all I needed.

When I get home, I find Dr. Rosen's number in an old address book and dial.

"This number has been disconnected or is no longer in service."

I try again and get the same cold reply.

I stand, holding the receiver to my ear, wondering how to proceed.

How long has it been since I last saw Dr. Rosen? Four years? Five? My prescriptions have been on automatic refill for so long, I finally stopped checking in, and he never reached out to check in with me. *Is that even ethical?* I wonder for the first time. I place the receiver back on its cradle, put my hands over my face, and breathe into my palms. Exhale, and then, hold. Wait, five, four, three, two, one. Wait again and wait . . . and then let the air swoosh in.

Would Dr. Rosen be retired? I remember iron-colored hair, furry ears, heavy skin around the neck. Would he be in his seventies now?

I call Lucy, tell her I can't get hold of my psychopharmacologist, and ask for a referral. She gives me the name of a doctor.

Dr. Steven Goya.

Dr. Goya, I decide, will be my savior. Dr. Goya will sort this whole thing out.

8

Broken Street Lamp

Sleep abandons me, chilled and fetal, to a sweat-soaked comforter; my wet T-shirt clinging to my chest, my scalp tingling, my heart pounding as if I've been crouched for the last eight hours beneath an extended barrage of artillery fire.

I am no longer entirely in control of my own brain. And my body knows it.

I think about my grandmother, who also lost control, rocking in that chair, staring at a television that wasn't turned on for thirteen years. I can't help thinking of the night my grandmother's mind unraveled, far away in North Carolina, during the winter when I was eight. When my father received the call, I watched his face fall and heard the timbre of his voice change. I remember watching out the window as my mother saw him off in a cab, handing his tidy overnight bag through the door before easing it closed.

He came back with my grandmother in tow, and she stayed with us after that. For thirteen years she watched that blank TV screen. In the bones of my arms, and my spine, and the length of my legs, I have dreaded such an end to my psychological struggles.

I still haven't told Jim. We've both been working a lot and I get up earlier than he does. I've been able to hide the excessive sweating because we've been sleeping with two separate twin-size comforters ever since we stayed at a hotel one weekend where the beds were made in what they boasted was "European style." In the mornings, I simply put my sweaty comforter off to the side in front of an open window and before Jim wakes up, it's already dry.

Gingerly, I slide out of bed and look over at him, still sleeping soundly.

"It" is always the worst in the mornings, I note, staring across the hours between me and whatever sweaty and haunted relief I'll get when I can finally go back to bed tonight. Dr. Goya will not be able to see me for three days. I have three days before I can get back on Paxil, and I have exactly four Klonopins in the little orange bottle by my bedside. I don't want to take one, though. I am still hoping "it" will pass. Taking a Klonopin would be admitting that this is more than just a blip, would be making it too real.

I remember Dr. Rosen suggesting morning ice-cold showers to stimulate the parasympathetic nervous system and reduce cortisol levels. Of course, the last thing I want right now is a cold shower, but I decide to give it a go. Walking into the bathroom, I peel the fabric of my shirt away from my skin and give it several rough shakes. *Only thirty seconds*, I tell myself on my way to the bathroom, *and then it will be over.*

In front of the shower, I pull my sweaty T-shirt over my head, wad it into a ball, and feel its weight in my hand. I marvel for a moment at how heavy it is. This tug toward the earth represents precisely the weight of my fear, and this physical manifestation of my terror somehow comforts me. It's validating in an odd way, like reading the thermometer and learning you have a fever, that feeling of *I knew it. I knew I felt bad.*

I drop the shirt onto the yellow marble floor—*plop*—peel off my shorts and underwear, and step into the shower.

"Okay."

I yank the knob all the way to cold and inhale sharply as the faucet opens with a whoosh. When the fierce cold spray slaps my skin, I am instantly angry, as if despite my mind's awareness that this is a choice, my body, in its language of seized muscles and goose-pimpled skin, is objecting to being wronged. I wrap my arms around my torso against the frigid assault and count (as slowly as I can manage) from one to nine, and—

"*Ten!*" I shout, jerking the water off.

My phone rings as if on cue. Shuddering and panting, I spring out of the shower, grab a towel, cinch the fabric above my breasts, and pad on the balls of my feet back to the bedroom.

When I pick up the phone I hear Joanna's unintelligible shouting. "Hi, Joanna," I say. "Slow down."

"—and all of my animals!"

"Animals?" I'm lifting up the bottom of my towel to dry my still-dripping hair.

"Remember my show, Maggie?"

"Yes—"

"And you remember all of the animals from my show?"

"All your mechanical animals, yes."

"The sheriff is going to put all my stuff out on the street. All the pictures of my mom with Gloria Allred-who-is-a-famous-lawyer and a sheriff came by. Eviction means—"

"Eviction? Did you get an eviction notice?"

"'*Notice of Eviction!*' It's red."

"Is the sheriff there right now?"

"No, not anymore."

Since Joanna always changed the subject whenever I brought up rent, I assumed there was an arrangement of some kind.

"He asked me who I was, and I said, 'Joanna,' and he said, 'Joanna Hergert?' and I said, 'Yes,' and he said, 'Do you know what this means?' and I said, 'No,' and he said, 'It means you have to vacate the premises,' and I said, 'What?' and he said, 'You have to get out of the apartment.' I have to vacate the premises. I'm in dire straits, Maggie. I'm in dire straits."

"Oh, wow. Shit. Okay, we—we will—we'll just figure something out. Okay?"

"I'm going to be out on the street, Maggie!"

"You're not going to be out on the street."

Joanna pauses, stunned. "Really? I can stay at Jim's house?"

"What? No. I'm sorry. I told you. You can't stay here."

Jim and I have decided Joanna can never come stay with us. That can never happen, we have agreed. We know it would be too difficult to ever ask her to leave and we weren't willing to take her on as a permanent addition to our two-person family.

"But temporarily?" Joanna asks.

"I'm sorry, but no."

"I stayed at Jim's house the night my mother died, and we watched the Kardashians. Remember that, Maggie?"

"Yes."

"And that was fine, Maggie."

"It was, but—"

"So why can't I stay at Jim's house now?"

"Joanna—"

"I'm in dire straits, Maggie. *Dire straits.*"

"I know. We will figure something out, alright?"

Joanna doesn't reply, and I take advantage of her silence to inhale and exhale a long, deliberate breath before adding sympathetically, "We'll find something less expensive for you to rent."

"But I can't pay rent. How can I pay rent without money?"

"We'll find something you can afford."

"Without money?"

"Well, Jim and I can help and with the money you have."

"What money?"

"The money from Social Security."

"What?"

"The disability checks from Social Security."

"They don't come."

"What?"

"They don't come anymore."

"You don't get your disability checks?"

"No."

"Since when?"

"Since my mother died."

"But why don't you get your payments?"

"I don't know. My mother would know, but she's not here. My mother had her mind. She always had her mind. My mother could ride the bus to anywhere in the city. 'From anywhere to anywhere,' she always said. 'Let's go for a ride' . . ."

"We'll just have to take it one step at a time, okay? I'll take you to the Social Security office, for one thing, right away Monday morning, and we'll find out about those checks."

I hang up the phone, grab a fresh T-shirt and underwear, and begin getting dressed. As I pull my jeans up over my hips, I realize I'm not feeling so anxious. Maybe it was the cold water? Probably not. It was probably Joanna. Her personal catastrophe pulled me out of myself. I notice that my mind is clear—but before I can savor the moment of peace, the question occurs to me how long such equanimity can possibly last.

Not long, probably, is the first answer that comes to mind. And with that thought comes a little shot of fear.

Then I get a bigger shot, which, as my heart rate increases, supports the idea that I am completely losing control.

I'm never going to be able to stop this, I conclude. *This is my new normal.* I might as well go buy a rocking chair and a broken TV. And that thought—coupled with the prickling sensation that crawls up my neck and turns into needles stabbing my scalp—is so properly terrifying that I start to feel dizzy and have to sit down on the edge of the bed.

"Just notice the sensations," I remember my Zen teacher Daishin telling me after I described my second break. "You don't have to control the world. There is no need to strong-arm the universe. Try something different. Try watching."

There's the tingling in my scalp and forearms.

There's the force of my heartbeat.

There's the dampness on the insides of my elbows.

It's just fear, I tell myself in an inner singsong as I pull a V-neck over my head. It's just my sympathetic nervous system kicking in and all my excited little neurons firing off their festive firework displays. La-di-da. That's all. Just a bunch of silly synapse activations making sparks. Hahaha. What a crazy crew.

My goddaughter Ruby has been learning the organs of the limbic system.

"The lizard brain," she says. "Thalamus, hypothalamus, and amygdala. It's a three-headed dragon!" A powerful dragon entirely impervious to the mollifying interventions of my reeling cerebral cortex. Then, without conscious forethought or choice, my body lifts from the bed, right arm outthrust, and a trembling hand picks up the orange pill bottle from my nightstand. Soon, one of the four magic tablets I have left is balanced on my tongue and I am taking a sip from a bottle of water and counting backward silently from ten.

There's a parking lot next to the putty-colored Social Security Administration building on Vine Street in Hollywood, but the parking lot is full, so I've left my car down the street in front of the bright yellow wall of the CA Surplus. Stenciled logos on the outside of the building advertise that you can buy a Coleman stove, or Timberland shoes, or a Maglite flashlight, among other items, or have a new set of keys made, or dog tags, or fit yourself for a gas mask.

As Joanna and I walk past the store's back entrance, I notice passersby struggling to make sense of our odd pairing. Their eyes dart from my manicured hands to Joanna's grimy nails and compare my well-maintained highlights with her thickly matted, auburn curls. Joanna is obviously struggling with a psychological condition. Her mental disability is on full display; her grooming, her gait, how she looks around as if she were in a forest and wild predators could come from any direction. Even from a distance, Joanna's suffering is apparent to all.

For a moment, I think there might be a little blessing in that, in appearing on the outside as you feel on the inside.

The bright yellow wall reflects a cartoonish cheerful wash of Monday morning sunshine: Hollywood, California, in all its unforgiving glory. It's a light suited to a *Thomas the Tank Engine* video or to one of those as yet un-disappointed aspiring actresses who seem to sprout like grass through cracked concrete everywhere I look, scarily convinced that visualization alone might at any moment vault them right out of the human condition and into everlasting success.

It's not a light for Joanna and me, though, not today at any rate, as we grimly make our way up the sidewalk. A better light for us would be the kind of broken streetlamp that jitters on and off all night long, never allowing your eyes to adjust to the dark and never illuminating the sidewalk quite enough to see whether or not you might be stepping in gum.

Inside the building, a short woman with broad shoulders and rough skin pulls a bandana tight over her forehead. I watch her step up to an X-ray machine and drop her bag in front of a guard. I step up behind her and am about to do the same, when the guard suddenly barks, "Behind the line!"

The guard's eyes remain focused on the woman's bag and so somehow I don't guess he might be addressing me.

"*Behind the line!*" he yells again, shooting to his six-foot, two-inch height as if I were brandishing a weapon and threatening to storm his post.

"What?" I say, widening my eyes in a startled and instinctively apologetic expression. "Are you talking to me?"

The guard jabs a finger toward my feet, and I look down to see the tips of my sandals crossing a piece of ratty red tape stretched on the floor.

"Oh my goodness, I'm so sorry," I say, jumping back.

The guard inspects my shoes to make sure the toes are now behind the tape.

"Sorry, again," I say, arranging my face in a rueful smile that reliably disarms hostility, which I've perfected for that purpose. "Where's the line for disability inquiries?"

"Go to the machine," the guard growls, uncharmed. "Get a number."

Waiting for Joanna on the other side of the metal detector, I feel my heartbeat against my sternum. Gently wiping the damp inside of my elbows down toward my wrists and up toward my shoulders, I deliberately extend an exhalation until my lungs feel completely empty. *Hold, hold, hold*, I say to myself in a little procedure I discovered years ago at Grace Point Hospital. Resist the impulse to breathe, and then . . . release. Fresh air rushes back in, bringing a portion of the minor relief I had been hoping for, and I lead Joanna over to a large touch-screen monitor mounted in the hallway.

Following the prompts, I tap in her name, then . . . "What's your birth date?" I ask.

Joanna whips her eyes down to her hands, which are urgently gripping each other, and presses her lips together.

"I need to enter in your date of birth," I repeat.

A teenage girl with long dark roots and a bleached ponytail impatiently bounces a bald baby on her hip behind us.

"Sorry," I turn and say to the girl, then back to Joanna. "I need to know your birthdate, Joanna. You know it, right?"

Joanna crosses her arms and rocks her weight forward onto the balls of her feet and then backward to her heels several times.

"The Golden Girls never tell their age. Sophia and Dorothy and Rose and Blanche *never* tell their age. Blanche says it should be a criminal offense—punishable by three to five years in prison. *Asking a woman her age*, Blanche says, *should be a criminal offense.*"

"Even Blanche Devereaux would make an exception at the Social Security office," I say, controlling my temper through the grip of my jaw. "Blanche Devereaux would realize, in order to get the money she wanted, she would have to type in her age."

Joanna stares at me, unyielding, her feet planted and her jaw set.

I turn back to see the mother and the baby on her hip, both looking like they are about to erupt in a wail.

"You do it, then," I say, backing away from the machine. "Tap the month, then the day, then the year. I won't look. Here"—I cover my eyes with my hands—"see? I can't see anything."

Joanna ponders for a moment, apparently weighing the risk. "Okay," she finally says, walking cautiously toward the machine, one foot directly in front of the other, as if out onto a diving board. I coach her from the side through the process of entering the appropriate digits. Then, after much review, she takes the plunge and hits enter.

A printout tells us to go Window 4, where a weary woman informs us that Joanna's disability payments have been suspended because she has no representative payee.

"I'm sorry," I say, "Could you explain what that means?"

"Payee deceased," she says, bleary eyes sliding from me to Joanna and back. "It's in the file."

Joanna's disability payments have stopped, apparently, because Sunny had been receiving them on her behalf. Now that Sunny has died, the administration cannot issue a check.

"Since Ms. Hergert is not competent to receive payment herself, she must have a new representative payee. Her representative payee will receive payment and then disburse the funds to Ms. Hergert."

"So will Social Security assign her one? How do I help with that?" I ask.

"Our offices do not assign representatives."

"Oh. Well, who does, then?"

"That's up to her," the woman says.

"So then, who can she ask?"

"It doesn't matter. She can ask anyone she wants."

Thumbing through the stack of paperwork I have brought home to facilitate my stepping in for Sunny as Joanna's legal representative, I learn that Joanna $1,200 a month in disability payments and conclude that I'll need to find her a substantially less expensive apartment than the one she will soon be locked out of.

Something under $900, I figure, will leave her what she'll require for other expenses, and if Jim and I help out a little, there should be enough for food, TV, movies, Cabbage-Patch-doll outfits, crayons, and construction paper on which to draw suggestive pictures for my husband.

I've just started browsing the listings on PacificRentals.com when an upsetting piece of information pokes through the surface of my Facebook feed. A woman I vaguely know from a yoga workshop I once took has just sold a screenplay to Hallmark. Why is this upsetting? Because *I* am not the one who sold a screenplay to Hallmark. I have, however, *written* a screenplay for Hallmark, one I labored on for months, but *my* script languishes on some mid-level development executive's desk.

I click the link to the *Hollywood Reporter* article helpfully provided in the post and read about the project. I grow dizzy as my anxiety escalates. It's a ridiculous physiological response, I have the presence of mind to observe. At this point, my career success or lack of it is far from my biggest concern. Somehow, though, this petty covetousness toward a fellow yoga practitioner I barely know has further dysregulated my already out-of-whack nervous system.

I find myself following determined feet down the hallway to my bedroom and watching as my hands pick up the orange bottle from my dresser and open its childproof lid and place on my tongue not one but two orange pills, which I swallow together.

I walk to the kitchen, open a bottle of merlot, and pour a generous measure into a long-stemmed glass. As the light passes through, it appears as a deep-purplish mixture of red and blue and green. The color of black roses, I realize.

I return to my computer, glass in hand, refocused on finding an apartment for Joanna, but I can't find anything for under nine hundred a month in the area. I'm hoping to find a place nearby. It will be easier to help her get set up and do . . . well, whatever Sunny used to do.

My boundaries expanded by Klonopin and wine, I try another site and feel good about locating a studio apartment in Silverlake for $825 a month, utilities included. Silverlake isn't walking distance, but it's also not a long drive, and the building is on the same street as a Buddhist meditation place I often attend. That qualifies as familiar turf. The rent is cheap because parking in the area is a nightmare, but Joanna can't drive, so it's not an issue.

Perfect, I think, and dial the landlord's number.

"This is Nazrini," a man's soft voice answers after two rings. "How may I help you?"

"Good evening, Nazrini," I say. "My name is Joanna Hergert and I'm calling about your apartment for rent." The call goes smoothly, and we agree on an appointment for the next day at 5:00 p.m. As I hang up the phone, I notice that I can no longer feel my heartbeat in my chest. Apparently I will be fine as long as I take twice the prescribed dosage of an addictive sedative and couple it with alcohol, which the pill bottle warns against.

"I think I found an apartment," I yell to Jim, who has not been informed that there is anything askew in my brain. "It's right near Against the Stream."

"Against the Stream?" Jim yells back from the kitchen.

"Yeah. You know, that meditation place."

"In Silverlake."

"That's right."

"There's no parking in Silverlake."

"I know that. Joanna doesn't drive. I told the landlord that I was Joanna. I'm going to meet him tomorrow at five."

"You told him what?"

"I'm going to pretend to be Joanna," I say, checking out the building on Google Maps.

Jim leans his head into my office. "Why did you do that?"

"No way a landlord is going to rent to Joanna once he meets her, so I'm going to check out the place and make a good impression."

"You can't do that."

"It's not going to be a problem," I insist. "I'll be paying Joanna's rent once the papers are filed."

"I don't feel great about this."

"Why not?"

"You'll be lying."

"Oh please," I say. "Rigorous honesty is important in relationship to oneself, but in relation to other people, it's overrated."

"He could sue."

"Not if he gets his rent."

"Anyone can sue any time they want, for anything."

"What could he sue us for?"

"Fraud, to begin with, and then diminished property values and who knows what else? The networks don't offer courses in real estate law."

"Fine," I say, grabbing a scrunchie from beside my computer and winding my hair into a tight ponytail. "I'll take Joanna with me."

"Why does it have to be tomorrow?" Joanna asks, alarmed.

I cradle the phone between my shoulder and ear and say, "Because I found a place that will fit into your budget. So, 5:00 p.m. tomorrow. And before that, I want to take you to get a"—I pause dramatically to let Joanna know the next words out of my mouth are going to be exciting—"to get a . . . *makeover!*"

I don't know why I expect Joanna to be happy about this proposal. The expectation is entirely unreasonable given past evidence, but still I somehow anticipate that she will squeal in delight and clap her hands in a small frenzy. *A makeover? Me? Just like on TV! Oh, thank you. Thank you!*

But there's no squealing, no frenzied clapping.

"A what?" Joanna asks flatly.

"A makeover! We'll get you a new outfit. We can go to the hair salon on Larchmont."

A sniff.

"Haas and Company! You can get a blowout."

"They'll try to make it straight. Jim likes my hair curly. He likes my curls."

"He does, but he'll like it blown out, too. It's fun to get a new look."

I really want Joanna to get her hair blown dry. But why? For one thing, a blowout is an established urban symbol of disposable income and will signal to the landlord that Joanna is more likely to pay her rent on time than someone who couldn't tame her hair with both hands.

I guess I'm also curious. I want to see what Joanna will look like with straight hair. Like when I used a flat iron on my life-size Barbie styling head, pulling the blond curls out into stick-straight icicles. The possibility of Joanna's physical transformation unfolding before my eyes is exciting. Also, I recognize there's an irrational hope that taming her hair could actually tame her mind, as if just seeing herself refreshed and nicely put together in a mirror might miraculously cause her to think, *Holy shit. Look at that. I can be normal. Forget all this "differently abled" bullshit. That's just a drag. It's time for me to sign up for GED classes and start making eye contact with others.*

But that's my own problem, I realize. Looking at myself in the mirror and thinking, *There's nothing wrong with that woman*, and supposing all my travails can't be real, that I'm making them all up in my head and could just as well unmake them if I simply chose to.

Though of course I'm not, and I can't, and neither can Joanna.

I'd also simply like to see Joanna happy and pleased with something new: a Larchmont blowout. Like a mother, I want to be able to say, "Look at this. Isn't this cool? Beauticians can turn your hair into a bolt of silk and then you can have fun swishing it around like a princess for the rest of the day."

For all these reasons, but mostly for the first, I try again to persuade her.

"It will be an adventure, Joanna. Movie stars change their hair all—"

"When I was baby at the hospital," she says, "the nurse told my dad she had never seen curls on a baby like mine. She'd never seen anything like it."

"Okay, okay. Fine," I say. "They'll just do a cut, and—"

"No!" Joanna yelps, "You can't make me cut my hair!"

"Why not?"

"It won't grow back."

"What?"

"It won't grow back."

"Of course it will grow back. Everyone's hair grows back."

"*My* hair hasn't grown since I was seven."

"Alright, fine. You're the exception to the human race," I say with a snarkiness no one should be proud of. "We'll ask just for a shampoo and style, then. How does that sound?"

There is silence on the other end of phone, which I take for assent. The Joanna-apartment-hunt-makeover plan is in motion.

"It's illegal to straighten someone's hair without their permission!" Joanna shouts before hair-stylist Larissa can invite her to sit down.

"What's that, sweetie?" the six-foot African American fashion plate purrs, unfazed.

"You can't make me have straight hair. You can't make me. It's illegal. You don't have my permission."

"Of course not."

Larissa reaches out to feel the texture of Joanna's hair. Her delicately painted, rainbow-colored nails stand out against its deep shades of reddish brown. "Such lovely curls."

"When I was born, the nurse said she had never seen curls like mine on a baby."

"Indeed." Larissa is nodding to Joanna, but one perfectly shaped, slightly raised eyebrow and a quick glance throws a subtle reality check out toward me.

"Joanna would like a shampoo and styling," I say, smiling and nodding to signify that I recognize that Joanna's behavior is not traditional behavior but that I *am* traditional and that at the end of this session she will be traditionally paid. "A shampoo and a styling, that's all."

"But you can't cut it," Joanna insists, pinning her gaze on Larissa and grabbing fistfuls of hair on the sides of her head, protecting her wares.

"She's not going to cut it," I say, but Joanna's fists only squeeze tighter.

"Just a shampoo and styling," I tell Larissa and then with an eye to placate Joanna. "Nothing more."

"Alright, then, sweetie. Come with me," Larissa murmurs, bending down to Joanna's eye level and offering her hand as if to a child.

Joanna crosses her arms over her chest and thrusts her lower lip out.

Larissa smiles, straightens, and gestures to her station, inviting Joanna to lead.

Forty-five minutes later Joanna steps through the archway, blinking. Larissa follows close behind, holding her arms in a presentational gesture that seems to declare *abracadabra* and *presto change-o* and *voila* all in one. The change in Joanna's appearance is indeed astounding. Her electrified mane lies soothed and grounded, frizz channeled into smooth waves that lap over her shoulders.

"Whoa," I say to Larissa, handing her the money with a tip. "You're a magician. Thank you so much!"

"You're welcome," Larissa replies, smiling. "Come back any time."

"Oh my goodness," I exclaim, turning to Joanna, spreading my arms wide. "Look at you!"

"I told the lady I didn't want it straight."

I hope to see a twinkle sneak into her eyes, but her gaze remains flat.

"Jim likes my hair curly. Jim likes girls," she says pointedly, her eyes pinned on my lank, fake-blond mop, "with *curly* hair."

Then, for the first time all day, she smiles.

Riding the escalator from the parking lot to the main entrance at Target, Joanna presses her body against the cold metal siding and white-knuckles the black handrail as if we were riding a rollercoaster about to zip into a gravity-defying corkscrew.

"Exciting, right?" I prompt, still hungry for a trace of excitement on her part. "Makeover Day! I've always wanted a makeover."

Joanna just stares at her feet. "Nobody shops at Target."

"What?" I furrow my brow in surprise and nod to the other shoppers ascending to the store. "Lots of people do."

"Celebrities don't."

"Celebrities?"

"The Kardashians don't."

"Well, you're right. Celebrities probably don't shop here."

"No!" Joanna erupts, then suddenly laughs with surprising force. "Celebrities definitely don't shop at Target. They probably shop at Chanel and Gucci. Celebrities shop on Rodeo Drive at Chanel and Gucci. We're not going to see any of the Kardashians at Target. That's one thing I know for sure. I may not be an aerospace engineer who worked on the moon landing like my father, but I know that."

"Wait, what? The moon landing?"

"Yes, my father," Joanna says, her chest rising, "my father worked on the moon landing. The big one, the big one where they landed all the way on the moon. My dad was an aerospace engineer—"

I marvel for a moment at how smoothly *aerospace engineer* flows off Joanna's tongue, not to mention her father working on, I guess, one of the *Apollo*s.

"My father was very smart. You don't get to work on the moon landing by not being smart."

I nodded. Undeniable.

Then her mood darkened. "The only person he ever hurt was himself," she said. "He wasn't a mean drunk. He wasn't a bad drunk. The only person he ever hurt was himself."

"Ah," I say, attempting to express sympathy while processing new information.

We turn the corner and get on a second elevator. As we ride up, I notice Joanna's gaze being pulled by something over my shoulder. I turn to see a thick bald man covered almost entirely in tattoos descend the elevator opposite us. Joanna nakedly scowls at him as he passes.

"Not a big fan of tattoos?" I ask casually.

"The Other One has tattoos. He has tattoos all over his face."

Joanna has not referred to her brother since the first time we met at Koo Koo Roo.

"Oh wow, a tattoo on his face? That sounds painful. What's he like—the Other—well, what's his actual name?"

"Phillip," Joanna growls.

"What's Phillip like?"

"Bad. Even my mother agrees. He goes to jail for methamphetamine drugs, then comes out, before he goes back. Sometimes he stays with me and my mother before he goes back."

"Is Phillip," I ask tentatively, "ever violent?"

Joanna stares straight ahead.

"My father was never violent. He drank alcohol but he never hurt anyone but himself. No one but himself. My father was an aerospace engineer. He worked on the moon landing. You have to be very smart to work on the moon landing."

"But was Phil—?"

"The Other One is bad," Joanna says, ending the discussion.

I lead Joanna off the elevator toward the red Target sign, possessed by the need to feel like Daddy Warbucks. "Whatever you want," I say, sweeping my arm grandly to the entire Women's Casual section. "Pick out whatever you want."

Joanna looks from me to the clothing racks and back to me again.

"Is something wrong?"

She crosses her arms and rocks forward onto the balls of her feet, then back to her heels.

"Joanna?"

She doesn't answer but stares at the floor and continues rocking.

I walk to a rack of brightly colored skirts. "What size are you?"

"I don't know."

"You don't know your size?"

"I lost weight," she says without looking up. "I lost weight. Since my mother died. I lost weight, but I'm not trying to lose weight, but it's what happens when your mother dies. It's just what happens."

Then she abruptly brightens. "My mother was always the same weight. She was always the same weight until she broke her hip, and she always had her mind. You have to admit that, Maggie. She always had her mind. She could ride the bus. She could ride the bus anywhere she wanted in the city."

"Yes, she totally had her mind," I say, rubbing the fabric of several skirts between my fingers before pulling out a blue A-line. "You're right about that. What about this one?"

Joanna frowns and shakes her head firmly. I lead her to the next section and pull a yellow romper pantsuit with oversized pockets from the hanging display.

Joanna squinches her nose in distaste.

"No?"

I suggest a purple cap-sleeve sweater, then a pale, silky blouse with large flowers, a striped pullover, a gray T-shirt that says AVOCADO-HOLIC in blocky moss-green letters.

No. No. No. And No.

Past the next rack, I notice a woman my age with a teenage girl. Both have slender necks, broad shoulders, and narrowly placed green eyes magnified like capers in a jar by the thick lenses of identical wire-rim glasses.

Look at that, I think. They are so undeniably mother and daughter, sole representatives of their own two-person species, belonging to-gether as surely as a duck with her ducklings or a bear with her cubs. It occurs to me as I observe them that the two are forever tied one to the other by those necks, those shoulders, those narrowly placed caper-green eyes. The mother stands with a stack of clothes, which appears heavy but not burdensome, slung over her forearm. The daughter hands her a denim skirt, she adds them to her collection, and the daughter runs off, back to the hunt. I remember once reading about attachment parenting and how securely attached children feel confident enough to go off by themselves on the playground, assured that the parent will be there when they return.

Joanna stays by my side, immobilized, as I watch the young woman sort through blouses, consumed by her mission, examining each piece of clothing thoroughly before moving on to the next. Suddenly she thrusts a purple sweatshirt emblazoned with a glittery unicorn and the words BE UNIQUE up overhead where it will catch the fluorescent lighting. With her free hand, she brushes off the sweatshirt, clearing off the dust so its subtleties can be illuminated, then runs back to her mother to present the unearthed treasure.

With Joanna at my side, uncertain, her arms crossed over her chest, I bring my attention back to the rack in front of us, where it comes to rest on a brown suede dress with brass buttons down the front.

"Hey Joanna," I say, holding it up. "How about this?"

Joanna looks at the dress, then bolts away from me like I'm presenting a court summons that she must not acknowledge.

"Joanna, why are you running? I'm just showing you a dress!" I trot after her. "It's pretty! It's a pretty dress!"

Joanna dodges past a rack of maxi-dresses and heads into Athletic Wear without looking back.

"Where are you going?"

I almost overtake her by a clothing stand of comfortable-looking velour warm-up suits, but she darts away into Lingerie and weaves through a collection of silky bras and cotton panties. I rush after her, narrowly avoiding slamming into a display case of thongs, until I finally manage to corner her in front of a display of flannel pajamas.

"Joanna, why are you running?" I say, panting. "What's going on?"

"Oh, I didn't see you."

"Of course you saw me," I say exasperated, raising my palms and karate-chopping them in the air in an absurd display of frustration. "I held up the dress and you jumped away like I was about to—"

"*I didn't see you!*"

"Fine," I say, dropping my arms, deflating, accepting the futility of making sense of the senseless and continue as if our chase through Women's Casual never happened. "I was just wondering what you thought of this dress."

Joanna grabs each of her elbows and starts rocking again.

"It's okay, I guess."

"You like it?"

"It's okay."

It's not the enthusiasm I was hoping for, but I'll take it.

"I'll be out here," I say, plopping down wearily outside the fitting room on a green faux-velvet chair. The hours with Joanna have drawn down my reserves. Rubbing my hands over my face, I find that the steady-state anxiety, buzzing since morning beneath the purposeful activities of the day, has begun to rise. I can feel my pulse in my forehead, hard and insistent. I press my fingers into my temples and massage the sheath of muscle that extends there from my jaw in small circles.

Breathe. One, two, three.

Then push my breath out through the bellows of my lungs until they are empty.

Hold, and hold, and hold, and inhale.

Cool air rushes in, and my chest rises on a tiny wave of relief.

Out again, two, three, four. And hold, and hold, and hold, and, wait for it, inhale.

Repeat, repeat, repeat.

After five minutes pass, I get up and knock on the fitting room door, my anxiety feeling as if it might soon spike.

"I'm changing," comes Joanna's voice.

"Okay, but we have to meet the landlord fairly soon. Can you go any faster?"

The caper-eyed mother—now with an enormous stack of clothing over her arm—and daughter approach the fitting-room attendant.

"Six items only," the red-vested employee instructs.

The mother counts out six items from her stack and hands them to her daughter. "I'll be out here if you need—"

"I don't," the daughter says, skipping to an open fitting room and clicking the door closed behind her.

"Uh-huh." The mother smiles, unoffended at being put off. "I'll wait."

Joanna, though, does need help.

"Come on," I say, knocking again on the door.

"I'm changing."

"I know that, but you're taking a really long time. What are you doing?"

"Changing."

"Can I come in?"

Silence.

I turn the handle, but the door is locked.

"You're going to have to unlock the door."

There's some knocking around inside, then a metallic clang on the floor, and I'm leaning forward to ask again if she needs help when the door flies out at my face. My arms shoot up to ward off the blow, but I'm not quick enough, and the wooden plank bangs first into my forehead and then my elbows.

"Ow," I cry angrily, rubbing my forehead. "Joanna!"

She looks at me, impassive. "Okay."

"Okay?" I huff. "*Okay?* You could at least say you're sorry."

"I didn't know you would be standing there."

"Sure you did. You just heard me knock."

"I thought you'd get out of the way. *I* would have gotten out of the way."

"You wouldn't have had time . . . nobody . . . oh, never mind." I sigh. "Let me see what's going on."

I step into the fitting room and look at Joanna. The dress fits reasonably well, but the buttons are off by two. "The buttons are in the wrong holes," I say. "Mind if I fix them?"

Joanna shrugs, so I do, and when I'm finished, I step back and take another look. Properly done up, the dress is actually rather becoming. It suits Joanna well. The only problem I see is that the material is thin, and without a bra, her breasts show through.

"Nice," I say to Joanna. "And how about a new bra?"

"A new bra? I don't know why I'd need a new bra. I've never had a bra before. I don't know why I'd need a bra."

Never had a bra? What kind of mother neglects to provide her extremely full-breasted daughter a bra? One who had her hands full just keeping her daughter alive, I suppose.

"You stay here," I say. "Let me get you one."

If I am a 36B, I think, *Joanna must be a 38D, or DD.* I begin hunting for a fifty-five-year-old woman's first bra.

I try to piece the together the puzzle of Joanna. Her father was an aerospace engineer, who worked on the moon landing, who drank himself to death. He left a decent pension to his wife and he wasn't abusive. Why didn't Sunny send Joanna to school past fifth grade, though? Was she scared Joanna would be diagnosed with a psychiatric illness and taken away? Was this before autism was a diagnosis? Would it have been considered something else? Or did Joanna just refuse so stubbornly to go to school that Sunny proved no match for her and eventually surrendered?

I return to the dressing room with a Maidenform underwire bra, size 38DD, and hand it over the door to Joanna. Then I sit down again and wait, again, for about five minutes until my patience flags, and my looping and anxiety rise, and I am once more knocking on the dressing room door.

"How's it coming?"

"Oh, okay."

"I'm coming in now. Unlock the door, okay?"

Having learned my lesson earlier, I catch the swinging door as she flings it open and then slide inside the dressing room.

Joanna is wearing the bra, but instead of snugging the underwire cups completely under her breasts, she has stretched them directly under her nipples, leaving two balloons of flesh hanging below.

"Oh, no, Joanna," I say. "These bras are designed to . . . You're supposed to put the wire . . ."

Joanna stares at me blankly.

"That looks really uncomfortable. Can I help?"

"Okay."

I reach over, take hold of the underwire, and attempt to pull the bra down, but I only manage to move it an inch of so, and it remains uncomfortably drawn over the meat of her breasts.

Next, I try pushing the flesh up from beneath. The skin is cold against my fingers, and I feel strange touching another woman's breasts, so I stop.

"You know what, Joanna, maybe you can bend over. That might work better."

Joanna bends over, placing her hands on her thighs, and I kneel down in front of her, squeezing myself between her shins and the chair behind me.

"Let's see," I say, and I reach up, hook my fingers around the bra's underwire, and yank it toward Joanna's waist. I manage to get the wire on the right side situated correctly beneath her breast, but her left breast has spilled out entirely.

"Shit. Sorry. Wait," I say, standing up and knocking over the chair. "I'm sorry."

Joanna stands up, and I pick up the chair, sit down, grab the left side of the bra with my right hand, hold her bosom in place with my left hand, pull the fabric over the left nipple, and secure the underwire where it belongs.

"There we go," I say, exhaling with relief, but then I see that her left breast is sitting significantly higher than her right.

"One more thing," I say, reaching up to tighten the right strap and overdoing it so that her right breast now sits just a little higher than the left.

"And this," I say, hiking up the left side to make the two sides even, but then both are too high.

"Well," I say, deciding this is good enough, "that's okay for now. Now let's get the dress back on, okay?"

Joanna steps into the dress and I help her button it up correctly. The bra makes a big difference.

"Joanna," I exclaim. "Look at you!"

With her hair shampooed and styled, and her new dress, her makeover amounts to a substantial accomplishment. She could pass for a slightly eccentric librarian, sporting an impressive rack. Or an offbeat med tech sporting an impressive rack.

I am pleased, and even though she won't say so, I can see that Joanna is pleased as well. Her gaze is fixed on the mirror, with interest, and she turns, first to one side to study her reflection, and then to the other.

"You look good, Joanna, don't you think?"

She nods ever so slightly.

We walk up the street toward the Silverlake address, Joanna trailing behind me, concentrating on her feet. As we walk past a storefront art gallery called Müsh, I drift into a little fantasy of Joanna receiving an exhibition at the hipster hangout for her penis drawings. It's a small-time gala event, and she becomes the toast of the Silverlake arts community.

Hergert's unjaded sensibility defies her fifty-five years, I envision reading in the *LA Weekly. Her drawings emerge from a powerful, deeply sublimated libido, fully erect.*

I imagine champagne bubbling in clear plastic flutes while talk of sales soaring into six figures buzzes in the background and aspiring collectors press to hear my tale of Joanna Hergert from Koo Koo Roo. The fancy set will examine me over studded vintage eyewear, their eyes a-glitter with fascination and greed. I will sell the screenplay to Hallmark, and the *Hollywood Reporter* will announce, "Woman Discovers Autistic Artist, Takes Bohemian Art World by Storm."

Past Müsh is an empty shop with a FOR RENT sign in the window, and my mind returns to its present errand. "So," I say to Joanna, stopping for her to catch up, "when we see the landlord, I'm going to say, 'Hello. You must be Nazrini,' and then he'll say 'Yes, I am,' and I'll say, 'I'm Maggie and this is Joanna,' and he'll say, 'Hello,' and then we'll both say, 'Nice to meet you, Nazrini.' Okay?"

Joanna continues to walk with her head down, but she also begins with one hand to pick at the hair falling about her shoulders.

"Stop that, Joanna. Wait till after we're done."

Joanna frowns, but her hands freeze.

"What are you going to say after Nazrini says, 'Hello?'"

"I'll say, 'It's nice to meet you.'"

"Yes, good, but don't forget to say his name, too. People like it when you say their names."

"I'm not good with names, though, Maggie. I forget them all the time. It's just what happens."

"Well, remember this one. It's important. *Nazrini.* Say it."

"Nazrini."

"Perfect! Alright. 'Nice to meet you, Nazrini,' and when we look around the apartment, find some things you like and point them out to Nazrini. It's his place, so if you say nice things about it, he'll like it. Say something like, 'Oh, what a nice view from the window,' or, 'I love that bathtub,' or, 'The refrigerator is bigger than I expected.'"

"The refrigerator is big?"

"I don't know."

"Does it have an ice machine?"

"I don't know anything about the refrigerator. The refrigerator was just an example. Just, you know, say positive things. Give him compliments."

We walk past Against the Stream, with its punk rock anarchic Buddhist aesthetic, and I suddenly wonder, *What if Joanna started meditating?* I imagine her blossoming into the darling of Against the Stream, or even a seminal teacher. "It's just what happens" will be her signature "punk rock" phrase, and her teachings will facilitate spontaneous awakenings among eastside L.A. seekers of all stripes. A contemporary Chance the Gardener, every comer will discern their own projected answers in the cipher of her blank personality.

The "it's just what happens" movement will point to the fact that ideas that seem disparate, or even opposing—like "everything happens for a reason" or "shit just happens" or "it's all part of God's plan" or "it is what it is"—are actually experienced quite similarly in different people's brains. What matters is that you stop objecting to what is and you shake hands with your own life. Joanna will point this out.

But why stop there? What if she genuinely pierces the veil of earthly illusion, and her equanimity, like the flap of the butterfly's wings, ripples across the world and alters the human experience?

"I'm not going to lie and say the refrigerator is big if it's not big," Joanna announces, puncturing my reverie.

"Fine," I sigh, "but try to say something nice."

An elegantly dressed Indian man is standing with his hands clasped behind his back in front of the building, and he smiles as we approach.

"You must be Nazrini," I say, putting on my most carefully constructed nice-and-reliable persona.

"Yes, good evening. And you are . . . ?"

"I'm Maggie Rowe, and this is Joanna Hergert."

"Nice to meet you," he says.

"Nice to meet you, too, Nazrini," I say pointedly, looking to Joanna. I try to make eye contact, but her focus is darting all about, as if tracking invisible mosquitoes.

"Thanks for meeting us on such little notice," I add, pressing my palms together in a prayerful gesture of respect before immediately dropping my hands to the side, thinking I must look like one of those white ladies I imagine he despises who reflexively offer *Namaste* to every brown-skinned person they encounter.

Joanna barrels past both of us and climbs three steps to the front door. She grabs the doorknob and pulls, and when the door doesn't give way, starts yanking at it with inexplicable fury.

"Let me get that for you," Nazrini says, politely ignoring Joanna's behavior.

He takes a key ring from his coat pocket and opens the front door, gesturing to a modest entryway. "Please come in."

Joanna and I follow as he heads into the building, and I squeeze Joanna's arm, probably harder than I should, and whisper in her ear, "Remember. Say something nice."

Joanna jerks her arm away and rushes ahead.

Nazrini stops and opens a door at the end of the corridor, and we follow him into a very small but clean room with recently painted walls and well-worn hardwood floors. Past the single room, we find a tiny checkered bathroom and a kitchenette with a compact stove and refrigerator.

"Oh God," Joanna declares in a volume more appropriate to public address than intimate commentary, "I really am in dire straits. Hard knocks. These are *very* hard knocks."

Nazrini looks at her, cocking his head to one side.

"Pretty colored walls!" I almost yell. "*Pretty.* I like this blue. Sky blue, right? Colors really make a difference, don't you think, Joanna?"

Joanna begins pacing the space like a caged animal, turning at sharp angles when reaching a wall and repeating under her breath, "Hard knocks, hard knocks, hard knocks."

I step in front of Joanna and put a hand on her shoulder. "Don't you like the color of the walls? Blue, *like the sky?*"

"It might be a nice color on the walls of Jim's house, where Jim lets you live," Joanna blares as if Nazrini were not standing six feet away, "but it's nobody's dream to live in a place like this. It's nobody's dream. And the refrigerator is not big like you said. It's small. Jim's refrigerator has an ice machine. This one doesn't have an ice machine. It's too small. It's way too small for that."

"Stop it," I mouth to Joanna, widening my eyes.

"Well, it doesn't have an ice machine, does it? It's way too small for that!" Joanna doubles down, impervious to my direction and oblivious to Nazrini's presence.

"Is she okay?" Nazrini asks politely.

I spin around and answer too quickly, "Oh, totally. She's just very picky. She's just—"

"You want me to lie and say nice things!" Joanna is shouting now. "But it's not your life, Maggie. It's not your life! Walk a mile in my shoes, then you'll see. *Walk a mile in my shoes, Maggie!*"

"I don't think this is going to be a good fit," Nazrini concludes with firm civility. "Thank you for your time. It was nice to meet you both."

I stride to the car in an angry silence, forcing Joanna to trot along behind to keep up. *What am I doing?* I think. Why am I trying to help this woman who won't make any effort to help herself, this woman unrelated to me whom I have no obligation to help, at all, by anyone's standards? This woman who is in love with my husband who wishes I would disappear off the face of the earth?

I should be concentrating on myself. I am in the middle of a mental health crisis, for God's sake. As I pull the key fob out of my purse, it occurs to me with a flash of horror that crises are by definition temporary, exceptions to the norm. And maybe I am not in the middle of a crisis at all. Maybe it's permanent. Maybe *it's just what's happened* to me!

Through a clenched jaw, I hiss at Joanna, "I asked you to say, 'Nice to meet you, Nazrini.'"

Joanna spits back. "You're not the one in dire straits, Maggie. It's easy for you to say when you live on Easy Street—"

"I *asked* you to say, 'Nice to meet you, Nazrini!'"

"You get to live in Handsome Jim's house. Handsome Jim married *you*, so you don't have to downgrade. You never have to downgrade. You don't know—"

"I don't know? *You* don't know, Joanna. You don't know anything about me. You don't know anything about my life."

"I know you live in a big house in Hancock Park with a pool and Handsome Jim on Easy Street. I know that. I know that much. I know you've never had hard knocks—"

I inhale deliberately, expanding my chest and drawing myself to my full height.

"I. DO. SO. HAVE. HARD. KNOCKS," I hammer in the deepest and most commanding tone I can produce. "IN. FACT. I'M. HAVING. HARD. KNOCKS. RIGHT. NOW! OKAY?"

Joanna scoffs. "I'd trade your hard knocks for my hard knocks any day. I wish I could. I wish I could. I'd trade you right now!"

She stares at me icily over the hood of the car, her neck thrust forward and her arms crossed over her chest.

"I've been really nice to you," I say, reining in my voice. "I spent my whole day taking you to the hair salon and to Target and driving you across town to see this apartment." I've succeeded in calming my tone, but I can't keep it up, and I explode at the end, "And you can't even say *Nice to meet you, Nazrini!*"

"I didn't want to say something that wasn't tr—"

"I'm doing a lot of shit for you, and the least you can do is be grateful and do what I say because, because, because for fuck's sake, without me you'd be fucking homeless, okay?"

Not a proud moment. Not a proud moment at all. A moment that will make it into no Hallmark movie, unless I write myself into it as the insufferable, self-important, overprivileged villain.

"I'm sorry," I say, resting my elbows on the hood of the car and collapsing my head to my forearms. "I shouldn't have said that."

My only accomplishment for the day was to be this one deed of helping out a soul in need, and now look at me. I've ruined it. My pulse bangs in my forehead and the familiar needling of tiny talons takes hold of my scalp.

Breathe, I silently direct, *out, out, out . . . and hold . . . and hold . . . and . . .*

I exhale and hold and inhale through a long silence before finally lifting my head to look over at Joanna.

"Will you tell Jim?" she asks calmly, looking at me as plainly as if our conflict had never happened. "Will you tell Jim that my breasts are bigger than yours? Will you tell Jim about my breasts?"

9

Body-Mind Organism

What if, as I leaned over the hood of my car, I didn't have to feel bad for attacking an underprivileged semi-dependent adult for behavior beyond her control because *my* behavior was beyond my control, as well as because everyone's behavior is beyond their control and no one in the entire world is responsible for anything? This is what author Wayne Liquorman, in his book *Never Mind*, asserts. Following Advaita Vedanta, a branch of Indian philosophy, Liquorman proposes that we are all just products of our genes and the environment, and so free will, from an ultimate perspective, doesn't exist.

I've been thinking about Wayne's ideas recently in relation to my looping, how it's possible to believe that rather than choosing to loop, I am instead looping's passive victim. "It" is some sort of glitch, just atoms or electrons or neuronal transmitters or something, dysregulating my nervous system via the operations of the universe, and not some kind of false flag mutiny going on, of me against myself.

I've been finding this perspective comforting, so when an email reminds me that Wayne Liquorman will be giving a *satsang*, or gathering-together-to-sit-with-truth, at his oceanfront condo in Hermosa Beach that afternoon at 3:00 p.m., I immediately click YES on the calendar invite. I'm hoping something Wayne will say might unlock the Chinese finger trap that has caught my brain.

Around twenty academic-looking seekers sit on cushions in the airy main room of Wayne Liquorman's oceanfront condo. Their attention is focused on the world's largest La-Z-Boy recliner. It strikes me as odd that Wayne is not occupying the spotlighted recliner, nor is in fact anywhere to be seen, considering he's the one who scheduled this event at his own place.

Then I notice a wide staircase—with glass treads, very modern, no handrails—leading down to the giant chair. Ah, Mr. Liquorman is going to make an entrance. Seems a little formal for a man about to sink down on a La-Z-Boy designed for Abiyoyo the giant, but I'm not averse to a touch of theatrics. Everyone has a right to a little Scarlett O'Hara in their own home.

Wayne does indeed make a grand entrance, but it's not the one I expect. I expect him to *namaste* his way down the stairs with a showy modesty in white kurta pajamas, guru-blessed prayer beads rattling around his ankles and wrists. When the great man appears, however, he is sporting a brightly colored Jamba Juice T-shirt and loose-fitting Hawaiian shorts. Full of brio, he spreads his arms and trots down the stairs as if expecting applause from a well-warmed-up studio audience.

Wayne settles his over-six-foot frame in the La-Z-Boy behemoth and I notice his flip flops, which reveal wiry black hair sprouting from the top of his feet and his toes. Then, because of the angle at which I am positioned, as I look up from Wayne's feet, I can't help but glance up through the wide flopping right leg of his shorts, past his inner thigh and at what I believe to be . . . yes, I think that is . . . a ball. But because I violently avert my gaze, I can't be sure. It could be ball-colored underwear.

Trust the message, not the messenger, I remind myself.

Then our guru announces the beginning of his lesson by leaning forward, pursing his lips, and inspecting his gathered acolytes. He makes eye contact with us, one by one, for about thirty seconds each, moving methodically around the room, and the whole thing seems both pretentious and uncomfortable until he gets to me.

Wayne's eyes settle on mine in a way that feels surprisingly intimate, as if he recognizes something deep within me, and for the first time I get a hit of the whole "young follower immediately falls in love with less-than-attractive but charismatic guru" cliché.

I want so much to believe that Wayne Liquorman's unaverted gaze has the power to cure me that all my faculties of critical attention switch off and I open to his influence with all the saucer-eyed hope of a Woodstock flower child. I hold my breath and plumb his gaze for the path to wellness I know must lie there. Then, just as I'm certain I'm about to grasp his golden key, Wayne's eyes shift left, and the customer next to me is receiving his shot of syrup while I find myself looking at the side of the guru's nose.

After engaging his last three students, Wayne presses his hands together in a final, wordless *namaste.* "Well," he begins, sagaciously, as I and my fellows bate our breath, "any questions?" Looking around the room, I feel as if I've stumbled into an ice-breaking mixer at the start of a graduate-level engineering program. Socially awkward acolytes wearing ill-fitting button-downs sport a selection of glasses that appear to be sponsored by Warby Parker's "Conspicuously Colored Wire-Rim" line.

A man as thin and wiry as his teal glasses raises a slender hand. "You talk in your book about the fiction of personal authorship."

"That's right. This"—Wayne gestures from the top of his head down to his hairy toes—"this body-mind organism called Wayne is nothing more than the product of a vast, interactive system of genetic and environment forces."

The wiry man nods, but his eyebrows pull together. "So there's no free will?"

"Well, sure, moment to moment people are making choices. Certainly choice is proximate to action, but pull back and you'll get the whole story, in which free will is determined by a variety of factors. You may be familiar with the work of Benjamin Libet." There is some nodding and mm-hmming as Wayne recrosses his legs, availing me of a sight I must whip my eyes down to avoid.

I listen, my gaze clinging for safety to the soles of my feet, as he continues, "Dr. Libet demonstrated the illusory quality of volition as early as the 1980s, showing how when an experimental subject, wired to an EEG machine for observation, reaches out to push a button, the action of his arm extending occurs several hundred milliseconds before the thought *I'm going to push that button* takes place. Do you see what I mean?"

The wiry man shakes his head.

"Dr. Libet's experiments," Wayne explains, "establish the sequence of causation. First, action takes place. Then, the ego jumps in to nab credit for an action already well under way. Egoic control determines nothing because it doesn't exist. Except as credit snatcher."

"I don't know, though," the wiry man presses. "I feel—"

Wayne cuts him off with a friendly reminder by way of cocking his head and looking out over invisible glasses.

"I mean," the man corrects himself nervously, "I mean the, uh, body-mind organism called Nathan feels this condition of being *I* very strongly."

"Yes," Wayne says, nodding vigorously. "Isn't it a fantastic illusion? *You* are illusion. *I* am an illusion. *This*"—his sweeping gesture takes in the students, the room, everything we can see—"is all a fantastic, mesmerizing illusion."

"Yeah. Okay. But isn't that very dangerous?"

"What?"

"The idea you're spreading? That choice is illusion? I mean, if there's no choice, what stops me, uh, this body-mind organism called Nathan, from flying a plane into a building and killing three thousand people?"

"Do you *want* to fly a plane into a building and kill three thousand people?" Wayne asks, a king on his La-Z-Boy throne, secure in his reign.

"No."

"Well, then I suspect that's what stops you."

Another sprinkling of laughter.

A man wearing round John Lennon frames, with one hand resting across his mostly bald head, raises his other and asks, "But if it's something you *do* want to do, not like flying into a building, but maybe like having an affair or something, what stops you if you're saying choice is just an illusion, if you're abdicating personal responsibility?"

"The question assumes you had responsibility to abdicate in the first place."

One of the two other women in the room raises her hand, revealing an intricately inked sleeve tattoo. "Okay, so I'm a mother," she says. "Are you telling me I should never punish my son? I should just say, 'Go ahead, Albert, and bang that block against your sister's head. That's what you're going to do anyway.'"

"No, no. You'll stop Albert from giving his sister a head injury because that's what *you* do. Just like Albert, you're an expression of the universe. You are what happens."

I think of Joanna's phrase, "It's just what happens."

"So if choice is an illusion," a man in a battery-operated wheelchair begins, "then guilt and blame are . . . what? Bullshit?"

"The Sanskrit word is *maya* but I like 'bullshit.' Yes, bullshit, I am saying guilt and blame are bullshit."

"Whew. That's a relief."

Laughter surges through the room, not the "I get the joke and need to make sure everyone else knows it" laughter of the typical California seeker, but laughter that seems to kick out spontaneously from all of these people's chests. It occurs to me that relief is what everyone is this room is looking for.

"Yes, that's right," Wayne says. "It is a relief, but pride is bullshit too, and most people, I find, are willing to accept limitless blame as long as they can get just a little credit."

"What about a Mother Teresa?" the man in the wheelchair continues. His lower body doesn't move, but his shoulders, neck, and arms twitch and sway.

"What *about* Mother Teresa?" Wayne asks.

"Without choice," the man asks, one hand tucked by his chin, fingers fluttering by his mouth, "how is someone like Mother Teresa moral? What makes her any better than Ted Bundy, for example?"

"Yes," Wayne answers, speaking to the rest of us, "Jerry here doesn't mind giving up pride. Right, Jerry? He's been put through an advanced course on the ephemerality of self and the illusion of volition. But what of admiration? Jerry isn't ready to relinquish his heroes."

Jerry closes his eyes and nods, and a murmur of appreciation for their guru's wisdom passes among the students.

"What I'm suggesting," Wayne continues, "is that the body-mind organism called Mother Teresa can be superior to the body-mind organism called Ted Bundy. We can have that inspiration. I don't want to take that away. But the 'I' of Mother Teresa, the self she experiences as choosing her path, is no more responsible for her good deeds than Ted Bundy is for his abominations. Who would choose to be a Ted Bundy instead of a Mother Teresa? I wouldn't. Would you? I doubt it. Nobody would, Ted Bundy himself least of all. Our actions are the result of genetics and environment. And there's no reason other than squeamishness to look for any other explanation."

"Why squeamishness?" Jerry asks.

"Well, the body-mind organism named Wayne has noticed that these ideas are a tough sell. People don't have the stomach for it. They get anxious."

Anxious. Yes. This is what I want him to talk about, and I decide to grab the chance to ask, undergirding my voice so it's strong and clear. "What about anxiety?"

Wayne's eyes do not stray from Jerry. I realize I have forgotten to raise my hand, so I belatedly shoot it up and pipe, in a voice frailer and more faltering than I'd hoped, "You were talking about anxiety and I guess I was wondering . . . what you think anxiety . . . *is*?"

Wayne turns his full attention to me, and I look back at him, fervently hopeful.

"Yes," Wayne says, leaning forward, considering, resting his elbows on his knees. Again, the students, the room, the condo fall silent. Any of Wayne's words could be the pointer that cracks open the mystery of the non-dual nature of the universe for any of us.

"I think," Wayne finally says, and then pauses again.

Nobody moves.

"I think that you already know what anxiety is."

Laughter washes across the room, and though it's probably less raucous than it sounds to me, it feels more at my expense than shared. Also, the light coming through Wayne's picture-glass windows suddenly seems overwhelmingly bright. I was hoping the simplicity of my question would seem profound to the group, but now I feel like I'm a sorority girl who has just asked, What do you think a snowflake is . . . I mean . . . *really*?

"What is it that you actually want to know?" Wayne offers kindly, picking up, I imagine, on the discomfort I'm trying to hide.

"Okay. Well, this might sound weird, but I have this thing, I mean this body-mind organism called Maggie—"

Supportive nods all around.

"This body-mind organism called Maggie has a thing which is

unwanted thoughts, or words that come into my mind over and over for no reason. I don't want to think them, but they still come, or I still think them, and I find it terrifying because I feel like I'm doing it to myself, but I don't want to, but I'm doing it anyway."

"Ah," Wayne says, "You *can't* be doing it to yourself, alright? You can't be because *you* don't exist. 'I' is an illusion. It's a curtain that, once seen through, dissolves. Do you follow?"

I'm trying to follow.

"And once one sees through the curtain, the seeking stops, and there is peace."

"But how can I do that?" I ask. "How can I see through the curtain?"

"You can't."

"I can't?"

"'I' can't. 'I' can't de-mesmerize itself because it is part of the mesmerization."

"So, all I can do is what, wait? Wait . . . and hope?"

"Waiting may arise, Maggie. Hoping may arise. *You* have nothing to do with it."

Mesmerize, de-mesmerize, part of the mesmerization. I mull over the words in time with my steps past the succulent gardens and drought-tolerant arrangements of sage plants and ornamental grasses on my way back to the car.

What does it really mean?

It means, I feel, that whatever is running around in my head, I, Maggie Rowe, am not responsible.

I can't be doing it to myself because *I* doesn't exist, right?

Right. That does make sense to me. It has logic and a conclusion I can grasp.

Drawing the sea-scented air into my lungs, I try to *de-mesmerize* myself. I feel—I'm not sure why—that if I truly understood that the repetitions in my mind were just *appearing* and not that I was *creating* them, if it weren't some kind of "self-assault" scenario, the whole looping phenomenon might cease to be problematic. That sounds strange and simplistic and an odd way to solve a mental health crisis, but I'm convinced that if I could just sincerely believe that I weren't in some way pitted against myself, I might be okay. Of course, from my early years in the church, I know how difficult it is to make yourself sincerely believe anything.

But maybe . . .

And you know what? I *am* feeling a little lighter. It's true. I'm not sweating at all, for the moment. My heart rate is reasonable. In front of one particularly well-landscaped yard, I pause to admire the colors of ice plant laid in along the sidewalk. There's orange. Purple. And there's yellow, and a kind of pink, and red.

Not red, though, but scarlet, I observe, softening inside. Soon, a cascade of color names pours through my mind. *That orange is really marigold; the purple, lavender; the yellow,* sun *yellow, no, dandelion; the pink like . . . like the palm of a baby's hand.*

A feeling of peace arises and a mood I can't quite name washes over me.

What just happens *can truly be amazing*, I think, and then . . .

Oh no. No. No. No. No. NO!

I feel a hell twinge and suddenly my mind is enflamed.

Auschwitz, Auschwitz, Auschwitz.

My heart rate soars, and I am drenched.

I don't fall to my knees, because the body-mind organism called Maggie Rowe is genetically predisposed and environmentally conditioned to not be publicly demonstrative, but a burning sensation does shoot up my spine, my scalp does prickle with icy heat, and I do have to force my stiffening legs to carry me back to my car one step at a time.

The looping continues nonstop on my drive home, punishing repetitions overtaking my thoughts, weaving serpentine through my brain, cracking open and rushing through deeply carved but dried-up rivulets. When I get home, soaked in sweat, weak-kneed, blurry-eyed, and nauseated, I can't keep my condition from Jimmy any longer. I tell him everything, starting with the Salinger documentary and including the looping and *Auschwitz* and the recurrence of the hell twinges and all the details of the whole embarrassing, shameful mess.

"I'm sorry, I'm so sorry, Jim," I say. "I'm sorry you got a bum wife."

"No, no, no," he said, of course. What else would he say? "You're not a bum wife. You're the best wife. You're the best wife in the whole world."

"Oh, please. You're stuck dealing with a mental invalid who suffers from disorders no one has ever heard of. It's not fair for you. I mean, you even said you married me because I was *sane*."

"Ah, c'mon," he murmured in his gentlest, it's-all-going-to-be-all-right voice. "Cut it out, Mags. This isn't anything new. You've had it before, and I haven't been wheeling you around in a chair ever since."

I smile.

"Who's that doctor you told me about? He'll tweak your meds just a little, and you'll be fine. You can go see him tomorrow first thing in the morning."

I am stuck in the slowest luxury-building elevator in the modern world.

Lucy has recommended Dr. Steven Goya, and I have made it across town without any delays from traffic, and now it seems as if I will never arrive on the seventeenth floor.

I haven't been able to eat for at least twenty hours, and I'm feeling lightheaded, so I hang on to a brass handrail as tightly as I can. The small chamber is gorgeous, with burl wood paneling rubbed as smooth as the dash of a Rolls-Royce, and a plush red-carpeted floor patterned with gold-threaded fleurs-de-lis, but it is going so slow, moving upward at a barely perceptible pace in quiet little jerks, that I can barely stand it.

As the doors slide open, I think how wonderful it will be to have another reliable advisor besides Lucy. I make my way down the corridor with a lift in my step. I push open the door to the waiting room, see there's a set of four switches on the wall, each next to the name of a member of the practice, and flip the switch with *Goya* under it.

I sit down in one of the waiting room chairs, which give the impression their designer lacked knowledge of the human form. I shift my weight to one hip and then to the other. I tilt forward slightly and then try leaning back. It's not long, thankfully, until the door by the call switches opens and a tall, noble-looking man calls me in.

"Please come this way," he says, gesturing past the doorway and standing aside. "It's just to the right." His office door is open, and the first thing I notice is a floor-to-ceiling view of the Beverly Hills hills and the Santa Monica mountains.

Dr. Goya invites me to sit. Once I do, he says, "Tell me, Maggie, what I can do for you."

"Thank you, Doctor," I reply right away. "I need a prescription for Paxil and a prescription for Klonopin. The last prescription I had was for 60 milligrams for the Paxil, daily, and 10 milligrams for the Klonopin, as needed, and—"

"Oh, whoa, okay," Dr. Goya interrupts, gently. "Let's back up, why don't we? I'd like to get some idea of your background to get started."

"Well," I say. "Okay, short version. I went off my medication several months ago, which I guess wasn't a good idea because it seems to have set something off in me or broke something, because now I'm having a really bad time. I'm hoping if I get back on the meds, that will fix everything, but I'm scared that what I've set off in my mind now has a life of its own."

Dr. Goya studies me. "Tell me a little bit about how you came to be on the medications to begin with."

I tell Dr. Goya about my previous doctor, my hell twinge, and about Grace Point Psychiatric Hospital. I explain my struggle with repeated phrases running through my mind, about J. D. Salinger and Auschwitz, about the panic that overcomes me and sweats my sheets every morning until they are several measurable pounds of misery.

"The worst," I say, "is this feeling that I am under attack from within, the idea that I am somehow doing all this to myself. I'm afraid it will drive me crazy, in an old-school *they're coming to take me away* style. I'm afraid, and I'm afraid of being afraid. A strange endless loop."

"But what kind of helps me," I continue, optimism straightening my spine. "Well, are you familiar with Benjamin Libet? Those experiments that showed how when you reach to press a button, the *action* of your arm reaching occurs a split second before you think the thought *directing* your arm to reach?"

"Yes, I believe I'm familiar with Dr. Libet's work."

"How could that be true unless our whole perception of the self is fundamentally flawed? Which is a fascinating idea, right?"

Dr. Goya lifts his chin slightly and wrinkles his brow in an expression that looks thoughtful and, I flatter myself, admiring of my knowledge of mid-1980s neuroscience.

I proceed with confidence. "Anyway, it makes sense to me, and helps me, to think of my repetitive thoughts as a computer glitch that just happens, a malfunction."

Dr. Goya smooths the wrinkles from his forehead with elegant fingers before offering his conclusion. "Well, but we're not robots."

I have to blink a couple of times before I can express what I'm thinking. "What?" I say, still without words.

"We're not robots. Robots are programmed; we have free will."

I shake my head, as if to ward off his dismissal of Wayne Liquorman's entire description of the universe, a description I have just the told this man has been of great benefit to me.

"Do we, though?" I ask. "What's the basis for saying that?"

"That people are not robots; we're more than that."

Of course we're more than that, I want to say, but that has nothing to do with my reasoning. Why does everyone jump to conclusions like this? It's like the Evangelicals who don't want to believe in evolution. *We're not monkeys!* they always yelp.

"I'm not saying we *are* monkeys," I protest.

"I'm sorry?"

"What?"

"You said 'monkeys.'"

"I did?"

"You said, 'But I'm not saying we *are* monkeys.' That's interesting."

"Oh, I mean robots. I'm not saying we're *robots*. I'm saying it's helpful for me to think that the sense I have of an 'I' inside this body-mind organism called Maggie could be an illusion."

Goya raises a very non-therapeutic eyebrow at that, but I haven't finished my point.

"That there's no separate little self running the show. It's just the universe playing out probabilities. There's nothing inside that's responsible."

"Yes," Goya responds. "I understand what you're saying, Maggie."

Good, I think.

"Though of course," he adds with a curt nod, "we do have a soul."

I freeze.

Are you fucking kidding me? I want to yell.

Now, this may seem to be a strong reaction. Certainly the word *soul* is not off-limits for a therapist, but the particular way Dr. Goya says the word *soul*, with the hiss and bite of certainty, makes me certain he is a particular type of Evangelical.

How dare you use the word *soul* with me? I want to carry on. You're a psychiatrist. I mean, the doctors at Grace Point used the word *soul*, but Grace Point was an *Evangelical* inpatient hospital. *Psychiatry where the Bible comes first.* It says it right there on all their literature and smack above the entrance when you go in. Here, though, here in Beverly Hills, the bastion of the secular, I should not have to unexpectedly duck because the word *soul* is hurled at me out of the blue. I should at least be given fair warning or a waiver to sign or something.

Instead of allowing my entire tirade to erupt and destroy my chance of getting the medication I need, I simply ask, "What?" hoping that somehow Dr. Goya will realize he has misspoken, feel profound shame, retract the entire thing, and replace it with "What an inquisitive lady you are. I don't often get a chance to discuss the convincing hoax of the ego with patients. What a treat."

"Souls," Dr. Goya repeats, sharing his wisdom with the good cheer of a grandmother passing out cupcakes. "Human beings have souls."

I know, of course, the word *soul* has different meanings in other religious traditions and that even within Christianity the word has been used to refer to the depth of connection with the inherent divinity of life rather than to a poor forlorn ghost-self that needs to be saved before the cosmic buzzer goes off. But the way this man says the word *soul*, the affronted confidence with which he feels compelled to defend his position to me, convinces me that his usage is of the latter, more primitive variety. An Evangelist in healer's clothing has ambushed me like an unsuspecting animal grazing the meadow.

"Robots run programs," he continues. "People are granted free will."

I stare hard, my body knotted into a stiff column of muscle. Then, through a clenched and quivering jaw, I ask evenly, "What religion were you brought up with?"

"I'm a Christian," he says with an unexamined pride that makes me want to give him a slanting smack across the top of his head.

"Is that okay?" he asks with a smile.

NO, I scream in my head. NO, no, it's not okay. It's not okay for you to foist your personal religious beliefs on a patient. I know I shouldn't care about this man's position but that would require confidence in my own position, and I can't be confident of anything at the moment. How could I be if I can't trust my own mind? And how can I trust a shifting and faithless entity that repeats unwanted phrases and throws up harrowing fears and seeds my body with obsessive anxieties that won't go away? Who am I, the disease-riddled patient, to question this tall, impeccably composed, obviously prosperous physician?

Logic follows logic and reaches its conclusions, and it's not long before I come to mine: maybe it really is true. All the things I've always been scared of are actually true.

I flash back to one of my earliest memories. I am walking into kindergarten cradling a handmade Christmas ornament for show-and-tell. The ornament is minutely crafted from a sugar-coated eggshell and shaped into a bassinet that contains a tiny baby Jesus covered in a blue satin blanket. I brought it to show-and-tell because I thought it was the most beautiful thing I'd ever seen. My mother warned me to be careful with it because it was so fragile, so, so fragile. And I was. I was so, so careful, but before I got a chance to show and tell about the sugary bassinet housing a miniature infant savior, five-year-old Eric Kirshner shot past me to whack Rob Martier on the head, knocking the elbow of my winter jacket on the way. I helplessly watched as my delicate ornament arced away from my mittened hand and smashed to pieces on the polished cement floor.

This is what Dr. Goya has done with my precious, fragile little comforting idea of no "I."

"I feel like I've upset you."

I stare at him in a way that I hope will communicate that not only has he upset me but that when I'm through with this whole thing I plan to sue him and get his license revoked. I narrow my eyes to add that I will also attempt to publicly shame him in way that causes him to lose his family as well as his job.

"I need a prescription," I state firmly, fighting the waver in my voice. "I need Paxil, 40 milligrams, daily, and 10 milligrams of Klonopin, as needed."

"I'm sorry if I said something—"

"Would it be possible for you to write me a prescription?" I ask, simply, icily, but with plausible deniability, maintaining the possibility that I am not castigating him, but rather simply getting down to business.

"Uh, let's see," he falters. "Uh, I can certainly write you the Paxil if that was working for you, but Valium might be a better choice right now than Klonopin."

"A better choice?"

"Valium breaks down more slowly in your bloodstream, so it has a longer-lasting effect. Klonopin works well in a pinch, but Valium gets better results with sustained anxiety, and your experience seems rather pervasive."

I'm thinking of *Valley of the Dolls* and of "mother's little helper" and Harper in *Angels in America* taking it in wee fistfuls and feeling worried about what accepting a prescription for Valium will mean in the movie version of my life when I say, "Okay, so let's try Valium then, Valium will be fine," and pull my checkbook out of my purse.

I clutch the brass railing in the elevator less tightly on the way down, grateful for the prescription in my purse. I think about the first psychotropic prescription I ever received. I remember walking out into the small courtyard at Grace Point, clutching the small piece of paper in my hand and heading to the pharmacy in the adjacent mall, feeling like Jack on his way to get his magic beans.

"And you shall have the beans," I say to the silent elevator, understanding that the Paxil probably won't take effect for four to six weeks, if it works again for me at all, but trusting that the Valium will work right away.

"How did it go?" Jim shoots up from the bed. "What did the doctor say?"

"Motherfucker told me I have a soul," I growl, unbuttoning my top and changing into my favorite pea-green sweatshirt, which I've dubbed Greenie.

"He said that? I mean, what's . . . uh . . . uh . . ."

"Maggie," I prompt helpfully, slipping Greenie over my head.

Jim, expressing his usual lack of amusement at my little joke, continues, "Maggie. What's wrong with him telling you that you—"

"Dude was an Evangelical."

"Really? How did you know?"

"He started going off about having a soul."

Jim does not quite understand how this follows but remains determined to support me. "Oh no," he says, gravely, as if I've just presented him the doctor's rap sheet.

"Yeah. Can you believe it? But it's fine. He wrote the prescriptions and I never have to see him again. I'll find a doctor who didn't skip the lectures on professional ethics."

"Sounds good."

"I just took the first Valium, which will work right away, so I should be fine for tonight, and—"

"Valium?"

"I know."

"Wow."

"I know."

"Okay, Mags."

"I won't get addicted. I promise. I just have to get at least a night off."

"And it's okay to take it with wine?"

He's referring to the glass of merlot I poured in the kitchen when I was taking the pill and am now holding in my hand.

"Just one glass. Just tonight."

"Uh—"

"It'll be fine. Can you find something on TV?"

Jimmy is still uncertain, but he dutifully scrolls through the shows we have recorded. "We've got a new *Dateline: True Crime*."

"Perfect, nothing calms my spirit like murder."

I climb onto the bed and get under the covers as Lester Holt begins the narration. "She had a smile that lit up a room."

"Dead!" Jimmy and I call out in unison, knowing from watching hundreds of these shows that nobody with a smile that lights up a room makes it through the first commercial break.

"Can I ask you a big favor?" he asks.

"Sure."

"Hug?"

I cuddle up to Jimmy, squeezing myself into his torso, my legs squashed up toward my belly, my head burrowed into his chest.

"Did you ever think you'd get a girl so tall she had to curl up to fit around you?"

This is another of my little jokes: asking Jim if he ever thought he would get a girl with characteristics I possess that would not generally be sought after in a mate. Often this little joke references my height. "Did you ever think you'd get a girl who could comfortably put her arms over your shoulders without shoes on? Did you ever think you'd get a girl who'll never ask for help getting the peanut butter down from the top shelf?"

"No, I didn't," Jim says, kissing the top of my head.

As the light-up-the-room-with-her-smile *Dateline* ingénue goes missing, I monitor my senses and flow of thought, waiting for the Valium to kick in.

"How's it going?" Jim asks with a squeeze.

My pulse is still racing, and it's still hard to take deep breaths, but it's been only ten minutes since I took the pill.

"Let's not pay attention," I say.

"You're going to be okay," he says, rubbing my back. His voice is soothing.

"Can I ask you something?"

"Yes, okay," Jim says, bracing for a tough one.

"Ever think you'd get a girl who'd give you such a first-class education in the effects of psychotropic medications?"

Jim does not laugh, but I've drawn a smile from his eyes.

"What a jackpot of mental health discovery you've landed in!"

We chuckle for a moment. Then, after a silence, I add a simple "Sorry."

"Don't be sorry."

After the third commercial break, as the once-smiling girl's body is being dredged from the lake, I still feel no effect from the Valium. *No problem*, I think. I've got until act three of the show. Forty-five minutes is still fifteen minutes away. Everything is going to be fine. *Fine, fine*, I play a little singsong in my head. *Fine, fine; everything is fine. Fine, fine; everything is fine.*

As the episode's initial suspect confesses to the crime, however, I note with alarm that nothing seems to be changing. *It's not working!* I think, and a burning sensation blazes from my stomach up to my scalp and back down to my stomach. "I have to throw up," I tell Jimmy.

Bethanie, my psychiatrist at Grace Point, diagnosed me as bulimic, but she wasn't right. I was never trying to lose weight. But one thing about the process of heaving the contents of your stomach out of your mouth is that you are guaranteed to feel different afterward than you did before—not necessarily better, but definitely different. If an emotional state is intolerable, throwing up can move you to a different intolerable emotional state. It's something, at least. A small mercy.

I pull the door to the bathroom closed behind me and cave to the floor, banging my knees on the cold marble and grasping the sides of the frigid porcelain. I want the relief of a big expulsion, but nothing more than red wine mixed with bile comes up. I heave again, but when I'm really anxious, I can barely eat, and there's just nothing there. And so, no small mercy.

I rinse my mouth at the sink, dry my watering eyes, and walk unsteadily back to the bedroom, wiping my cheek with one hand.

"Are you okay?"

"I don't know," I say, my heartbeat accelerating.

Jimmy's eyes are steady, comforting.

I want to be fine, but, "No," I say. "I'm not."

Jimmy takes a step toward me, but I shake my head.

"The Valium isn't working. It isn't working. It's not going to work. Nothing's going to work." Sweat gathers on my forearms and shoulders, and I can feel it dripping toward my hands. "I'm burning, Jimmy. I'm burning up."

"Lie down, Mags. Lie down," Jimmy tells me with an assurance he can't possibly feel.

I nod and lay myself down flat on top of the covers, arms tucked to my sides, as stiff as a corpse in a coffin. I look up at the ceiling and wait, but my heart continues banging in my ears so strongly I can feel the beats in my eyes, so I shoot back up and begin pacing in front of the television. "I feel like it's getting hotter," I say, stroking my face and then looking at my hands wet with sweat. "I feel like it's hot. It's so hot. I feel like it's getting so hot!"

Jim watches me, covering what I recognize as his own rising panic.

"Do you want to go for a walk?"

"I don't know."

"What do you want, Mags? What can I do? I don't know what you want me to do."

"You don't have to do anything!" I snap. "This isn't about you!"

Jim freezes.

"I'm sorry. I'm sorry. Turn off the TV? Maybe you could turn off the TV."

Jimmy springs to the remote and hits a button. There is silence.

"I think—I think—I don't know. I don't know." The house is an oven. "Okay, then. Okay. Let's go for a walk. Let's get out of the house."

"Yes, let's go," Jim says, grabbing a coat from the closet and me around the waist.

"I'm burning up. Fuck. I'm burning up, Jim."

There are always a few genuinely cold days to a Los Angeles winter, and on this moonless January night, I brace against what feels like Chicago wind whipping off the icy lake. As I welcome the frigid air into my lungs, walking past one dark house, then another, and then another, the pounding of my heart softens into something more like a tap.

Tap.

Tap.

Tap.

After several more blocks, I lean my weight into Jim's and ask, "Did you ever think you'd get a girl with such a complicated inner life?

"No," he says, giving me a kiss on the forehead. "No, I did not."

10

Road to Nowhere

I don't have it, Maggie, I don't have it. I'm in dire straits!"

"Hello, Joanna," I grumble into the phone, the right side of my face still pressed into the pillow. "You don't . . . you don't have what now?" Without lifting my head, my eyes search out the clock: 5:07 p.m. Three weeks have passed since I resumed taking medication, and now apparently I've taken another mid-afternoon Valium-and-merlot-induced nap. The Paxil should have kicked in by now, but it hasn't.

"Six hundred and twenty-five dollars! I don't have it."

I spot a small purple drool splotch on the white fabric in front of me. And another, slightly larger, a couple inches over, from the day before. And another. The wine. And maybe that should worry me, but instead, I think that if I can just manage to lift my head and turn the pillow over, the spots will be gone. Problem solved.

I must deal with problems in the order and extent to which I can handle them. I have started back to work in the writers' room after a hiatus and have been able to function adequately. I can do the tasks that need to be done despite the disruption of my mind, despite my body's all-day alert to my grave and immediate danger, despite the disconcerting side effects of my medications. I can do it. And no one, for the most part, can tell anything is amiss. I do not appear haunted or tortured or rattled or afflicted.

"What do you need six hundred and twenty-five dollars for?"

"My mother. I need six hundred and twenty-five dollars for my mother, Maggie."

Oh shit. I sit up. Is Joanna hallucinating? I've been scared of this exact thing ever since the Social Security clerk told me about Joanna's disability qualification.

"Paranoid schizophrenia?"

"Yup," the clerk had said.

"But I've never seen Joanna see or hear things that weren't there," I objected, as if the sweet, acne-scarred twenty-year-old before me had anything to do with diagnosing Joanna when she was eighteen, two decades before he was born. And as if I knew anything about schizophrenia.

I had gone back to Social Security to get Joanna's disability qualification for a group home application form after several more landlords told us, like Nazrini, "It's just not going to work out."

"Maybe it's for the best," Jimmy had offered, taking the bright side. "She'll have someone to be accountable to, someone to make sure she bathes and eats more than Oreos and hot sauce."

"Maggie!" Joanna's scream into the phone pulls me back to the moment. "Are you there?"

"Yes," I say, drawing the receiver back from my shocked eardrum and standing up.

"Oh, I thought you weren't there anymore."

"No, no," I say, "I'm here."

I examine myself in the full-length mirror across from my bed and take in the slackness around my eyes and the purple stains on my lips. "So," I cautiously probe, flinching from my reflected image, "you've seen your mother, or, um, you've been talking to your mother recently, and she needs six hundred and twenty-five dollars?"

"What?"

"Your mother asked you for money?"

"My mother's dead, Maggie," Joanna states matter-of-factly.

"Oh, good—I mean not good, I was just—"

"How could you forget a thing like that? How could you forget my mother—?"

"I didn't forget. I was just making sure that you weren't having . . . never mind. What do you need the money for?"

"To dispose of it."

"Dispose of what? What is 'it'?"

"My mother's body."

"Joanna," I say with complete focus. "What do you mean by dispose of your mother's body?"

"They sent me the certificate. The death certificate. 'Sunny Hergert,' it says, 'deceased.' It says I have to claim the remains of Sunny Hergert, deceased, and pay six hundred and twenty-five dollars to 'dispose' of them. 'Remains' means her body, Maggie. It's her body, Maggie."

I had just assumed that Sunny's body had been taken care of by, well, somebody associated with the state. I haven't really thought about it beyond this very general idea. She died two months ago. Where has her body been this whole time? You can't just keep a body lying around, so it must be refrigerated, or is it frozen? Are there freezers of bodies somewhere waiting to be disposed of, tossed out like a couple of poached eggs? I think of all the morgue scenes in *Dateline* episodes, with that same stainless-steel drawer sliding out a body with a tag on its big toe. I picture Sunny sliding out on that drawer and a tag on a bunioned toe.

But why wouldn't the coroner's office contact Joanna before now? Two months seems like a long time for a body to sit on ice.

"It came in the mail?" I ask, walking to the bathroom, picking the sleep crust from the corner of my eyes.

"Yes. In an envelope."

"*When* did it come?"

"Today. I just got it today."

I tick through the facts in my head as I wet a washcloth in the sink and rub it over my dehydrated lips. The state—or is it the county?—having identified Joanna as the deceased next of kin, is asking her to pay for a cremation, or burial, or something. If Joanna claims the body, will she have to *see* the body?

I've always been uncomfortable seeing a dead body, scared I would begin contemplating its former soul, its eternal soul, its perhaps luke-warm soul, perhaps in jeopardy, perhaps condemned to hell. I did not go to my grandmother's funeral when I was twenty-one, which my mother and father kindly told me they thought wise. It wasn't worth the risk, they assured their strange, troubled daughter.

I don't think a coroner would be showing Joanna Sunny's body, though. They already know it's Sunny. They're probably just trying to extract a fee for something they're going to do anyway. I mean, they can't just leave unclaimed bodies stacked up in the morgue forever. They'll have to dispose of Sunny's remains in any case. Joanna doesn't know that, I figure, and maybe she imagines $625 will buy Sunny dignified treatment.

"I can pay the money, Joanna. She can get a proper—" I falter, unsteady talking about something so primal and tender and tragic. "A proper . . . burial."

"*Proper?*" Joanna interjects, incredulous. "She's already dead, Maggie! What does she need to be proper for?"

An excellent question, of course, but one I'm surprised to hear Joanna ask.

"Oh, no," I say. "Of course. Of course it doesn't need to be proper. I just was trying . . . I just wanted . . . I just *didn't* want you to have a picture in your mind of . . ."

"Of what?"

It's hard for me to say anything directly on this subject, it seems.

"Of your mom, or . . . of your mom's body being treated—"

"My mother's not in her body, Maggie. I'm never going to see my mother again," Joanna says with biting lucidity. "She's not going to come back. She's not going to ride a bus anywhere she wants in the whole city."

"Yes," I reply, thinking how sturdy Joanna sounds, sturdy enough to attend a grandmother's funeral at age twenty-one, anyway. "You're right. So then we can ignore the notice; the state will just take care of it."

"But they'll send me to jail. They'll send me to jail for not claiming the body. This is dire straits, Maggie. I'm in di—"

"They can't send you to jail, Joanna. Is that what you're worried about?"

"But I have to pay, Maggie. I have to pay six hundred and twenty-five dollars."

"No, you don't. I don't know what that letter is, but it's not a tax bill or a citation or a summons or anything like that. You can just leave it alone. You can just not respond if that's what you want to do."

"They won't send me to jail?"

"Definitely not."

"With no hope of parole? They won't send me go to jail with no hope of parole?"

"No," I say. "No jail. No need for parole."

"What a relief!" Joanna says with a profound sigh. "That's a very big relief, Maggie, a very big relief. I thought for sure I was in dire straits."

"Nope, " I say, feeling like a divine magician. "You're doing just fine."

In the empty moment following her call, I realize I have not been monitoring my anxiety, or my anxiety about anxiety, for the length of the conversation, which I realize has lasted almost an hour, a relief from what feels like my own dire straits.

"The diagnosis is out of date."

I squeeze the phone against my left ear with my shoulder and empty the last of a bottle of merlot into a glass from the sink.

"We would need a current diagnosis for Ms. Hergert," the group home worker goes on. "The one on record is from 1983. You'll need to make an appointment to have her evaluated."

I hang up, wondering how in the world I am going to get Joanna, who is terrified of all doctors and has refused to see one the entire time I've known her, to agree to see a psychiatrist. I decide to address the issue head-on by taking an especially long, slow sip of merlot and making plans to definitely call Joanna first thing in the morning, when my phone buzzes on the counter.

Zzzzzt, Zzzzzt.

JOANNA, the call screen tells me. "Hey, Joanna," I say into the receiver, "I'm glad you called."

"Forgery!" Joanna shouts in lieu of hello.

"I'm sorry?"

"It's a forgery! Forgery, Maggie! He didn't sign it!"

"Who didn't?"

"The doctor."

I sit at the kitchen table, take another sip of wine, and remind myself to be a good listener.

"What doctor, Joanna? Tell me the whole thing."

"Dr. Reed. My mother's doctor. He didn't sign my mother's death certificate. Dr. Reed never *went* to Pure Hearts Home Care. He never went there, so how could he know her cause of death? It says 'cause of death: cardiac arrest,' but how could he know about cardiac arrest if he wasn't there? Dr. Reed never even went to Pure Hearts Care Home. He never went there once."

"How do you know that?" I ask.

"Because he didn't even know she was dead. That's what I'm saying!"

"He didn't know she was dead?"

"Dr. Reed, my mother's doctor, he's been her doctor for years, he called *this morning* to say my mother missed her scheduled exam. What does that say, Maggie? What does that say?"

"I don't—"

"It says he thought she missed her scheduled appointment because he didn't even know she was dead."

I lift my forehead from the table, thinking that does sound somewhat suspicious.

"It's proof! It's proof my mother was murdered," Joanna says with the flourish of a triumphant lawyer wrapping up a slam-dunk argument. "It was murder, murder in the first degree!"

"Oh, Joanna," I say, "I really don't think it's likely your mother was murdered."

"YES, SHE WAS!" Joanna shouts. "You have to call Dr. Reed and tell him."

"I really don't feel comfortable accusing—"

"I would do anything to see Reyna go to jail, Maggie, go to jail without parole. Anything."

And there, right there, I see my opportunity.

"Okay, okay," I say. "I'll call Dr. Reed. But I need you to do something for me. I need you to talk to a psychiatrist."

"But I've always had my—"

"You just said you would do anything."

"But I have my mind, Maggie."

"Joanna, I'm trying to get you into this nice place that I think you will like, but have to talk to a psychiatrist first."

"But I have my mind, Maggie. I've always had my mind just like my mother."

"I know that, Joanna. You totally have your mind. It's just for the paperwork."

"But I'm not crazy. I'm not crazy, Maggie."

"No. You're not crazy. Seeing a psychiatrist doesn't mean you're crazy. I've seen lots of psychiatrists."

Silence.

"In fact, I'm seeing a new psychiatrist tomorrow morning. His name is Dr. Frank Nestor."

Silence.

"You? *You*, Maggie? I never would have guessed."

"Yeah, well, lots of people get psychiatric help—"

"But you live in a nice house. You live in a nice house in Hancock Park with Handsome Jim! I'm very surprised to hear that, Maggie. I'm very surprised to hear that you're going to see a psychiatrist especially because . . ."

Joanna's voice trails off, uncharacteristically, and she leaves her thought hanging.

"Joanna?"

"Especially because your mother," she continues in a tone I've not heard from her, softer, younger-sounding than the voice I'm used to, before trailing off again, "you still have your mother, Maggie."

I think of my mother and her slender fingers and how she would tap them on the steering wheel as she drove me to school. How impossibly lovely her fingers seemed to me. I remember wondering if all children think their mother's fingers are beautiful or whether my mother's were exceptional. Now, an image of Sunny's hands, her fingernails and the thin black line, spread beneath the quick flashes in my mind.

"That's right, I do. And I can't imagine how hard it is for you to not have Sunny around. I sure know how much she loved you."

"Okay." Joanna slices through the softened mood. "Okay. So you'll call the doctor?"

"Yes," I concede, but then add pointedly, "*if* you'll see the psychiatrist, I'll call the doctor."

"You will call the doctor and report the murder?"

"Yes," I sigh. "I will call the doctor and report the murder."

I'm generally not comfortable challenging authority and I definitely do not like the idea of calling a doctor's office to question the validity of a death certificate, but this is exactly what I'm planning out the following morning when I drive into the parking garage of Dr. Nestor's building. In the waiting room, I see six of those little I'm-here-notification switches stacked in a neat array near the entrance. I flip the one next to Dr. Nestor's name, then sit down on an unyielding leather-covered couch. Two large paintings, depicting two sleepy pastel towns, loom over me on the opposite wall. The roofs of the houses in both paintings appear to shine, as if from reflected moonlight or an evening glow from the wide skies, and in the skies hover . . . skeletons?

I lean forward to double-check.

Yes, I'm pretty sure. That's strange.

In the wide skies above the towns, barely perceptible skeletons float like wispy constellations against the purple night.

I rest my elbow on an end table displaying not one or two but three boxes of Kleenex, a gesture that seems rather dear but also a little overanxious. I fight the urge to take a Kleenex simply because they are so extravagantly offered. What if waiting rooms were places where people came to cry? As I look up again at the skeletons drifting lightly in the night, I imagine a chorus of loud sobs, soft whimpers, and wet sniffles, comrades nodding to each other while politely passing boxes of Kleenex to and fro.

Then, all at once, without the warning of a footfall or the click of an opening door, Dr. Nestor is standing there in front of me.

Whoa, that was like a magic trick, I want to say, but instead I just smile and try not to look startled.

"Maggie?" he asks, pointedly. I nod.

"Please come in." He gestures to the door with a well-manicured hand.

Something about his precise features, pressed clothing, and swift movements speak to me of more than the typical practitioner worn down by the shuffling of insurance papers and the parade of unliftable depressives. *He could be the one,* I think, the one with the grand and gleaming answer. I sit down on a couch, put my hands on my lap, and look up. Everything about Dr. Nestor is pointy. His nose, his chin, and the line of his jaw seem drawn by a draftsman's pencil, and his elbows and knees seem to have been shaped in the tool-and-die shop of a mechanical engineer.

"What brings you to my office, Maggie?"

I tell him my story and end by explaining that the Paxil I'm taking is not working, that Klonopin taken at twice the dosage with alcohol helps, but not much, and that Valium taken with alcohol puts me to sleep—which works out great until I have to wake up.

Dr. Nestor gazes past me, face slack and eyelids half closed; searching, I imagine, through the stacks of some inner library. When his face reanimates, I know he must have located his idea, and I feel a surge of excitement. *He's going to propose the cure for my illness, and I will have reached—finally!—the end of this crazy journey.*

Dr. Nestor's eyes come back to rest on mine. Lifting his chin, he asks, "Do you know . . ."

"Yes?" I reply, my wide eyes and the upturned corners of my mouth declaring to him that I will faithfully adhere—for the rest of my life—to the next thing that comes out his mouth.

". . . the Talking Heads song 'Road to Nowhere'?"

I resist the urge to kick Dr. Nestor in his precise, pointy kneecap. He's asking me about the Talking Heads? Those guys from the eighties with the shoulder pads who sang "Burning Down the House"? Sure, David Byrne may have been a delightful lyricist and the band may once have had mind-boggling cachet, but I've been hanging on the edge of his austere cowhide sofa for something along the lines of "You need to try Miracuwonderlum, a new drug chronicled in the medical journals I keep myself extremely up to date on, coupled with a groundbreaking form of talk therapy I practice which has been established through rigorous peer-reviewed, double-blind studies to be 100 percent effective with tall, facially asymmetric blond women suffering from OCD who grew up scared of going to hell and are currently suffering from a rarely described form of obsessive-compulsive disorder."

"Wait, what now?" I ask, still processing, "'Road to Nowhere'?"

He nods, widening his eyes like a child about to open a present. And then Dr. Nestor has shot to his feet, and before I can chart his journey, he is typing away at a computer and a document is being printed out and with almost no time having passed, I'm now holding a piece of paper in my hands with the lyrics to "Road to Nowhere."

I stare at Dr. Nestor in shock for an instant, then down at the paper, then back up to him.

"What should I—? Do you want me to read it?"

He nods.

"Out loud?"

"No, no. To yourself is fine."

Dr. Nestor stays standing there, pressing his palms together and holding his fingers up to his lips, clearly anticipating that the words I'm about to read are going to blow my mind.

Okay, I think. *Let's give it a go.*

I read opening lyric, about knowing where we are going but not knowing where we've been but then . . . all I can hear is *Auschwitz, Auschwitz, Auschwitz.*

I try the chorus.

"*We're on a road to Auschwitz. Come on inside. Taking that ride to Auschwitz, Auschwitz, Auschwitz.*"

Now I can't even read! I wail in my head, as my face becomes hot and a blaze of fear runs behind my sternum.

Auschwitz, Auschwitz, Auschwitz.

I smooth the drops of perspiration that have appeared in the crooks of my elbows down my forearms toward my wrists and focus on the page that is now shaking in my hands.

"*We're on a ride to nowhere. Come on inside. Auschwitz, Auschwitz, Auschwitz. Time is on our side.*"

Why is this happening? Why am I doing this? Why am I doing this to *myself*?

Auschwitz, Auschwitz, Auschwitz.

"I can't," I finally squeak, my scalp ablaze with Billy Graham tingles but somehow managing to keep the tears forming in my eyes from falling down my cheeks.

"The looping is going on right now, and it's making it difficult for me to read."

Dr. Nestor's hands fall limply to his sides and his face loses expression, but he rallies. "Okay," he says. "Well, you can keep that." He resumes his seat as instantly as he abandoned it and offers, "Let's talk about medication. I'd like to be rather aggressive about it."

"Great. Aggressive is great." Then I add, "Because . . . I'm really not doing so well."

"Yes, I see. Well, I'd like to see you keep up the Paxil and Valium, start you on Remeron and Seroquel, which you will find, if you look them up, categorized as antipsychotics, but don't let that scare you. Also, I'm thinking propanolol will help with the rapid heart rate and tremors you're experiencing. How does that sound?"

"Okay!" I say, overly bright, covering the terror of being prescribed a wee fistful of drugs suitable for someone running around a blazing schoolhouse with a gas can in her hand shouting, "Fire is fun!"

"But no alcohol with these," he says. "Okay?"

"Yes," I say, "of course," but think, *Well, that seems a little extreme. But I can* definitely *cut down.*

"Are you seeing a therapist?" Dr. Nestor asks.

"Yes, a woman named Lucy Rosenthal, who I love."

"Good," Dr. Nestor says. "What kind of therapy does she practice?"

"Narrative."

Dr. Nestor frowns with a barely detectible eye roll, but one which still manages to inform me that I might as well be consulting a past-life regression therapist with a degree in "candles" who specializes in working with troubled cats.

"Hmm," Dr. Nestor says. "Narrative therapy can be a fascinating intellectual pursuit, and for many it holds value, but I think you might, for the time being, benefit from the attention of a specialist."

"I see."

Dr. Nestor again stares past me, his eyes dimming as he consults some inner file, but then life is restored to the windows of his soul as he claps his hands together and actually says, "I've got it!" He pops to his feet again, dashes to a bookshelf by the window, and calls over his shoulder, "Have you heard of a type of therapy called ACT?"

"No, what is it?" I ask, sitting up sharply on the edge of the hard couch.

"ACT, acceptance commitment therapy," he clarifies, plucking a book from the shelf and walking over to ceremoniously place it in my hands.

Get Out of Your Mind and Into Your Life, the blue and gold hardcover reads in an ornamented typeface. *The New Acceptance and Commitment Therapy.*

Dr. Nestor taps the cover with his finger. "It's an approach that emphasizes accepting whatever happens to arise in your mind and whatever sensations happen to pass through your body without trying to block out or get rid of anything."

That's perfect, I think. *ACT* is perfect, and it's perfect for a person just like me. What I need to do is *accept*. I need to accept all the looping going on in my mind instead of trying to get rid of it.

"And committing to what really matters to you and enriches your life," Dr. Nestor continues.

That seems good, too. I mean, those are all good words in that sentence, but mainly I'm excited about not trying to root out the looping and all the feelings of anxiety. ACT is going to be my thing. I'm certain of it. Dr. Nestor is a genius-saint.

Grateful, reverent, I hold my holy book, part it in the center with my left hand and riffle through its hallowed pages with my right, feeling the edges with my fingertips. I will read every word of *Get Out of Your Mind and Into Your Life: The New Acceptance and Commitment Therapy* tonight in one consecrated sitting. I will pour a glass of merlot, and that will be fine since I'll only have one. I will settle in under my blanket, Holly will curl next to my hip, a warm lump of dog, and I will savor every word of my new Bible.

"Thank you," I say, resisting the urge to clasp the volume to my breast like a junior high school girl trying to pull a love letter into her very heart. "Thank you, Dr. Nestor. I will read this tonight."

"Oh, good," Dr. Nestor says, blinking. "But, um—that's my copy."

I shake my head. "Huh?"

I think he's telling me that the *Get Out of Your Mind and Into Your Life* clutched to my chest is his and that he wants me to give it back. That can't be right.

"What?" I say, affording the doctor the opportunity to clarify.

"That's my copy of the book," he says.

I look at him in disbelief. "Of course, totally, but can I . . . borrow it?"

"I'm sure it's available on Amazon."

My mask of unflappable niceness drops. I don't pretend that everything is fine while internally rehearsing some rage-fueled revenge fantasy.

"Do you know?" I say in a clear and matter-of-fact tone. "That seems unkind, Doctor. I want to read this book tonight and the thing is that I am in bad shape, truly. I am truly in bad shape, and I am your patient, and I think it would be unkind of you to not loan me this book."

"Oh, uh, of course," the doctor says, glancing at his shoes, perhaps somewhat chastened. "Just bring it back next week."

"Definitely," I say, still wounded by his sudden stinginess, but pleased I addressed it and got what I needed. "Thank you."

Joanna is standing five feet away from me in my kitchen and yelling into a wireless phone handset I have just given her.

"Can you hear me?" she shouts, looking me right in the face.

"Yes," I say at a conversational volume, into an identical handset. "I can hear you, Joanna. It's the same phone line. It's just two handsets."

"I can hear you, too!" she yells.

"Good. Okay, so when the doctor calls back, we'll both be able to hear what he says and talk to him together."

"When we report the murder."

Maybe Joanna's not being paranoid, though. Maybe she's on to something. I review the facts as I turn off the receiver and lay it on the counter. First, Reyna asks Joanna, who controlled Sunny's checkbook under Sunny's guidance after her surgery, to pay a higher monthly rate for Sunny's care. Then, Joanna says no, they can't possibly afford that. And then, subsequently, but like right-away subsequently—the next day, in fact—her mother turns up dead. Finally, her physician somehow signs her mother's death certificate without knowing she's even deceased.

Is it possible that Reyna didn't actually murder Sunny outright, but *did* delay responding when Sunny went into cardiac arrest? I mean, that's plausible, right? But could she have actually forged the signature on a death certificate? No, that's ridiculous, unless . . . somehow she arranged to have the signature forged? Do paramedics sign death certificates? Could she have convinced or bribed a paramedic to forge a signature? That's even more ridiculous, but it's equally ridiculous for a doctor's signature to appear on a death certificate when that doctor doesn't even know the person has died. And Joanna said Sunny's doctor called because she had missed an appointment, so he must not know she's dead, right?

"The doctor's receptionist said he'd call in the afternoon," I tell Joanna, "but she didn't say exactly when. Do you want to swim in the pool while we wait?"

"What if he calls while I'm in the water?"

"Well," I say, walking outside and placing the handset by the edge of the pool, "the phone will be right here, so you can just swim over and answer it."

"Like a mermaid," Joanna says brightly. "I can swim over like a mermaid and answer the phone."

"Perfect," I say.

Two hours later, Joanna, white-faced with sunscreen, is still bobbing in the water, held aloft by Ruby's bright yellow arm floaties. I lean out the kitchen door, my mind swirling with loops, and call to her, "Wanna sandwich?"

"Okay."

"Turkey?"

"Okay. Do you have mayonnaise?"

"I do."

"But not mustard."

I walk to the refrigerator, imagining Josie Rose and little Babette bobbing in the pool instead of Joanna, buoyed by matching yellow floaties. Would they be yellow? *Yes,* I think, *bright dandelion yellow.*

I imagine the two girls, my two girls, swimming with their friends while the sun plays on the palm trees and reflects off the water. Josie and Babette are older now, but I can still see all the many incarnations they've been through as they splash around before me.

I deliver the sandwich, with potato chips and four Oreos, on a plastic plate.

"Okay," Joanna says, swimming toward me and sitting on the steps. "You found mayonnaise?"

"Yes. It's in there."

She accepts the plate without looking up at me.

I stare at her for a moment. "You know, *thank you* is a great thing to say after someone brings you a sandwich with chips and Oreos on a plate."

"Thank you," she tosses out as she peels the bread back. "Is that mayonnaise?"

"Yes, I told you it's mayonnaise."

I return to the kitchen, feeling ridiculous for my absurd demand for gratitude, and am twisting the bread bag closed when the phone rings and the caller ID displays KAISER PERMANENTE.

"Pick up your phone," I yell to Joanna, reaching for the handset I've left on the counter. "Pick up your phone!"

"Now?"

"Yes, now! Press the green button."

I press my green button and say "Hello."

"HELLO!" Joanna shouts into her receiver from the side of the pool. "CAN YOU HEAR ME? CAN YOU HEAR ME?"

"Yes, Joanna," I say, covering my receiver. "We can hear you."

A disoriented male voice inquires, "Uh, is this Maggie Rowe?"

"Yes, this is she," I say, too formally.

"Hello, Maggie. This is Dr. Reed returning your call."

"Hi, Dr. Reed. Thank you so much for calling me back. I won't take up much of your time. I know you're busy." I have a thing about doctors where I'm hyperaware of wasting their time. I'm pretty sure for every minute they talk to me, ten people die.

"I am here with Sunny Hergert's daughter, Joanna. Sunny Hergert was your patient?"

"Yes, I have her file right here," Dr. Reed replies.

"Okay, great," I say. "Well, so here's Joanna's question. You signed a death certificate for Sunny Hergert on October seventeenth citing cardiac arrest as the cause of death, and I was wondering how you were able to determine that."

"Let's back up a moment, Maggie. Tell me, how are you related to Sunny Hergert?"

"Oh, sorry, I'm not . . . I was a, uh, friend, but now that she's gone, I have become her daughter's—Joanna Hergert's—legal representative."

"But not with power of attorney!" Joanna shouts into the call. "She doesn't have power of attorney over me!"

This detail had always been quite important to Joanna, making me wonder if someone had exercised power of attorney over one of Joanna's two brothers in a way she found frightening.

"Hi there, Joanna," Dr. Reed says warmly, undisturbed by her outburst. "I remember your mother talking about you."

Joanna is silent before mumbling through a bit lip, "No one has power of attorney over me. No one."

"It's good to meet you over the phone, Joanna."

"Okay."

"So, now, Maggie, you were asking about the cause of death?"

"You didn't know she was dead!" Joanna erupts. "How could you know how she died if you weren't even there? *How could you know?*"

"Ah. Well, Joanna," Dr. Reed answers with a surgeon's calm. "It was the paramedics, in this case, who determined the cause of death—cardiac arrest—based on their evaluation when they arrived on the scene."

"But you signed it! You signed it, and you weren't even there!"

"No, I wasn't. That's right. The death certificate was sent to me at Kaiser, as her primary care physician, for my signature. I was sorry to hear about your mother's passing, Joanna. I always liked her jokes. She was a very funny lady—"

"But you didn't know she was dead. You didn't know it. You called and said she missed an appointment. How could she miss an appointment if she was dead?"

"I called?"

"You called from your office, the office of Dr. Reed, that's you, and you left a message on the machine about her annual appointment. You didn't know she isn't here anymore."

"Ah, I see. That must have been my receptionist. I'm sorry about that. Sometimes it takes a while to update records."

"But they murdered my mother!" Joanna screams. "Plain and simple. It's an open and shut case."

"No, the paramedics are very thorough. You can be quite sure nobody murdered your mother, my dear."

"It was Reyna! Reyna murdered my mother!"

"No, Joanna. Your mother was not murdered." Dr. Reed repeats, in a sterner tone, attempting to set the question to rest. "I was treating Sunny for heart disease."

We both hear a crash.

"Joanna?" Dr. Reed asks.

"Oh no," I say, looking out the door to where the handset lies on the bricks, battery cover open and lights no longer blinking. "I think Joanna has . . . hung up," I say. "Thank you for your call, Dr. Reed. Thank you for taking the time."

"Poor girl," he replies. "I'm sorry I couldn't be of more help."

I think how the word *girl* is actually appropriate for Joanna despite her fifty-five years.

Of course it was his office that called. I didn't think to ask if it was his receptionist who called. I didn't think.

I walk outside and see Joanna, standing perfectly still in the shallow end of the pool, water up to her waist, elbows and yellow arm floaties pinned to her side. Her eyes are squeezed shut. She is shivering but is not trying to get warm.

"Oh, Joanna," I say, "let me get you a towel." I look around the patio for a stray that didn't make it to the washer and find one in a sun-dried orange mound by the kitchen door. "Here," I say, shaking it out. "Why don't you get out of the pool?"

Joanna shakes her head.

"I'm sorry, " I say, squatting by the water and spreading out the towel to receive her. "I guess physicians don't have to be at the scene to sign a death certificate. I guess they just send it back to the office. And I should have asked what you meant when you said Dr. Reed called."

Joanna opens her eyes but looks past me, immobile, oblivious to the fact that her lips are quivering and blue.

"Come on out," I say, standing up and shaking the towel as if I were enticing a reluctant bull.

Joanna complies, sloshing over to the steps and climbing out, her face drained and vacant. "Places like that are supposed to take care of people," she says, turning around to let me wrap the towel around her as if we have done this ritual a thousand times before instead of just this once. "Pure Hearts Care did the opposite of that. Reyna did the opposite of that. It wasn't taking care of people. It was the opposite."

"I know you must be disappointed," I say, pulling the towel tight around her shoulders, thinking of the little Anna and Ruby and Nerys wraps I used to make when they were small, those damp, squirmy little-girl burritos.

"She's going to get away with it," Joanna whimpers to the late afternoon sky, her arms swaddled into her torso with the orange towel. "She's going to get away with it. And there's nothing I can do."

That night I lie flat on my back, perfectly still, because my nerves are hyper-tuned and any new contact with the bed or Jimmy or Holly will give me a jolt. It's like that game at the carnival where you have to weave the metal hoop around the spiral without touching it to avoid getting zapped.

Joanna is still on my mind, but Auschwitz has returned with all its power, punishing me for straying from my task.

I simply need to remain steady. *Just breathe*, I tell myself. *Sleep will come.*

I think of how Joanna once said her body has always *taken* to sleep. My body has always taken to sleep too. *But neither of our bodies*, I think, *are going to be taken away easily by anything tonight.*

And then *zap*. Holly has poked my thigh, sending what feels like electricity stinging through my body.

I flash to a memory of shaking my classmate Eric Kirshner's hand in fourth grade, the weird metal nugget in his palm and the buzzing that started in my hand and shot to my heart.

I think of my grandmother in the hospital after her shock treatments that one Christmas, gumming a candy bar, a strand of caramel dangling like tinsel from her mouth. I think of images composed by my ten-year-old self that now feel to me like fact, of her being wheeled into a hospital, of her wrists muscled into restraints, of her blue eyes searching up into the harsh fluorescent lights above for some sort of explanation, with her trademark red lipstick smeared across her cheeks and chin, slashing her face like a scar.

I see the nurses put grease on her temples before they place the electrodes.

"Ah," I yelp.

Jimmy has rolled over and shocked me by flopping his arm over my chest.

"Sorry," he says, rolling back.

"Don't be sorry. *I'm* sorry. I'm just going to try to go sleep in the TV room," I say, standing up, pulling a blanket over my head and staggering down the hall, feeling a zap that goes from my heel up to my skull with each step.

11

What a Pair

I thought you said your psychiatrist was a boy."

"Well, the one I saw last week was a man," I say, easing my Camry ten feet forward in the Beverly Boulevard stop-and-go traffic that is mostly stop, "but the one I'm seeing today is a woman."

"*Two psychiatrists?*" Joanna's scream pierces though the Camry's hands-free phone system. "You see TWO PSCHIATRISTS?"

"Well, actually one is a psychologist and one—"

"*Two psychiatrists?* I can barely believe my ears, Maggie. I can barely believe my ears."

"Well, it's true. You can believe it."

"But *you've got everything*! You've got everything a person could *want*. You live on Easy Street with Handsome Jim in his house he bought before he even knew you."

"Joanna," I spit out, only able to pull forward another ten feet before having to press the brakes again, "I don't have it as easy as you think, okay?"

Joanna's silence pointedly informs me she finds my assertion ridiculous.

"Okay," I say, my frustration with her, and the West Hollywood traffic, rising. "I've got to go. I'll meet you at my place at three, and we'll go to Kaiser."

"Okay. Three p.m. At Jim's house."

"It's *my* house, too, you know."

"Two psychiatrists," I hear Joanna mutter, astounded, under her breath before the click of the phone.

Whoa, I am so tired, I suddenly think.

And then, *whoa, my eyelids are anchors.*

Whoa.

The cocktail from Dr. Nestor has definitely started to take effect.

I need to keep all of my concentration on the road, where the cars around me seem to be sailing on an ocean, swaying up and down. I'm managing the seas fine, but I'm desperate to pull over, dock, and take a nap.

I think of the story of the tortoise and the hare and how I've always wondered: Why in the world would the hare choose to take a nap right in the middle of a race that he had clearly staked much of his personal identity on winning? What was the hare thinking? Apparently the missing puzzle piece was that the hare was taking a cocktail of Seroquel, Remeron, Viibryd, Lexapro, and propranolol and was really fucking tired!

But I can't pull over. I need to get to this appointment.

I can do it. I can stay awake. I have only ten blocks to go. I need to meet Kalene Hale. Kalene Hale is an ACT therapist who Dr. Nestor says is at the very top of her field. Kalene Hale could be the one who saves me. So I do what I always do when I'm driving and I need to stay awake.

I scream. I hold on to the steering wheel, hold my eyes open wide, and I scream. Loud and wild.

One block at a time.

At every stoplight, I scream.

Dr. Kalene Hale's waiting room is long, narrow, and unpromising. The carpet is thin and hard under the fluorescent lighting. The pictures on the walls are aggressively corporate with generic ponds and paths through nondescript woods, which communicate the sentiment, *Wouldn't it be great if we didn't work in an office?* It's the type of holding area I imagine I might be sitting in if I were applying for a job at a Holiday Inn. It makes me feel like I should be holding a resume and rehearsing a speech about how much I love being a part of the hospitality industry.

Kalene's door swings opens almost as soon as I sit down on the cold metal chair. It takes me a moment to realize that the woman standing in front of me is meant to be my therapist. Her hair has been bleached to a desperate fragility, leaving but a few clusters of strands loyally clinging to her scalp. She is wearing a jeans miniskirt, no nylons, cowboy boots, and a halter top.

"Maggie Rowe? I'm Kalene. Please come in." I follow Kalene into her office and take a seat on another cold folding chair to begin my story, a story I've gotten down to a tight seventeen minutes. Kalene nods, tucks a few embattled blond hairs behind her right ear, then wordlessly reaches down to open a drawer by the heel of her left cowboy boot and retrieves a two-foot length of white nylon rope. She firmly wraps a fist of cherry-red acrylic nails around one end and, smiling gently, offers me the other.

Oh come on, I think, unable to prevent scorn from narrowing my eyes. *Just tell me the point you want to make.* Stay open, I remind myself. Don't let fears become prophecies. Maybe Dr. Kalene Hale's rope trick, whatever it might turn out to be, is good for more than I imagine. Maybe something magical will happen. Maybe this sorceress disguised as a woman who wants nothing more than to make offerings before the gods and goddesses of spring break will be able to break the spell that afflicts me.

I reach out with my right hand, grasp the rope firmly, and nod. Kalene begins pulling on her end, and I match her force. For a moment nothing happens except the two of us sitting on matching metal chairs in a demoralizingly generic office, playing silent tug-of-war with a two-foot stretch of soft nylon rope.

"What do you feel?"

"Tension."

"Tension," Kalene repeats, "that's right. Now, what would happen if you dropped the rope?"

I allow a moment to pass before observing dryly and with a bit of an edge, "I would no longer have a rope in my hand."

"Aaaah," she says, as if she expects waters to part before us and my mouth to gape.

"What would happen if you stopped attempting to get rid of your anxiety? What would happen if you"—Kalene pauses here for dramatic effect, widening her eyes, allowing her spidery lashes to crawl up toward her overplucked eyebrows—"just . . . dropped the rope?"

Kalene glances pointedly at the rope between us, and I look down as well, then back up at her with anger I attempt to disguise as confusion. "You mean, literally? You mean literally drop this actual rope we're both holding onto right now?"

"Why not?"

I raise an eyebrow to let her know I'm not exactly besotted with her clever little exercise and open my hand. The rope swings down and away from my hand and over toward Kalene.

Kalene, impervious to the articulation of my eyebrow and my tone of skepticism, looks at me eagerly. "How does that feel?" The rope sways back and forth in diminishing little arcs before coming to rest below her hand.

"Yeah," I say, "that would be great if I could do that with my anxiety. If I could just drop the proverbial rope and be done with it, but I don't know how—"

"Value-based living. You focus on value-based living."

"What do you mean by that?"

"Focus on the values that our life is based on," she says, unhelpfully rearranging the words in her original statement.

"Okay . . . well . . ."

"What matters to you?"

"What matters to me is that I stop walking around terrified of the contents of my own head."

"What if you were fine walking around terrified of the contents of your own head?"

But who, I think, *could be fine with walking around terrified and living on the verge of a panic attack from the beginning to the end of each day?*

"Is it going to hurt?" Joanna asks flatly.

"Is what going to hurt?" We are driving down Sunset Boulevard toward Kaiser Permanente hospital. I am sipping a triple cappuccino to stay awake.

Joanna holds on to her seat belt as if it is not up to the task. "When the psychiatrist examines me?"

Suddenly the car in front of me is inches away and I must slam on the brakes.

"Aaargh," Joanna yelps, her body jolting forward, her hands flying up to the dashboard.

"Sorry, Joanna," I say, "And no, of course nothing will hurt. He's just going to talk to you."

"But what about . . ." Joanna releases her hands, pulls back to her seat, and adjusts her seat belt. "What about . . . what about . . . what about *the diagnosis?*"

"Oh," I say, feeling a wave of empathy, "the diagnosis is just . . . he's just going to ask you questions and you'll answer them and . . . and you can talk about anything you want with him. About your mom, if you want—"

"But how are they going to measure my brain?"

I realize Joanna thinks she's going to be getting some sort of neurological examination. "No, no, Joanna, it's not like that. The measuring is just by talking. He's just going to get to you know you a little bit."

"But they shock your brain."

"Oh my goodness, no, Joanna that's—"

"When they measure it. They shock your brain."

"Where did you hear that? That's something else completely. That's *electroshock* therapy. That's absolutely *not* what you're doing."

I lose focus on Joanna for a moment because of my own rising anxiety and when I continue speaking, I hear alarm in my voice. "And even electroshock therapy probably isn't like you think, anyway. It's called it electro*convulsive* therapy now and they've made incredible advancements, actually, in the practice. The whole thing is way better than it used to be. It's much more precise than when your grandmother got it."

That stops me. I know nothing about Joanna's grandmother, or whether Joanna ever met or was even told anything about her grandmother. I'm talking about my own grandmother. I'm talking about her early-generation electroshock treatments, her blank eyes and her listless body collapsed on a folding armchair in the Forest Ridge Hospital family and visitors' lounge.

"Anyway," I continue, shaken by the memory and my classically Freudian slip, "I promise there will be no shocking." I expect Joanna to be relieved, but she looks down at her lap, grabs two fistfuls of hair, and pulls down, violently straightening her curls.

"What's the matter?"

Joanna pulls the frayed ends toward her mouth and bites at different clumps. "They can't take away my money?"

"No, I promise. The only purpose of this appointment is to get an up-to-date diagnosis so you can stay in a nice board and care—"

"Board and CARE!" Joanna bellows. "Board and CARE? I'm not going to a board and care! My brother was in a board and care before he died, he was on dialysis, and they took his entire check. They took his *entire check*! He didn't even have enough money to go to the movies. He only ever knew about movies from billboards. *From billboards*—"

The light turns green, and I focus ahead. "No, no, this isn't like that. I'll be paying your rent out of our account. You'll be able to see movies. I promise."

"They won't take my whole check?"

"No."

"Because I want to see movies."

"You'll always be able to see movies."

"Movies on billboards?"

"Movies on billboards," I promise.

As I sit next to Joanna in the waiting room at Kaiser—held together by a magical medical mixture that weighs me down as if gravity's force has been heightened, causes my hands to shake, dries out my mouth, and I would swear makes it possible for onlookers to observe me getting fatter in real time—Joanna checks out a man seated across from us. I follow her impolite stare to an Ichabod Crane–looking fellow drumming spindly fingers into hollow of his right cheek and speaking into the air.

"Streetwalkers aren't always prostitutes," he's proposing to no one. "Sometimes they're people walking on the street. I walk on the street, but I'm not a prostitute. I'm not a prostitute, but I walk on the street. I'm a streetwalker, that's all. Streetwalkers aren't always prostitutes."

Joanna listens to this for a moment and then looks over at me, arching an eyebrow and gesturing toward the man with a conspiratorial thumb as if to say, *Whoa, check out the crazy dude!*

I can't contain an explosive laugh, and Joanna thinks it's funny that I'm laughing with such force, and soon there we are, two middle-aged female mental patients—one with cognitive incompetence and the other drugged to the gills—perched on uncomfortable plastic chairs that conform to the shape of no person's body, in the Kaiser Permanente waiting room, laughing our asses off.

What a pair are we, I think, blinking back tears. *Send in the clowns.*

A doctor's assistant with a name tag that reads LINETTE comes to the door and says "Joanna Hergert." Joanna pretends as if she hasn't heard and stares straight ahead.

"Joanna, that's you," I say, gently placing my hand on Joanna's shoulder and nudging her.

"What?" Joanna asks, defiantly oblivious, pulling her chin sideways to inspect her armpit.

"That's you."

Joanna, her gaze locked into her armpit, asks, "They won't take my check?"

"They won't take your check," I say, squeezing the hand of my comrade.

"Joanna Hergert," Linette repeats, insistent, staring at Joanna, holding a folder at her hip like a gun in a holster.

"I'll be waiting for you right here," I assure Joanna, thinking about the broad-shouldered, caper-eyed mother at Target with her daughter, her daughter who walked, confident, with her stack of clothes into the dressing room, not looking back.

"My brother moved into a board and care," Joanna says through pinched lips, "and they took his entire check."

"We can talk about the board and care later. This is just a diagnosis," I assure her. "It's just talking."

After several moments of consideration, Joanna gets up, takes two steps, but then turns back to me.

"They can't take my check?"

"Nobody can take your check."

"Okay, okay, okay," Joanna mutters, walking toward Linette.

"Oh." I leap up. "Make sure you get something in writing from the doctor, a paper with your diagnosis. I told them on the phone, but just in case he forgets."

"Okay, okay, okay," Joanna continues, miserably pulling on her hair with both hands, pushing past the woman and going down the hallway by herself.

I watch as the door closes and think of my mother watching me as I went down that first hall in Grace Point. I remember her telling me the fear she felt when my therapist, Bethanie, closed the door behind me and locked it.

Linette looks back toward me, uncertain. I know she is wondering who I am. A sister? A niece? A social worker? Assuredly not the wife of a man who twelve years ago met a pair of surprisingly engaging women outside of Koo Koo Roo panhandling for change.

With Joanna gone, my focus turns back to myself, specifically to my face and why it is so hot. Like I'm running a fever, but only in the face. I wonder if this could be a side effect of one of the newer medications. After four weeks, the Paxil had not kicked in and rectified the situation in my brain like I hoped it would, so Dr. Nestor has switched up my cocktail.

I bring my palms to my cheeks, which do indeed feel hot to the touch. My insides feel parched and hot with a different kind of heat, a dry heat, ready to be sparked into flames.

Twenty minutes later Joanna returns.

Wow, that was quick. I smile at Joanna until I notice she doesn't have a piece of paper in her hands.

"Oh, Joanna. Didn't the doctor give you a diagnosis?"

"He said I didn't have to tell anyone what we talked about. That's what he said, Maggie. He said it was confidential."

"Fine, but—"

"I don't have to tell you anything."

"No, but we need to get a diagnosis. That's the whole reason we came here."

Joanna stiffens herself and stares at me blankly.

"Did you ask him for your diagnosis in writing?"

Joanna crosses her arms across her chest, then says matter-of-factly, "I told you I'm not going to a board and care."

"What?"

"I'm not going to a board and care. They take your entire check."

I whip around toward the receptionist behind a glass screen.

"Hi," I say, sharply, "I came here to get an evaluation for my friend Joanna Hergert. She needs a recent diagnosis for a supportive housing situation, and the doctor didn't give her something in writing like I had requested."

Joanna crosses past me and directly addresses the receptionist. "The doctor said I didn't have to tell anyone what we talked about."

The receptionist looks to me, suspicious, then back at Joanna. "That's right. Everything you discuss with the doctor is confidential."

Joanna smiles, satisfied.

"This weekend," she informs the receptionist, "I'm going to go see *Mamma Mia*."

Part Three

2016-2020

12

It Is Well

T hat's it," I say, marching into the bedroom where Jimmy lies propped up, asleep with a script on his chest. "I'm done!"

Jimmy takes a sleepy stab at emotional support with a knee-jerk "That's great. Good for you."

"Let her live on the streets!"

Jimmy's eyes pop open. "What?"

"I am out of the Joanna game. I'm out. *Out!*" I slam my purse down on the bed and kick off my shoes.

"Oh, no. What happened?" Jimmy asks, removing his glasses and rubbing his eyes.

"She wouldn't go in." I unzip my pants and yank them down to my ankles, desperate to get out of my "see the world" outfit and into Greenie and my Capezio shorts. "I found a place that doesn't require a psychiatric diagnosis, a diagnosis which Joanna has been given, it's on record at Kaiser, but of course she still refuses to allow me access to it." I pull my blouse over my head with an angry flourish.

"So, Joanna and I go to the place. Seems like a nice place, there's a nice lawn that apparently gets mowed once a week and everything's going quite nicely until Joanna sees the name of the place written on a sign, Stanley Board and Care, and she completely freaks out."

"Why?"

"*Board and care.* Her brother."

"Oh, right. They took his whole paycheck."

"Right. So then she scowls at me like I'm some kind of witch who's trying to lure her into a dungeon, like my whole goal for the last eight months has been to slam a heavy board-and-care doorway shut behind her and throw away the key. And then she starts shrieking at me right there on the sidewalk, 'I'm not staying in a board and care, Maggie! You can't make me! *You can't make me!*'"

"Does the place actually take the disability check?"

Greenie is not in the drawer where it's supposed to be, so I go to the hamper.

"I don't how they work it." I flip up the hamper lid, yanking items out and flinging them to the floor. "We were supposed to learn that at the orientation meeting. I tried to explain to her that it was just a meeting, but she just kept saying she won't go to a board and care. She hates board and care. Won't go inside a board and care."

Greenie is not in the hamper.

"Shit," I say. "Shit, shit, *shit!*"

"What's the matter?"

"The matter is," I say, slamming the hamper shut and whipping around, "Joanna is taking up all my time. All I'm doing is thinking about fixing Joanna's problems and talking to Joanna on the phone and taking Joanna all the places she needs to go, when I should be working on book promotion stuff and finding a new therapist before the writers' room starts up again next month because I'm going to need to act like a human being and ya know what? I hate Kalene. I fucking *hate* her. I've tried three times a week for a month to not despise that woman, but I've failed. I've failed spectacularly at the Grand Endeavor of Not Hating Kalene."

I stomp over to the bed and yank up the comforter. No Greenie there either. "Damnit!" I say, throwing the comforter back down with enough violence to back Jim up off the bed and against the wall to stay out of my way. "I would have stopped seeing that dimwitted dodobird after the first session, but every time I bring it up with Dr. Nestor he says to give the dimwitted dodobird another shot. He says the dimwitted dodobird is good with my sort of dysregulation. What *is* my sort of dysregulation?" I drop to my knees and crane my neck to peer beneath the bed frame. "Is it the 'repeat word in your head, freak out for no reason, scared of going to hell, Paxil no longer works' dysregulation? What kind of fucking dysregulation is that?" It's like I have this weird beast of a mental illness few have encountered, which morphs into different horrific forms to avoid naming or taming.

Why can't I have a regular psychiatric disorder? Why couldn't I be beset by a dime-a-dozen depression or standard-fare addiction or run-of-the-mill mania? Why do I have to be one of the weirdos torn apart by disruptions of the mind not well documented, with system glitches that possibly evade all forms of treatment? I stand up and look again under the comforter, and when I see there are still only dog chews there, begin thrashing it up and down. "Where is fucking Greenie? Where is Greenie? Where is it, Jim? Fuck, *fuck*, *FUCK!*"

Finally, I sit down on the end of the bed and slump over with my elbows on my knees and my head in my hands. Jimmy sits down next to me and asks in a gentle tone, "Maggie, are you sure you're okay with my leaving?"

I whip my head toward him and notice, over his shoulder, a small black rolling suitcase with a winter jacket lying on top.

"I leave for New Jersey tonight. I'm going to see my dad, remember?"

No, I do not remember.

But then, "Oh, yes," I say, locating a hazy wisp of a memory of Jim worrying about leaving me alone and me assuring him I would fine. "You gotta go see your dad," I recall saying. "I'll be fine."

"Right. Yes, I totally remember."

"I could postpone the trip. My dad would understand."

"No, no. Don't do that." Jimmy's father is ninety-four years old. I cannot ask my husband not to visit his ninety-four-year-old father. During football season, no less. "Go. You should go."

Jimmy searches my eyes. I know he would stay if I asked, but I want him to be there with his dad watching football on that familiar corduroy couch and not have to play nursemaid to a dysregulated wife, so I consciously engage the tiny muscles around my eyes and ever so slightly lift the corners of my drooping lips.

"Go," I say, lightly. "Go and have a good time. I'll be just fine."

I wait with Jimmy in front of the house for his Uber. When the car arrives, I promise to call if I need him and give him a cheerful peck on the lips before closing the door. Then I head to my computer, determined to find a therapist (or physician, or life coach, or necromancer if that's what it takes) who can help me with whatever this morphing beast of a condition is that I must grapple with.

I start by searching "word stuck in head" and learn about earworms, "a word or phrase or snippet of a song that repeats in one's brain, often to the point of exasperation." When I google "earworm cure" I find three pieces of advice: (1) Chew gum. (2) Try a puzzle. (3) Let it go, *but don't try.*

I doubt this cheerful 1-2-3 advice will be any sort of match against the life-consuming science-fiction monster of an earworm burrowing through my skull, so I try "earworm mental illness" and learn about earworms and their relationship to OCD and bipolar disorder. None of the articles mention any form of treatment, so I search "earworm mental illness therapy," which leads me to an article on NLP, neuro-linguistic programming. I learn about the NLP "swish" technique, in which you picture troubling psychic material floating in front of your face, large and looming. Then, physically, with your hand, you "swish" it to the lower right quadrant of your visual field.

The idea is to begin to see yourself as the maître d' of your own mind, whose job is to determine where to seat the guests. The guests are your various ideas and thoughts, good or bad, comfortable or disturbing, and you get to decide what to do with them. You might have a troubling guest, let's call him Larry, whom you have to seat, but you don't need to give him a prime table. You can seat asshole Larry at the table with a busted leg, for example, way back in the corner by the bathroom, under a ficus tree. But if you try to kick Larry out altogether, he'll have a fit. He'll never let up, banging at the door, demanding a table. *I'm a VIP!*

Yes! I think as I read about the swish technique. Exactly! This is *perfect!* I feel flooded with a sensation not unlike falling in love. *I've found my match!* I think, elated. NLP is the one for me. I love NLP. NLP understands me. NLP knows perfectly well I can't let my troubling thoughts go . . . *without trying!* or rid them from my mind with bubble gum or sudoku or banish them outright with a call to security, just like a maître d' can't throw out a paying customer from his restaurant. I shall be the maître d' of my thoughts, I decide, and the NLP *swish* will be my deliverance. I am certain.

I search "NLP practitioner +Los Angeles" and within six or seven clicks I find my guy, Baruck Saraf of Beverly Hills, who not only practices NLP but also trains and educates up-and-coming NLP practitioners and even writes articles about training and educating up-and-coming NLP practitioners. Needless to say, I do not look any further than Dr. Baruck Saraf.

Dr. Saraf's prices are exorbitant, I notice with some dismay, and my insurance will reimburse only a portion of the bill. But since the man appears to be the grand wizard of NLP in Los Angeles and I'm desperate for the grandest wizardry one could possibly conjure, I email his office. I describe my earworm affliction and the anxiety it provokes and inquire whether he thinks NLP might be helpful in such a situation. I press send and close my eyes and lean back in my chair with a sigh.

Good, I'm thinking. *What should I do now?* when *ting!* My laptop notifies me that Dr. Saraf has replied. It's as if he's always been my guardian NLP angel, standing by, waiting for me to reach out and make contact. "Yes," Dr. Saraf has written, "I have treated many patients in situations such as yours, and they have found NLP not merely helpful, but an eradicator of their problems altogether."

I am generally suspicious of the inflated language of self-marketing and sales, but . . . *"eradicator* of their problems *altogether?"*

How great would that be?

Plus, Dr. Saraf writes that for situations like mine he can boast a 98 percent success rate.

Those are excellent odds.

There is an incredibly good chance that I will fall into that 98 percent. And only a 2 percent chance that I won't.

This man is going to save me. I know it. All subsequent pets, I decide, will be named either Baruck or Saraf. I fall to sleep at night with maître d's dancing like sugar plums in my head and wake up certain that Dr. Saraf will soon make my vivid terrors seem like a distant dream, a wispy dream of an offensive but unimportant guest off in the distance, seated at a shitty table, mostly hidden by a ficus.

A sapphire building, constructed of glittering blue glass, slices upward in front of me into the darkening sky on Rodeo Drive in Beverly Hills.

Wow, I think. *Look at that.*

White marble steps lead from the sidewalk to tall glass entry doors. I walk up with something like reverence, as if approaching a temple. The door with its impressive brass handle looks heavy, but it swings open smoothly and silently with surprising ease.

My sandals slap against an inlaid parquet floor as I walk past art deco murals of patterned pyramids.. I decide that once NLP has cured me, I should look into getting certified to practice NLP. *It might even be able to help Joanna*, I think. *Maybe she will be my first client.*

One plush elevator ride later, I enter Dr. Saraf's waiting area and take in an opulent space accented with intricately tiled floors, burgundy velvet seats, and a tiered chandelier that drips leaves of glass from its golden boughs.

Dr. Saraf opens the door on the opposite side of the room, then pauses a moment in the doorway, as if knowing I will need a moment to take in his striking physique. He is well over six feet tall with a square jaw, far wider than his cheekbones, and shoulders that even for a superhero would be considered broad. He is completely bald, I notice, with the darkest, most luxurious beard I have ever seen. His appearance makes me think of a magnetic toy I used to have called Wooly Willy, where you could arrange iron shavings on a printed face any way you chose. You could give Willy a handlebar mustache or bushy eyebrows or dreadlocks, or a dense, primeval forest growing on his face.

I follow Dr. Saraf into his office and sit down on a chair upholstered in white fur. Horsehair? I wonder. Albino camel? Snowbird?

"Maggie," Dr. Saraf begins, sitting down across from me with a soldier-straight spine. "I'd like to start with an exercise. Are you willing to jump right in?"

"Yes, definitely."

"Good, then. Now, this is a very basic exercise. I'm going to have you visualize a timeline of your life, a timeline which includes your past, present, and future. Do you think you can do that for me?"

"Yes!" I snap back, a cheerful and obedient cadet.

Dr. Saraf tilts his head a little, as if surprised by my hyper-responsiveness. I've got to get a hold of myself. NLP is going to be my salvation, for sure, but I've got to be a little more chill about it.

I visualize a path behind me starting from when I was baby in

Anchorage, meandering through my childhood, and stretching out in front of me to the unknown future, to where it bends in the undergrowth. I give the doctor a nod.

"Good, then. That's very good, Maggie. Now I want to ask you something about your timeline. Is that okay?"

"Yes."

"Are you imagining the timeline going from left to right, from back to forward, or from bottom to top?"

I consider, and then reply, "From back to forward."

"That's very good, Maggie. Now I'd like you to picture a time in your life when you were angry."

I don't know why he's asking me about anger, and I start to worry he might be confusing me with another patient, so I clarify, "Oh, sure, but you know, anger isn't so much my problem. I was the one who emailed you about the earworm thing?"

Dr. Saraf's lips curl up but the smile does not reach his eyes. "I know who you are, Maggie. Now, do you think you can you picture a time when you were angry?"

"Sorry. Yes, of course," I say cheerfully, hoping we'll get through this exercise quickly and move on to the swish.

As Dr. Saraf nods, I picture the time I confessed to my youth pastor Dale that I was scared of going to hell. I was twelve, and it took a leap of faith for me to trust an adult outside my immediate family with such an intimate fear. Pastor Dale rewarded my confidence by informing me that the fear I suffered confirmed in itself that I was indeed in danger. I still feel a small shot of anger on behalf of my credulous twelve-year-old self.

"Are you picturing a time when you were angry?

"Yes, I am."

"Good. Now, I'd like you to keep holding that time in your mind. Let me ask you a question, and you don't have to answer right away."

"Alright," I say.

"Was this time," he begins, leaning forward, slowing down his speech and dropping his voice, "before, during, or *after* your birth?"

"Excuse me?"

He repeats his intonation exactly but raises the volume as if the only problem in my comprehension might have simply been that I was slightly deaf.

"Was this time before, during, or *after* your birth?"

This question guts me. I know in an instant, from the pit of my hollowed-out stomach, that NLP is not the savior I had been counting on. I wouldn't trust a man who asks me a question like that to recommend a slice of pie, much less solve my mental health crisis. My scalp burns with the familiar hell twinge and I think about walking out the door and speeding back home, where a friendly bottle of merlot sits on the counter patiently awaiting my return. But I don't want to give up on this man who, not fifteen minutes ago, was my beloved savior and guru.

"Was this time before, during, or *after* your birth?" Dr. Saraf repeats.

"After," I say, finally, letting him know with a flat voice and sharp look how ludicrous and discrediting his question seems to me and how much I resent having to answer it. "It was definitely not before, or during, but *after* my birth."

"After," Dr. Saraf confirms, somehow not picking up on my hostility. "Good, then. That's very good, Maggie."

I continue the session, but I'm no longer really present for the exercises. Instead, my mind spins with all the negative information I came across while researching NLP. "Extravagant NLP claims not backed by persuasive evidence," I remember reading on one site. And on another: "Convenient, online, NLP Practitioner Certification Training for only $100."

I hear Dr. Saraf ask me how old I was at the time I pictured, and hear myself answer twelve, and that on a scale of one to ten, the memory is at a level six of distress. I hear him saying I should tell that twelve-year-old girl she doesn't have to be angry anymore.

"Tell her she can let go of that anger," he's saying, "and let it float like a balloon up, and up, and up, and far, far away."

I'm picturing a version of myself, permed hair, permed bangs, braces, leg warmers over jeans, letting go of a balloon.

"Far, far away into the sky," he continues. "Tell that young girl the anger doesn't serve her anymore. Tell that young girl she can now give up her anger. Tell her you're going to go back to the future where you and she will both be relieved of the distress."

I am trying to talk to the girl in my mind's eye, but my voice is drowned out by a terrible thought: *What if I am un-helpable? What if I may be beyond the reach of aid? Irremediable?* Now, thanks to Dr. Baruck Saraf, I am one more tried-and-failed solution closer to that fate. What if I fall into that slice of the pie chart of the mentally ill whom no medication or technique or insight—or anything at all—can help? What if I am doomed, or damned, even? *Damned. Damned.* The word loops in my mind.

Dr. Saraf asks how distressing the memory of anger is *now* on a scale of one to ten. I say, still six, and he is not pleased. He says I'm blocking the treatment, that I'm not cooperating, and that I can't expect to achieve a positive result if I'm not really willing to try. I object, telling him that this is just my first visit, that I can't all of sudden let go of some anger I felt thirty years ago after one exercise with an imaginary timeline and a balloon.

"I'm pretty sure my problem doesn't have much, if anything, to do with anger in the first place," I say.

Dr. Saraf's face flushes. For the first time, I notice how cold and hard and dark his eyes are. "I can't help you if you don't give yourself to the method," he huffs, as if we'd been locking horns for months.

"I've worked with Iraq war vets with PTSD, vets who when they hear fireworks feel like they're back in battle with bullets flying, vets who dive under the couch when a doorbell rings, vets who have seen and done and been subject to unspeakable things, but *these* men and women, these *brave* men and women have been willing to give themselves to the method. And because of that commitment, they've been able to cut through the initial layer of their issues in the first session with me."

As Dr. Saraf lectures me, I scold myself for being impressed by a dumb chandelier in a pretentious waiting room on stupid Rodeo Drive and even more for thinking I'd find a cure by searching "earworm treatment" on the internet.

The first glass of wine goes down like water as I stand over the kitchen island, then refill it from the bottle still in my hand. I reach into my purse, which remains slung over my shoulder, for my small orange bottle of Valium. I unscrew the top and shake out two pills, which I place on my tongue and wash down with another swallow of wine.

Twenty minutes later, I am still standing over the island, my elbows pressed into the cold marble and my face in my hands, but now a warm tingling flows from my heart up to my head and back again, coating my fear with a thick, syrupy calm. The fear till lurks there, somewhere, but it has thankfully become much harder to locate.

Ah, I think, *this is fine*, and I press my hands into the marble and push myself up, feeling only a little woozy and only slightly unsure on my feet.

Looking out the kitchen window to the sky, which is deepening from lavender to purple, I am suddenly possessed by a desire to be out there beneath it, so I grab my hoodie from the chair by the door, pull it over my head, and soon find myself walking down the driveway and turning right onto the sidewalk in front of our house.

The air is suffused with a fine mist, which blends the shades of the night and cools my face. I walk up one street and down another, marveling at how simple moisture in the air can soften so many boundaries. It blurs the distinct lines that separate bush from lawn, flower from stem, my foot from the sidewalk. With an assist from the syrup of Valium and wine, it smudges the border between myself and my fear.

I am the only one out walking this evening, and it seems strange, like a dream, as if I am the only one who has slipped into this milky plane of experience. I feel small here, or slight, a nothingness, almost. Not being able to see more than a few yards in front of me, I imagine the milkiness stretching out for miles, like in a Japanese landscape painting, the kind with a vast sky or towering mountains or an endless road dwarfing the one or two lone human figures, who are seen to be, from the perspective of the painter or the admirer of his work, no more significant than a leaf in a forest or an individual cloud in a stormy sky.

I wipe my hand across my forehead and when I realize it is damp, I think of Zen master Suzuki Roshi's description of enlightenment.

> You are walking through a fog
> and without realizing it,
> suddenly you are soaked through.

I drift along until seemingly out of nowhere, a girl, or maybe a petite woman, appears ahead of me in a skirt, rain boots, and hooded raincoat.

She holds a red umbrella, which she tilts slightly back like a parasol. *Why is she holding an umbrella?* I wonder. Is she shielding herself from the mist or just prepared for rain?

Something about that red umbrella carried by this quiet figure on this quiet, misty night in Los Angeles strikes me as heartbreakingly poignant, so much so that I momentarily lose focus and trip on a tree root that has lifted the sidewalk. I barely notice and continue walking.

When the girl with the red umbrella turns a corner, I follow, feeling like Alice chasing her white rabbit. The girl crosses a street and so do I, determined to not let her slip from my sight.

I follow her up to Melrose, towards Pavilions, our local grocery store, then turn and walk through a strip of stores, neon signs blurred by the mist, that have remained unchanged since I moved here in the late 1990s. These are not the "fancy-but-pretending-not-to-be Larchmont" type stores. There's nothing couture, or artisan, or vegan, or farm-raised about these establishments. I follow the girl past a tattoo parlor "of the stars," an establishment I've never seen anyone enter or exit, an iPhone repair shop not authorized by Apple, and an upholstery business with an ancient sofa yellowing in the window.

The woman with the umbrella stops before the entrance to Iglesia Pentecostes, a storefront church I've passed many times on my way to Pavilions to buy donuts in the morning or pick up late-night snacks when Jim and I have nothing in the fridge. I've gathered (from peeks I've taken through the open doors) that the services are less ceremony and more party than anything I grew up with. At all times of day and evening, I've caught glimpses of swaying shoulders and rattling tambourines and the raised hands of congregants shaking toward the ceiling.

The girl collapses her umbrella into a red baton and tucks it under her arm. Then she reaches up and pulls back her hood, revealing the face of a middle-aged Hispanic woman. I stare at her features, disoriented, feeling even more now that I am in a dream, a surreal landscape where faces and identities can morph in an instant. I watch as the woman steps into her church, begins clapping to the beat of the music, and takes a seat in a pew by a group of similar ladies.

I am possessed by a desire to follow and sit there beside her in the pew among her friends, but of course I can't. I'm a white woman who barely remembers how to say "My name is Maggie Rowe" in Spanish. I am not part of this congregation. I've donated to none of their collection plates. I have no tie to this place other than that I followed a lady with an umbrella here because she looked strange and pretty in the mist. Not to mention the fact that I have avoided all places of Christian worship, both grand and humble, since I was nineteen years old for fear I would hear "gnashing of teeth" or "unpardonable sin" or "depart from me I do not know you" and stop being able to breathe. Symbols of the cross, raised above buildings and painted on doors, have for two decades warned me of danger within, an inversion of Dante's *abandon all hope, ye who enter here.*

Now, though, standing outside Iglesia Pentecostes, I feel no danger. I won't understand the words spoken inside, for one thing, and also, what I can see through the doorway looks nothing like any church I have known. There are none of the freighted symbols, no crucifixes, no lost sheep, no pierced hands or feet, no shepherd's staff, no bejeweled gates, no Jesus with flowing, Pantene-washed hair, whose kind-seeming eyes feel as if they could turn on unsuspecting followers in a condemning instant. All I see is a room full of people singing and looking like they are having a really great time. Plus, it seems to be warm under those lights and I'm suddenly very cold. My hoodie is chilled and damp and, I realize with surprise, almost completely soaked through.

My body has started moving forward before I've actually decided to enter the chapel and a surge of adrenaline washes through me. As I step forward, I find myself tucking several stray strands of blond hair beneath my hoodie to hide my whiteness. I brace for heads to turn toward me with suspicious eyes as if I'm an outsider who's just sauntered into an Old West saloon with a menacing jangle of my spurs. As I walk toward an empty pew, however, heads do turn, but with smiles that seem to bid me welcome.

As I take a seat, an elderly woman with slight shoulders and wide features slides in next to me. She is plain and unassuming, the type of woman I could have encountered a hundred times and never noticed in the frozen foods section at Pavilions or at the pharmacy, looking through cough syrups.

"Bienvenido," she says as she squeezes my arm.

"Gracias," I reply with a nod, exhausting my Spanish vocabulary and feeling strange at having a stranger touch me so intimately, and stranger still when that stranger loosens her grip but doesn't let go of my arm. Instead, her small hand just stays there, curled around my bicep as she begins to sing along to the music.

I look over and smile.

She smiles back at me, and I feel grateful we don't speak the same language and she can't ask me what's wrong. I don't need her to know my story or what I believe, and I feel no urge to understand the nuances of her faith. But as I absorb the beat of the drums and the sound of the voices filling this modest room, the presence of her hand on my arm comforts me.

The two of us watch a well-groomed gentleman at the front of the room, a preacher or a song leader, maybe, guiding the congregation. His dark, lacquered mane and the way he swings the cord of his microphone makes me think he's spent some time on cruise ships or fronting a lounge act, but I also discern genuine devotion under his slick surface. He's accompanied by two men behind him, one standing with an electric guitar, the other perched on a folding chair and pressing the keys of a small Casio keyboard. All three are dressed in nicely pressed but well-worn suits, and it seems as if they've been playing their songs on some eternal plane of storefront Christian-service music and lifting up small congregations together for generations.

A slender woman with long, unbound hair rises from a pew in front of us, walks toward the preacher, and kneels. For a blessing? A healing? I'm not sure.

The way her loose hair flows around her shoulders makes me think of Mary Magdalene washing Jesus's feet, and I picture this woman lowering her neck before the preacher now and gathering her dark hair in her hands while he gently touches her head with an outstretched hand, but she remains upright and he continues to hold the microphone, swaying and snapping its cord.

I wonder what might happen next, but for a long moment nothing does. The bandleader-priest alternates between song and a sort of rhythmic intonation that would remind me of an old-school Southern Baptist evangelist were he not speaking Spanish. His accompanists accompany him, the congregation sways and claps, and the long-haired woman kneels. Then, responding to a cue I don't see, several members of the congregation get up from their pews at the same time and join her, some standing and some kneeling beside her, and place their hands on her back and shoulders and arms.

This tableau plays out briefly while the music continues, then another unseen cue and the assembly stands and returns to their seats, original petitioner and all, without saying a word. The ritual repeats again and again with different congregants. They approach. They kneel. They are joined. Hands are placed. All return to their pews.

After several minutes—six or sixteen or sixty, I couldn't say—bathed in the unfamiliar sound of the preacher's exhortations, I find myself rising from my pew, walking forward, and standing at the front of the room. I pull my hood back and let my hair fall around my shoulders. The preacher's voice, alternately husky and singing, incants a stream of words of which I understand only *corazón*, but that's enough to make me drop to my knees as several of the faithful gather by me, place their hands on my shoulders and back and arms and head and sing along to the portable keyboard, which is playing a melody I eventually recognize as the hymn "It Is Well."

Once I identify the tune, the words easily come to mind even though I haven't thought of the song in decades.

It is well, it is well with my soul.

The word *soul* does not seem frightening to me now, as the voices rise around me.

Maybe someday all will *be well with me,* I think, *maybe even with that something some others might like to call my* soul.

I think of Christian mystic Julian of Norwich's phrase.

"All shall be well, all shall be well, and all manner of thing shall be well."

I've loved the phrase since I encountered it in a female mystics course several years ago. It feels to me as if Julian has crafted her words specifically to answer the objection or soothe the fear of a troubled questioner, someone who she knows will press. "Julian, I know you said *all will be well* and then you said *all will be well* again, but are you sure everything is going to be well for everybody, I mean, throughout everywhere, throughout all the galaxies, I mean what about—"

"*All manner of thing* shall be well," comes the assurance.

I sigh deeply and feel the warmth of the many hands against my body, and then, without so much as a twinge of advance warning, something hooks into my belly and pulls toward my throat and it is as if the contents of my stomach are being reeled back up my esophagus to my mouth.

I am suddenly so sick that all I can think is, *Don't vomit. Don't vomit. Don't vomit on this preacher. Don't vomit in this church.*

I look up at the people around me, straining to arrange my face in a way that communicates gratitude, and I head to the door as fast as I can, but keeping my legs straight so I don't look like I'm running.

Outside, the mist and cool air soothe my nausea just enough to keep me on my feet, and I shiver as I walk home, chilled by my now cold and heavy sweatshirt. All I want to do is get back to my house and my bathroom where I can drop to my knees and wrap my fingers around the toilet seat. *I just need to get there*, I think, stumbling forward. *At least then— At least then— At least then, nothing.* I'll feel different, I guess, than I do now, awful, still, but a different awful.

I think of the phrase "God will not give you more than you can handle" as I walk past the tattoo parlor.

Right.

Whenever I hear somebody say that phrase, I want to choke them with my hands and see how they handle it. The phrase is not, as most people think, Biblical. It's a misquote of Corinthians 1:15, which instructs, "God will not tempt a man more than he is able," which I'm not fond of either but don't find quite as hateful, because, consider:

Okay sure, say that God, or *life*, or the *universe*, if you prefer, will not give you more than you can handle.

Sure. Fine. Unless, of course, you happen to be one of the two million people across the globe who are going to commit suicide this year.

Or what if you're one of the many committing slow suicide right this minute, via alcohol or drug use or binge eating or binge working or unconscious reckless driving or refusing to take necessary medication? Or what if you're one of the mentally debilitated, convicted felons languishing in prison, minds drugged to stupor or, worse, denied medication and yelling all night at the steel gates of their cells?

Or—and this I bet speaks to a much broader constituency—what if you're among the ranks of the persistently disappointed multitude pantomiming their way through this badly written show of life until they can finally get out of their contract and be forgotten forever? If so, you probably already know that God has given you more than you can handle, maybe much more, and the only thing you can't tell is whether or not he did it on purpose.

My nausea has subsided by the time I get back to the house, so instead of going to the toilet, I head straight to the phone and call Jimmy.

"Hey, husband," I say, folded over in bed like a paperclip, head pressed against my knees.

"Hey."

Holly pokes her nose into my neck with concern.

"I'm not doing so well."

"You want me to come home?"

I am silent.

"I'll be on a flight tomorrow," he says.

13

Centipede's Legs

'll take six" is what I want to say.

It's nice the way the little bottles knock against each other in their tray as the flight attendant rolls her cart along the isle. Six of red, if she has them—any red, cabernet, merlot, pinot noir, shiraz, it doesn't matter—will be perfect.

I'll put on my noise-canceling headphones. Maybe they can dampen the cacophony of my shrieking thoughts and the nagging voice of responsibility: we need to find Joanna a place to stay very soon. I will jam my travel pillow against the bulkhead and vibrate to sleep on a warm wine buzz. By the time I wake up, we'll have begun our descent and the pilot will be telling us about the weather in Newark and thanking us for flying United.

But since I've done what I should I have done long ago and sworn off alcohol while taking medications that explicitly state on their bottles they are not to be taken with alcohol, I order a hot tea. I've started drinking tea almost constantly. I've always thought people who drink tea seem generally more satisfied with their lives than those imbibers of other substances and I'm hoping to sip my way to the same satisfaction.

Jimmy asks for a coffee and graciously lowers his tray table to share. "You want a snack box or something?"

"No."

"You should eat."

I groan and look out the window. Below us, successive ridges, pow-dered winter white, separate a seemingly endless series of dun-colored basins. Over there is what looks like a road drawn ruler-straight across one of the wider basins and winding onto a ridge. It might be a sign of life except that it peters out along the ridge and never makes it down to the next basin, which is completely empty except for a large, irregu-larly round white patch toward the middle.

Looking down and sipping my tea, I imagine a lost traveler coming across the ruler-straight road and feeling a rush of hope. "I am saved!"

How does she become lost on that expansive waste in the first place? It doesn't matter. That part of the story is unknown. She buys a ticket to a movie and then waits in line for popcorn and simply finds herself there, alone on a dry plain. She's terrified, but she wants to live, so instead of giving in to the weight of despair, she picks her way across sandy washes and stony banks until she reaches the road.

Over the last few weeks since I yanked Jimmy home from his trip to see his dad, I've been that traveler lost on a rocky desert, striking out as blindly. I've continued to see Dr. Nestor and Kalene but also ex-perimented with acupuncture, behavioral activation, biofeedback, and hypnotherapy before trying out a hospital day program for sufferers of OCD. But these attempts lead only to further basins of anxiety-filled afternoons and looping-stricken nights, costly steps closer to the pri-vate doom of permanently suffering from a weird mental affliction no one can seem to understand, much less identify with, and which I wouldn't even believe was real myself if it hadn't already almost com-pletely destroyed my life.

With the jet's airframe softened by the pillow and gently buzzing the side of my face, I replay in sequence all the ineffectual therapists and crackpot interventionists I've visited over—I want to say these past several months, but the truth is more like several years—or, if I'm going to be completely honest, more like a quarter of a century. When I count it up it gives me a bit of a start, not because it's such a long time but because a human lifespan seems so short.

The addresses, waiting rooms, faces, and soft-spoken greetings of my many therapists play through my mind like sheep jumping over a fence: not too many to count, but enough to ease me to the verge of sleep before I reach the most recent.

I've never met anyone who loves falling asleep like I love falling asleep. That long moment when you're slipping away feels like a kind of euphoria to me, so much so that I've been known to take interrupted naps, waking myself over and over just so I can experience that warm sensation again and again. On this night, the pleasure of releasing all my anxious ideations and psychosomatic stresses, with our jetliner pushing through the air at five hundred miles per hour over the midwestern states, is particularly welcome.

It starts with a smell of sandalwood and a feeling of familiarity I can't quite place.

I am walking down a narrow staircase, which opens into what looks like a Japanese sitting room: a floor covered in tatami mats, Zen calligraphy paintings scrolling down the walls, and two zafu cushions facing a bronze gong. The smell of sandalwood is coming from a stream of smoke spiraling out of a ceramic incense bowl placed on a carved wooden altar next to the gong.

What an attractive room, but why am I here?

Then I see the perfect picture of a Zen master sitting in a leather swivel chair beside the altar, and—ah, yes—I realize, this is the home of my former Zen teacher Daishin, and I'm here because I've called him for help.

I open my eyes, click a fingernail against the airplane window, and watch the wing-light blinking in the sky. I'm not dreaming. I'm remembering visiting Daishin last week. *It feels like a dream, though*, I think, noticing ice crystals on the outside of the window.

Last week had been going particularly badly. All day every day I felt like I was a boxer taking a beating in a ring I just couldn't manage to get out of. Whenever the phrase "the new normal" occurred to me (which it did, over and over), I felt socked in the stomach. Could this be my new normal? Could my new normal be this horribly dysregulated nervous system with its shakes and sweats and banging punishing heartbeat? The concept seemed to punch me in the solar plexus and ring in my head until I wanted to stagger over to the corner, spit out my bloody mouth guard, and crumble into a ball.

There, crumbled in my psychic corner, although looking fine by all outward appearances, it occurred to me that I could try calling Daishin.

I hadn't seen Daishin in years. He was my therapist for a bit, but when I stopped seeing him professionally, I still saw him all the time the time at the Zen center where I attended his every lecture and took each opportunity to speak with him one-on-one through a Zen practice called dokusan. But then, as Daishin got older, he came to the Zen center less regularly until finally I stopped seeing him altogether. Five years ago, I heard through the Zen community that he had been struggling with early-onset dementia and did not often leave his home.

Years went by, enough that my phone no longer held his number and I had to search for an old notebook to find it written down, enough that I felt nervous when I dialed the number, wondering if it would still be good, and more nervous still when someone picked up after three rings but then remained silent.

"Daishin, this is Maggie Rowe," I said tentatively. "I was wondering if I could possibly see you. I mean, if you remember me."

"When would you like to come?" he answered without a beat, his deep, easy voice instantly taking me back to years of sessions on Wednesdays at eleven.

"Whenever you have time."

"I have time, now."

A very Zen statement, I'd thought.

"Oh, wow, that's amazing. So I'll come over now then. What's your address?"

A hard silence followed, interrupted by a weak faltering voice. "Um . . . can I call you back?"

My body became very still as I realized Daishin couldn't tell me his own home address. It felt like a stairstep giving way under my foot.

I expected the worst but when I met him later that afternoon, I found him to be alert, aware, and very much Daishin.

There is a bit of turbulence on the plane. I squeeze Jimmy's hand to let him know I'm okay, then slide the window shade down, adjust my pillow, and think back to the afternoon of my visit. There's the stairs and the smell of sandalwood, the decorated room, and my old advisor sitting before me, as peaceful and silent as the gently rising incense and unstruck gong, inspiring a flush of warmth to fill my chest.

Daishin has always reminded me of one Zen master in particular: the sixth-century monk Bodhidharma, popularly depicted in artwork as a serious-faced thinker, bald, broad nosed, fully bearded, with wild eyebrows and characteristically bulging eyes that droop down at their corners toward his earlobes. Daishin might be his spitting image.

"It's nice to see you, Maggie," he says, hands resting on top of his round belly, the outer corners of his eyes turning downward slightly more sharply than I remembered.

I sit down on an empty chair across from him.

"Thank you for seeing me right away."

"Still sinning bravely?" he asks.

"Yes," I say. "I'm still working on it, anyway."

"Patti Smith, right?"

No, I think. *Sin bravely* is not a Patti Smith lyric. It comes from Martin Luther, his idea of *pecca fortiter* or the brave sin: "Sin bravely in order to know the forgiveness of God." But I don't for a moment consider correcting this remarkable man, who doesn't remember his own address but can somehow recall details from a conversation the two of us had over a decade ago.

"How have you been?"

I close my eyes and my hands reach up to cover them. I rock.

"Bad, Daishin, really bad. The old looping stuff is back—not explicitly the hell stuff, but the panic and then the words, the repetitions— but it's worse than ever."

"I'm sorry to hear that, Maggie."

When I look up to catch his eyes, he meets mine, and I know that he is indeed sorry, and I feel what Holly must feel when I pet her head after fourth of July fireworks have shocked her body into a steady tremble.

Daishin sits for a long moment in an easy stillness, just like he used to do, and when he finally speaks, his head tilting slightly to the right, the shift from silence to words is seamless.

"You've tried allowing it to play out like a little show in your mind and just watch?"

"I have." I allow my shoulders to collapse forward and shake my head. "I feel like I've tried everything, and I'm getting really scared that nothing is going to work."

Daishin falls into silence again, and as I wait, I realize I've never once seen this man fidget or rock or even tap his fingers.

"How would you feel about sitting for a little bit?" he asks, by which I know he is inviting me to meditate with him.

"Yes, absolutely."

I scoot up in my chair, lengthen my spine, and let my breath fall deep into my abdomen.

I haven't meditated in a long time. After my second break, I had begun practicing diligently, both on my own and with a local Zen community, but once I began feeling better, my daily practice became a weekly practice and then I stopped sitting altogether. I hadn't renewed my practice this time, partially because Kalene discouraged formal meditation in favor of general mindfulness of one's value-based life, and partially because I'd been too scared to sit with the material emerging from my mind.

I relax my shoulders, soften my jaw, and let my gaze fall down toward my lap as I continue to breathe. Rather than seeming strange or distant, It's comforting to find that the physical sequence feels as familiar as if I'd never stopped.

Observe, I think. *Let the breathing find itself. Where does it begin? Where does it end?*

I sense Daishin's eyes resting on me. Am I supposed to be looking him in the eye? I've sat with him at the Zen center, on our zafus in the Zendo, but never one on one, never facing each other like this. I decide to return his gaze.

After a minute or so, without any advance sensation to let me put up my guard, tears appear in my eyes and begin to stream down my face. I lift the sleeve of my shirt up to press into each cheek, first left and then right. Daishin says nothing, and we sit together in this way for five or six minutes more, my tears steady. Finally, Daishin breaks the silence by screwing his mouth to the side and saying in the voice of a raucous cartoon bird, "Here and now, boys! Here and now!"

I laugh.

"You remember?" he asks.

"Yes," I say. "Aldous Huxley's parrot!"

Years ago we talked about Huxley's vision of a utopia where trained parrots caw on citizens' shoulders, reminding them to pay attention to their lives.

"Maybe your looping could work for you like a call to presence. Maybe you could think of it as a parrot on your shoulder."

"Here and now," I say.

"Right," he says, nodding. "Just a reminder."

I like that idea and tell him so, and we talk for a while more until I decide I'm going to ask if I can start seeing him again on a weekly basis. I don't have any more illusions about a cure, those have been pretty well disabused by now, but Daishin knows me—better than I imagined—and that counts for a lot, and I feel like even just sitting with him might help.

"I was wondering," I say, "if you think it would be possible for me to see you again? I mean on a regular basis for, you know, treatment?"

It's strange, then, but I feel as if I can hear him think. *It would be nice to have a patient again*, his thoughts seem to say. *It would be nice to have someone with whom to share the store of wisdom I've been collecting all my life—before it sifts away. I am a caregiver, though, a caretaker, responsible to those who come to me, and specifically to this seeker, this sufferer, whose younger face I can still see.*

After the long moment onto which I have foisted this story, Daishin blinks, takes in a sharp breath, and says, "I'd be glad to see you anytime you want to come—talk."

The certain wistfulness that colors the word *talk* tells me this may be the last time I ever see Daishin. He's saying *Yes*, in a way, but I hear *No* ringing softly underneath the words like a gong.

"I can recommend someone, though. She's very good. Eleanor Calabrese."

Daishin once described himself as being in a final stage of life, the stage in which you turn back to take one last look at this wonderful world. Watching him reach for a pad of paper from the table beside him and pick up a pen, I think about those Tibetan sand paintings the monks make, painstakingly created only to be wiped away.

Daishin writes Eleanor's name down and then looks through a small address book for her number. I wonder if I will ever come back here. *If I do*, I think, *how will Daishin be?* What will he remember? And if nothing or not much, *who* will he be? Still himself? What, for that matter, is a self except a painting made of sand?

Daishin hands me the piece of paper and I thank him, then think, *If this ends up being the last time I ever see my teacher, is there anything I want to ask? Now that I have the chance?*

"Daishin," I ask rather abruptly, "do you ever worry about going to hell when you die?"

"No," he says, without even a sliver of hesitation. "Never."

I am so deeply, deeply pleased with this lack of a pause. Even a millisecond of a delay would have betrayed an insecurity, a need to formulate an answer to assure me of something.

"Really?" I ask, the tears flowing again. "But you had the same ideas drilled into you that I did. You memorized the same verses. I can't imagine someone could ever shake that. I mean, aren't you sometimes worried about the life to come?"

"Never."

"Really?"

"Really."

His answer feels to me like a benediction.

"Goodbye, Daishin. Thanks again for seeing me."

"Here and now, boys," he says in his parrot voice. "Here and now."

"Pretzels or peanuts?"

The flight attendant has returned to offer snacks, and I look over while removing my headphones.

"Pretzels," Jimmy says. "Mags?"

I search my body for an appetite but can only shake my head.

"Let's take some peanuts, though," Jimmy says, "in case you change your mind."

Our pilot lands his two-hundred-ton Dreamliner with a soft thump, and we taxi toward the gate.

I called Dr. Eleanor Calabrese from my car parked in front of Daishin's house and she had been able to see me the following day.

Eleanor struck me immediately as a woman who might have been a great Italian stage actress in her day. Not that there was anything especially dramatic about her presentation—her clothing and jewelry were

modest and her hairstyle conservative, a square cut with even bangs—
but her strikingly large turquoise eyes and the articulation of her hand
movements made me think she could have once captivated an audience
at the Arena di Verona and carried off the great heroines with ease.

After saying hello and offering a seat and the standard HIPAA no-
tification form for me to sign, Eleanor skipped the introduction of her
approach to therapy and questions about why I was seeking help at this
point in my life and whether I slept well or poorly at night. She began
our first session with three simple words.

"So, tell me," she said.

Her invitation seemed like an extension of Daishin's benediction,
warm, familiar, tender, and I felt at once as if I were a child in the care
of a trusted adult. *How easily she does it*, I noted to myself, how different
than Kalene, or any of the others who in all our sessions had never
managed to communicate such uncomplicated concern.

The FASTEN SEAT BELT sign blinks off and before Jimmy can rise to get
our bags from the overhead bin, I take his hand.

"I'm glad I'm coming with you to see your dad this time," I say.

I like Bill Vallely, and I always enjoy our visits to Jimmy's home-
town. The days are soothingly predictable. Weekday mornings at
eleven, for example, we will reliably watch *The Price Is Right*. I will
express my opinions about which of the models are decent human beings and which are monsters, information I'm convinced I can divine
from how the young women open a refrigerator or run their hand over
the hood of a brand new car.

In the afternoons, the three of us will place bets on various sporting events, including ones depicted in movies and on television shows,
always hoping to reach the height of excitement we experienced one
afternoon when the betting got out of control, when dollar bills were
flying and quarters clanking, as wagers were doubled and tripled and

quadrupled while we watched, with bated breath, the Golf Channel special "Go Down Swinging: The 1999 Open at Carnoustie" as if it were a live event.

Jim and I and his dad will eat together; three friendly, chatty meals a day. I'll try to eat, at any rate. Or sip an herbal tea. Then Jim and I will sleep in the guest room side by side on twin mattresses, I on the main bed, draping an arm down to Jimmy on the trundle below. When we pull out the trundle I will, as always, think of Wynken, Blynken, and Nod. *And the wooden shoe that sailed the skies is a wee one's trundle bed.*

Baggage claim goes smoothly, which feels like good luck. Having run out of midsized sedans, Hertz offers us an upgrade to a powder-blue Chevy Malibu and we feel happy to have been given something for free, even if we didn't want it. We ease over the WARNING, SEVERE TIRE DAMAGE bump, and as Jim follows the turns dictated by the navigation app, I feel a welcome lift.

Then, about a quarter mile down the road, I see the golden arches of a McDonald's lifting into the sky and feel a lurch in my gut that I recognize only after several seconds of investigation as hunger.

I'm hungry!

I experienced a similar appetite awakening one time on a group outing from Grace Point to McDonald's. I hadn't eaten properly for weeks, but then either the new medication or cognitive techniques I had begun to practice, or maybe both, kicked in that afternoon and inspired a meal that to this day I consider the most satisfying of my life.

"Jimmy," I shout without warning, "pull in there."

"Where?"

"McDonald's."

"Really?"

"I'm hungry!"

Jimmy reacts to my cry as if I've just announced that I'm about to give birth rather than merely feeling a basic urge most human beings experience three times a day. He swerves off the street in front of a small red car and cuts into the drive-through line.

"What do you want?"

"A plain hamburger," I say.

"That's it?"

"That's it."

Five minutes later I'm asking Jimmy to pull over.

"I need to throw up."

Eleven that night. Jimmy and his dad are together on the brown corduroy couch watching a film, which I could tell from a quick glance on my way out of the room involved men riding on horses, saying goodbye to women who love them but are agreed on by all to be replaceable, getting shot at, shooting at others, and wearing hats not required by the weather.

I am in the spare bedroom of the condo seated cross-legged on the top part of the trundle bed. I am reading three books at the same time: *Consciousness Speaks*, by Wayne Liquorman's guru, Ramesh Balsekar, which understands the self as complete illusion; *Opening the Hand of Thought*, by Kosho Uchiyama, which conceives of the self as a mirror; and Jack Kornfeld's *Wise Heart*, which describes the self as compassionate wisdom. My project is to figure out a way to describe what is going on in my brain, and since the idea that "I" am inflicting the looping and all its attendant anxiety—and scalp tingling and loss of appetite and midnight sweats—on myself is just really too horrible to accept, I'm hunting for a better understanding of what it means to have a self, or be a self, or what a self might be.

I'm switching from book to book, reading brief passages, comparing the different frames for consciousness, and taking notes in the books themselves when Jimmy pokes his head through the door. "My dad's asleep. I'm gonna go outside and smoke some pot."

"One second. I want to join."

This may seem an odd decision, given my delicate neurochemical state, but marijuana has never seemed to affect me as much as it does others. Mainly it just feels like a sedative, and I think, *Who knows? Maybe it will help.*

Jim and I pad past his dad's bedroom, silently take our boots and winter coats from the front closet, and wrap ourselves against the New Jersey winter. A blast of frigid air smacks me as I step out after Jimmy. "Yikes!" I say, wincing and tensing all my muscles against the assault, my mind for a moment wiped clean. It occurs to me that if I had more outer problems, my inner life might not seem so distressing. If I had to battle the elements, for instance, and hunt for food, or vigilantly avoid becoming food myself, these little squiggles in my head might not matter to me at all.

Jim sits down on a white bench in front of the condo, a bench he purchased for his dad after seeing it on sale at the Cracker Barrel Old Country Store the last time we visited New Jersey. We'd gone out to Cracker Barrel for a reason I can't remember, with some friends of Jim or his dad I don't recall, and eaten a meal that has slipped from my mind, but what does stand out clearly is the moment my husband saw this bench. The man had been struck. It was as if a light from heaven had illuminated the faux-weathered, shabby-chic arms and backrest and a voice from above had proclaimed its excellence. Never has a creature been so enthralled by the sight of a bench.

"Great bench, right?" Jimmy says now, gesturing for me to join him and opening the Tupperware container in which he keeps his green glass pipe and a small bag of ground marijuana.

"Spectacular," I say as I sit, wrapping my arms around myself and burrowing my head into my jacket. "Sublime. Best bench on the Cracker Barrel menu."

"You don't have to be sarcastic," Jimmy says, smiling, as he loads and hands me the pipe.

"I do though, I think," I say, inhaling carefully and then exhaling on a vocal fry. "Cracker Barrel, the best farm-fried steak and country-style benches between here and the Rio Grande."

At the street corner about twenty feet away, I notice a stop sign the size of a billboard. Each letter, S-T-O-P, is the size of a toddler.

"Whoa," I say to Jim, beginning to feel an easy buzz. "That is the biggest stop sign I've ever seen."

"Well, it's crafted for a community of people who have to start guessing after the first line on the eyechart."

I hand the pipe to Jimmy and find my thoughts swirling through all the versions of self spread out on the top mattress of the trundle bed. No self, big self, wise self, and small self stream in rainbow spirals as I try—truly, urgently try—to locate a genuine self in me, out here on the Cracker Barrel bench in the freezing night with Jimmy blowing ashes out of his green glass pipe.

What am I? I ask myself with complete sincerity and a hard agenda.

I asked the same thing while looking into the bathroom mirror that day in grad school, after walking in the sculpture garden on campus. Who is this person that is looking back at me with that birthmark one inch below her right eye and a quarter of a centimeter to the left?

I squeeze myself more tightly to keep the swirling cloud from blowing me apart. The puffs of philosophy abruptly vanish and all I can clearly see, as transparent as the air, is that I have no idea. If you asked me what "I" means, I'd have no answer. I can't even form the question. At once, a certainty pierces through me that having no answer is not okay.

It's not okay at all! I shout in my head as terror flushes through my body and hell tingles on my scalp turn into painful stabs. I feel loosed into dizzying free fall and desperately cast about for a thought to seize on to, a solid concept to arrest my descent. What if, I reflect in horror, I've pulled apart my entire ego? What if I can never get it back? What if I'm like one of those partygoers in the desert whose bad trips permanently destroy their ability to experience happiness or simple cognitive integrity ever again?

Images of Pink Floyd album covers kaleidoscope around the face of Syd Barrett, whom I heard went crazy on stage one night from acid while playing the guitar. He stopped playing the notes of songs that night the way they'd been rehearsed—stopped playing, in fact, all the notes on his guitar except for one, an E flat on the first fret of his lowest string. He plucked that same E flat over and over. *E flat, E flat, E flat* that single solitary "E," until an ambulance arrived to take him to a place in Cambridge with lovely lawns and very nice nurses, where he remained under caring surveillance for the rest of his life.

"There's something wrong with the pot," somebody says in a whispery voice.

"What, Mags?" Jim asks.

I'm rocking back and forth and my heart is beating loud and insistent and frantic in my chest, like a panicked neighbor banging at the door. "There's something wrong with the pot!"

"It's working great for me," Jim says, interlacing his fingers behind his head and leaning back.

Frosted tree branches outline against the lights along the street. I feel myself floating up toward them, my limbs about to be mangled in theirs. "No, Jim," I manage to pronounce, every syllable a challenge. "I. Am. Do. Ing. Bad. Ly."

"Oh shit," Jimmy says, catching my distress and popping to attention.

"I don't know how I'm coming up with the words I'm saying right now," a voice that seems to have borrowed my mouth meticulously articulates. "I don't know how I'm doing it. I don't know how I'm making the words I'm saying. I don't know who is talking right now."

"You're just having a reaction to the pot. You're just really high right now. In a little it'll pass."

I sway forward and backward on the bench, forward and backward over and over until I realize, with horror, I'm *rocking!* I'm rocking *just like her*, just like my grandmother. It's happening! It's happening! It's happening to *me!*

"Maggie?"

I have to stop rocking, but I don't want to stop.

"Maggie?"

The rocking is keeping me together.

"Maggie?"

It's the only thing left.

Jim is now squatting in front of me with a hand on the bench on each side of my knees, but I can barely see him. I feel myself rocking in my grandmother's chair, that exact chair, that black leather chair, the one with the crack in the middle of the seat. I feel the edges of the leather poking against my thighs as if I were wearing shorts.

But then a thought stops me.

How could I know there was a crack in the middle of the seat, a crack with yellowed stuffing showing through the split? How could I know that? When could I have seen it? My grandmother never got up from that chair. Am I making it up?

Except she did get up to go to the bathroom. She would have had to, and I could have seen the crack in the black leather seat cover and the stuffing underneath when she did. That makes sense. But how would I know that the leather feels jagged and scrapes against your thighs if you sit in the chair wearing shorts?

I must have sat in the chair. But when?

When my grandmother went to the bathroom, I posit. But that would be weird. Would I just run to the chair as soon as I saw my grandmother walk down the hall to urinate, just for a few back-and-forths?

Jimmy is saying something because I can see that his mouth is moving, and I want to listen, but a picture flashes through my head and grabs my attention: ten-year-old Maggie in shorts, rocking, holding the libretto from the 1970 cast recording of *Jesus Christ Superstar* in front of her face. I see myself listening to the album, reading along with the libretto, sometimes singing and sometimes not, but always rocking, rocking and rocking. I see, too, my mother watching me with concern on her face.

"Why don't you go outside to play?" she says. "You need to run with your friends and get some fresh air."

"No," I say. "I want to stay here. I want to listen to the music. I just want to rock in the chair."

Am I remembering that right?

Yes, I am. That black leather rocking chair with the rip in the middle was in the living room at our old house, off to the side of the picture window that faced the street.

The family rocking chair. Except nobody rocked in it except me.

And then in the new house, that chair was in my grandmother's room.

Suddenly, I realize. It was mine before it was hers.

"C'mon!" Jimmy suddenly shouts. "Maggie!"

"How far away is the nearest hospital?" I ask, holding my head, which now feels like someone is stepping on it.

"What?"

"I need to go to a hospital. I don't know how I've been doing it all this time. I'm like that centipede—"

"We're not going to a hospital. You're going to be fine."

"That centipede . . ." I repeat, trailing off while trying to manage my heart rate, which is accelerating like I'm driving a race car around a hairpin curve.

"What are you talking about?" Jimmy barks, his fear escaping as anger.

"That centipede that when someone asks how he keeps all those hundred separate legs working together like that says, 'Oh no!' and is never able to walk again."

"That's just a—"

"He's never able to walk again," I say, trying to relieve the pressure in my head by pressing the heels of my palms against my cheekbones, my fingertips resting on my eyebrows. "Like my grandmother. I told you she rocked in that chair for the rest of her life, but I didn't tell you I rocked in that chair, too—just like her, but before she ever did. I rocked in the chair and listened to *Jesus Christ Superstar* and read the libretto and sang along with the cast and rocked and rocked until my mother said I should go outside. But I didn't want to. I just wanted to rock and rock."

"Let's go inside," Jimmy says, sliding next to me on the bench.

"I need to keep rocking."

"That's fine."

He lifts my left arm over his shoulders, wraps his right arm around my back, and hoists me up, taking most of my weight as he guides me to the condo steps.

"Wait!" I say, thinking of his father waking up to find both us and the sky-blue Chevy Malibu gone. "What are we going to say to your dad?"

"Just give it a little time."

"What did you tell him when you had to fly back to Los Angeles all of a sudden the last time you were here?" I ask, pushing Jimmy away and making an effort to take a couple of steps on my own. "What does he think is wrong with me?"

"He doesn't think anything."

"We have to give him a reason why you're taking me to the hospital."

All of my attention is now focused on Bill not discovering my secret and thinking his son made a terrible choice in marriage. "What are we going to say about it? We have to figure something out. What are we going to say?"

In the kitchen, Jimmy helps me into a chair before beginning to search through the cabinets. "There's some chamomile tea in here somewhere," he says. "I remember seeing it the last time I visited.

You're drinking tea now, right? You're into tea, right? Because tea drinkers are happier, right? Isn't that what you said?"

As I watch my husband hunting for the tea to ease the bolts of lightning arcing through my nervous system, a picture forms in my mind, so vivid and so detailed I'm convinced the mists of time have actually parted to permit me a glimpse into the future. I see Jim years from now, weary and joyless, worn to a nub by the invalid wife he's had to move from institution to institution following the treatment programs covered by his Writers Guild insurance package, until eventually there's no more talk of treatment and he's resigned me, after much heartache, to a home, someplace with lovely lawns where docile patients dot the fields like dandelions.

The images are so specific I lose track of where I am, forgetting that I'm not, in fact, one of those dandelions on a lawn that spreads around me, nodding in my outdoor rocking chair, until Jimmy handing me a mug of tea jerks me back to Bill Valley's condo kitchen.

"What?" I say, disoriented.

Jim has looked through the cupboards, found the tea, and steeped it during what I experienced as just a couple of seconds.

"I'm sorry you got stuck with me for a wife," I say, gulping the tea I wish were wine and looking up at him, anxiously examining his response. I'm certain on some level that if he tersely replies, "I didn't get stuck with you," or murmurs, "You're not always going to be like this," or offers any number of other responses that fail to cover his simmering spousal resentment, my guilt for what I am putting him through on top of my rising panic will explode the pressure in my head.

Instead, however, my husband breathes the following carefully constructed seven-syllable poem.

I have never loved you more.

I know this cannot be true. I mean it would be weird, and frankly troubling, if a man's ardor for his wife were increased by witnessing her mentally disintegrate in front of him. And there's nothing remarkable about the words *I've never loved you more*. They are words that I'm sure have been printed on every country's drugstore greeting cards. Before there were drugstores, I'm sure the sentiment was painted in caves. But when Jimmy says these seven words to me, it's as if a cool mist were sprayed on my feverish psyche.

"Thank you," I say, reaching my arms around his neck and resting my forehead onto his shoulder. "I'm sorry. I know . . . I know you got an Edson when you married me."

"An Edson?"

"The car from the fifties that was a lemon."

"*Edsel*, you mean. I got an Edsel."

Jim and I are sitting on his father's sun porch, perched on rattan deck furniture usually reserved for the summer, in our winter coats and boots. Jimmy's ski cap is pulled down over his ears, and he's maximized the effectiveness of his scarf by securing it directly over his face.

"Are you sure this is okay?" I ask.

"It's great," Jimmy says, his voice muffled by the scarf.

My pulse is elevated, but no longer racing, and I can still feel the beating, but not like a janggu drum inside my ribs.

"The air helps."

"Excellent."

Its cold sting doesn't so much relieve the sensation of heated needles stabbing my scalp and arms as distract me from it. "And I don't feel like my head is being compressed to an infinitely dense point in space."

"That's an improvement."

I talk—chatter, really, babbling on about anything that comes to the top of my mind that isn't me. I talk about Joanna and how we've got to work on getting her a place as soon as we get back; I talk about how I feel wicker furniture is the worst kind of furniture, how it's preposterously uncomfortable, and wonder why old people, who are prone to hip replacements and general aches and pains, embrace it so fanatically and without seemingly any knowledge of alternatives. I prattle on about how the billboard-sized stop signs in front of the facility should blare prerecorded announcements when cars approach at appropriate decibel levels for ancient ears to register—things like *Stop! Stop! Vehicular manslaughter gets fifteen to life.* I natter conversationally about the *Price Is Right* models, informing Jim you can tell that long-timer Rachel really cares by the way she hesitates for a fraction of a second before turning a cube to reveal *the actual retail price* of a toaster or a can of baked beans, if she knows the price will be a disappointment to the contestant. Newcomer Jacqui, on the other hand, in the same situation, will frown ostentatiously, making a big show of her compassion, but then whip that cube around without the slightest hesitation of remorse. Jacqui doesn't fool me. I see through her act.

Jimmy is yawning behind his scarf, and I can tell that he's exhausted. It's well past midnight and we should go to bed. I think I can fall asleep, but am terrified of the inevitable waking up, so I keep talking, opining about nothing, dropping scattered observations the way Holly sheds fur, procrastinating sleep to push back waking up.

Jimmy's eyes ease shut and blink open again and again as he shows me he's listening to my talk, and even though I know he can't possibly be following everything I say, I recognize the difficult patience expressed in his pretending to understand. Finally, at one in the morning, I tell him he can let go of his watch and we can go to bed, one foot apart on the levels of the trundle bed.

"You're not worried about the morning?" He knows my waking up can be hard, and though he's tired and cold, still wants to cushion the blow. "Do you want to call Dr. Nestor or Kalene before we go to sleep?"

"It's almost 10:00 p.m. in California," I say.

"You've never called their urgent lines before, right?"

"No."

"They gave them to you, right?"

"Yes."

"So use one."

"I don't know."

"Go ahead."

"Maybe I can just ask them if we can talk in the morning."

"Good idea."

"Okay, okay. I'll do that. You can go to bed."

"You sure?"

"Yes. You're freezing. I'll come in a minute."

Jimmy heads in. I stay out on the porch and call Dr. Nestor. He doesn't answer, so I email to ask if he can call in the morning. Then I try Kalene, who doesn't answer either, so I email her as well, but just after I press send and turn to go into the condo, my phone gives a ping, and I see that Kalene's responded right away. This gives me hope, but then I read that she does not have time tomorrow, or for the rest of the week, but is looking forward to discussing what is troubling me at our appointment next Monday. The fact that she says she is looking forward to an event she could make happen earlier makes it clear to me that I should pay off the balance I owe this woman and never see her again.

Who can I call? I pace around a wicker chaise.

Lucy?

I haven't talked to her in months. I had felt, because of the severity of my problem, that I needed to seek out an expert specifically in the areas of OCD, pure O, intrusive thoughts, scrupulosity, or even just generalized panic and anxiety. Lucy, lovely as she was, was an expert in none of these things, so we had parted ways one brisk November morning. When Lucy had started the session with her usual attempt to make sure the temperature was to my liking up to the very degree, I tearfully told her I would be ending our sessions. I had a history of intrusive thoughts, I explained, from my childhood. I wasn't trying to hide anything, I had clarified. I simply had wanted to leave my past troubles in the past and focus on the everyday ordinary problems which, for a time, I had been fortunate enough to have be my only concern.

At the end of the session, I had stood up and, my face wet with tears, had done a truly terrible Arnold Schwarzenegger impression.

"I'll be back. Lucy." I had said, in a not-at-all uncanny Austrian accent, "I'll be back."

Daishin?

No, I shouldn't wake up an eighty-year-old man suffering from dementia who isn't even my therapist anymore.

What about Eleanor?

I'm not sure. It seems outrageous to call a therapist I've met only once. Surely she will immediately peg me as *that* kind of patient and slot me into the must-manage-boundary-issues file and possibly regret having taken me on as a favor to her colleague in the first place.

I decide to call anyway, and risk the blowback.

"Hello?" Eleanor answers after one ring, catching me off guard.

"Oh, I, um," I stutter, not sure what to say.

"Maggie?"

She must have my number in her contacts, and I wonder if she adds all her new patients as a matter of course.

"I'm so sorry to bother you. I know it's late. I was just—I wanted to see if we could talk tomorrow, sometime, whenever you have time. *If* you have time, that is. I can work around your schedule."

"Yes, of course. We can schedule something, but we can also talk now if you'd like."

"But isn't this a bad time for you? It's late at night."

I picture her in bed, taking off a sleep mask and rubbing her large turquoise eyes.

"I have time now, Maggie."

"Really?"

"Yes," she says. "Tell me."

14

Good Shepherd

As if my dicing the elements of my inner life into a thousand pieces and dumping them out on the winter veranda of Bill Vallely's New Jersey condo weren't enough of a crisis, the day after we get back to Los Angeles, Joanna's landlord finally drops the axe. It has been two months since the eviction notice and since there had been no further contact, I had put my head in the sand a bit. I'd been hoping to delay the whole process of finding Joanna a place until I had some sort of handle on my mental health crisis. Or until I had more time. Or Jimmy had more time. Or until someone or something somehow swooped in to save the day.

"Fuck!" I cry after hanging up the phone in the kitchen.

"One second," Jim calls back. "Be right there."

"Fuuuuck!"

I march into the bedroom to see that my husband is making no effort whatsoever to "be right there," but is in fact watching MSNBC, leaning forward and focused, as always, with the intensity of a man who will himself soon have to address the nation.

"Can you please put that on pause?" I say.

"What's going on?" Jim asks, the flicker of television glinting in his eyes.

I stand above him, my hand on my hip. "The landlord's locking her out."

Jim remains incapable of hoisting his gaze from Rachel Maddow over to me, but now he begins patting his hands on the bed to let me know he is looking for the remote.

"Today?"

"Friday."

"Shit."

I spot the remote peeking out from under a pillow, grab it, and shut off the TV. "What are we going to do?" I demand.

"Well, she can't stay here."

"Did I say she could?"

"No."

"Then why did you say it like that? Like *I* was for some reason suggesting she stay here? She *cannot* stay here."

"That's what I just said."

"No. That's what *I* told *you*."

Then there is a deus ex machina, as if lowered by Euripides himself upstage right from a crane. A phone call from Jim's first wife, Myra, rescues us from useless bickering. Myra had worked for many years with an organization called Good Shepherd, a transitional residence for women experiencing housing insecurity. Good Shepherd, Myra had called to tell us, had an opening.

"First wife?" Joanna shouts, though we're sitting right next to each other within the quiet confines of my car. "I didn't know Jim was married before you, Maggie!"

"Well, it was a long time ago."

"I thought you were the only one!"

"It was years before he and I even met."

"But I didn't know Jim was married before you at *all*! I'm surprised to hear that, Maggie. I'm very surprised to hear that."

"Yeah, but like I said, Myra and Jimmy got divorced many years before he and I even met, so it's not—"

"I thought you were the only *one*, Maggie," Joanna interrupts, urgently pursuing her point. "I thought you were the only *one* for Jim. I never knew he had *multiple* wives."

"One other is not multiple wives."

"If he has two wives, he can just as easily have three. He can have as many wives as he wants—"

"Joanna—"

"As many wives as he wants!"

"*Joanna!*" I snap, whipping my gaze to my right and biting out the words. "My husband does not have *two* wives. He has *one* wife, okay? That's *me*."

Gazing forward across the intersection, Joanna nods as if in agreement, but the private smile that plays across her lips suggests she's agreeing with her own conclusion rather than my straightforward statement of fact.

As the light turns green, I return to the business of driving, keeping a lid on my irritation. "Anyway. The important thing is that Myra called this morning with some absolutely amazing news."

Joanna folds her arms across her chest and stares blankly forward, but I press forward with my pitch.

"She found a *place* for you!" I enthuse.

"What place?" Joanna grunts, cramming herself back into her seat.

"It's called Good Shepherd Center."

Joanna, I believe, opposes any housing possibility I come up with not just because she's terrified of change, but also—I'm convinced—out of a secret hope that if Jim and I *can't* find her a place before the sheriff dumps her things out on the sidewalk on Friday, we'll finally feel compelled to take her into our home. I'm afraid that if I can't sell her on this new (and likely last) chance, she really will wind up on the streets.

"It's a place especially for women transitioning into living independently, like you, Joanna, nice women who are just, you know, in between one place and another."

I glance over and see Joanna's arms crossed and her lips pressed into a thin, defensive line. Her eyes narrow into a squint.

"You'll have a room to yourself, and they'll help you get ready to live in your own place again, as soon as we can find one. It just might, um, it takes a little time." I want to be honest with Joanna, but truly, it's hard to imagine her ever satisfying the requirements of a traditional landlord. "But for now, Good Shepherd sounds amazing. And the staff will teach you how to shop for food, and how to cook for yourself and use a computer and ride the bus to get—"

"My mother could ride the bus anywhere in the city."

"I know she could. And so will you. You'll be able to ride the bus anywhere in the city, just like your mother."

"She always had her mind."

"Yes."

"You have to admit that, Maggie."

"I do, I do. She definitely had her mind."

Despite appearances, I think, *it's me who doesn't have her mind.* I'm the one whose cognitive integrity was blown up by a single puff of well-cultivated pot. Nonetheless, I'm also the one who must gently cajole—or hector and goad—the resistant being next to me toward making an appropriate choice.

"Anyway," I say, moderating my tone, "today we're going to meet a woman named Aliya. I think you're going to get along with her."

Aliya was clear and direct when I talked with her earlier. She spoke in a no-nonsense manner, but with a kindness that assured me Joanna would be in good hands at Good Shepherd. The fact that she called Good Shepherd residents "the ladies," instead of "women" or "girls" struck me as tellingly sensitive. Such a slight difference, but one that nevertheless spans the vast distance between dignity and its lack.

"Good Shepherd is run by a group of nice nuns and you'll have your own nice room," I tell Joanna. "All the rooms are decorated by interior design students from USC, so your room will be special, not like any of the others."

"And it's not a board and care?"

"Nope," I declare, ignoring the fact that Good Shepherd offers exactly *board* and *care*, but assuming as long as it's not in the name, Joanna won't be put off.

"And . . . and . . . um . . . and they won't take my whole check?"

"No. They'll only take a third."

"A third?"

"Yes, four hundred dollars. Plus, they have a food pantry and a large kitchen where you can cook your own meals."

"Jim says you're a bad cook. He says the kitchen is your café. He calls it Maggie's Lousy Café."

The idea of Maggie's Lousy Café generally makes me laugh. Sometimes I even sing along with the theme song, "The toast is burnt, the potatoes are gray, at Maggie's . . . at Maggie's . . . Lousy . . . Caf-ay-ay-ay." But I don't like that Jim has shared our little joke with Joanna.

"That's true," I manage to acknowledge. "Maybe after the lessons you get at Good Shepherd, you might be better than me."

Joanna's eyes glisten, and for the first time she seems to lean forward toward the plan. As we continue driving, however, I notice with some anxiety the streets getting narrower, the storefronts grimier, bars appearing on windows, and 99-cent stores and bail bondsmen's establishments replacing personalized perfumeries and boutiques selling whimsical socks. Joanna also appears increasingly somber as she takes in the neighborhood.

"So," I say, attempting to rescue the slipping mood, "Aliya's going to give us a tour of the facility, and she'll answer all your questions, and then we'll get to meet the director and take care of paperwork and stuff. Jim can't come on the tour because it's a women-only facility, but he'll join us after, and—"

Joanna's face bursts into sunshine. "Jim's going to join us? Handsome Jim's going to join us at Good Shepherd?"

"Yes," I say, "Handsome Jim is going to join us."

Exuberance lifts her voice a pitch. "I'm pleasantly surprised, Maggie. I am pleasantly surprised."

"Maggie Rowe, with Joanna Hergert, for Aliya," I articulate clearly into the speaker by a large metal gate at one side of a narrow alley that is marred by several large dumpsters overflowing with garbage. Everything around us looks greasy, and there is a sour smell, pungent in the way you notice only after you've already inhaled it all the way and it's too late to hold your breath. *This is awful,* I think. *Am I dumping Joanna like a leaky trash bag?*

If I can just get her settled and safe somewhere. *Ensconced* is the word I keep using with Jim: If I can just get her ensconced, then I can feel good about what I have done, helped get a woman onto her feet, and can feel free to move on and focus on my own crisis.

When the intercom buzzes and the heavy gate clicks, I lean into it and push through, and my anxiety dissolves into a feeling of honest wonder. A secret garden! The type of haven I would be lured to by a glossy brochure advertising a spiritual retreat: "Our captivating gardens offer seekers countless nooks and picturesque alcoves for serene and uninterrupted contemplation." A winding brick path guides Joanna and me past plantings of gladioli and cheerful morning glories, meditation benches set next to bubbling fountains, and stone statues of the Virgin Mary. "Oh my goodness, Joanna," I say, genuinely feeling as if we've passed through a lucky portal into some unknown, private oasis. "Look at this place!"

Joanna lets me know she is not impressed with a simple grunt.

As we pass a small bakery on the grounds—run, Aliya told me, by the residents—a scent of cinnamon and baking pastries wafts through the air.

"Mmm," I say. "Smell that? What do you think? Cinnamon buns, I bet."

Joanna says nothing, and when I look over, I see that she's fallen several steps behind and is stooping to pull up her socks, which have puddled loosely at her ankles.

To the side of the path a small play area, featuring a modest climbing structure, a metal slide, and swing set, has been set in a bed of wood chips. A vigorous red-haired girl whizzes down the slide, whips around, bounces up the steps on hands and feet, and whizzes back down.

"Look," I say to Joanna. "Some of the residents here are moms with children, so kids will be around the place. Won't that be nice?"

The red-haired girl stops at the top to peer down a yellow, plastic telescope, which she directs at our position on the path, and I wonder what she thinks about this odd couple that has stopped to watch her play.

I have an impulse to wave to the girl but think better of it, and with a sharp breath I'm back on the path. "C'mon, let's go."

Aliya is a tall and athletic, with a smooth complexion that almost shimmers. The primary colors of an enameled flower pendant stand out against her skin, and the casual formality of a pressed blouse tucked into comfortably fitted jeans projects warm authority. "Welcome to Good Shepherd," she says with a smile that is broad, extending to the corners of her eyes and offered exclusively for Joanna. I feel shunned by the narrow greeting, but then I imagine this is exactly how Joanna must feel when she meets people with me: slightly beside the point.

Joanna is wary, but she meets Aliya's gaze. "So . . . you're . . . then you're . . ."

Aliya nods, with a complete lack of Los Angeles speediness, waiting for the words to come to Joanna.

"Then you're . . ." Joanna seems to internally review the recon I've given her on Aliya. ". . . you're a nun?"

"Oh no, Miss Joanna," Aliya answers, without judgment or personal offense, "I'm not a nun, but I *do* work with the sisters here at Good Shepherd."

"Oh." Joanna taps her fingers one at a time with her thumbs as if counting, reviewing, figuring what this might mean.

Aliya allows time for Joanna's process to unfold.

Past Aliya's shoulder, pale, skinny fingers wrap around a doorframe. A knife-blade-thin woman with stringy, sand-colored hair swings into view. "Look," the woman pipes sweetly. "I know I didn't sign up for stove privileges tonight and all, but I just wanna cook some noodles. It's not like pasta or anything, just noodles, so—"

"If you didn't sign up, then no privileges," Aliya responds decisively and without hesitation.

"Oh c'mon," the woman pleads with a flirtatious smile, making no effort to hide two missing front teeth. "You're my girl. I got these noodles at the pantry, and I just wanna cook 'em tonight real quick."

"Next time put your name on the sign-up sheet, and then you can prepare your noodles. You know the rules."

The woman groans, her chin thrust toward the ceiling, before staggering dramatically from the office like a teenager protesting her chores.

"Have a nice night, Miss Sarina," Aliya calls with good humor.

"'Night, Aliya," Sarina grumbles without looking back, her sneakers sliding on the linoleum into a squeaky complaint.

Aliya is not a people pleaser. She did not take a job at Good Shepherd for these women to love her. She took it, I assume, to serve, and this commitment affords her a clarity and firmness that ironically *does* win their love, or at least respect. In her place, in my anxiety to please, I'm sure I would have put on a cutesy, sympathetic face and caved. "Oo-oh, okay, Sarina, but you'll sign up tomorrow, right? Enjoy your noodles," I would have said, and then Sarina would fail to acquire the essential life skills I had been tasked to impart. She would fall back on old habits when her time at Good Shepherd was up, and eventually lose her way completely before dying somewhere outside, alone—all because a self-involved people pleaser couldn't stand to experience herself as someone that might not be nice.

Aliya interrupts my self-critique by suggesting we take a look at the room they have for Joanna, "just to see if it seems like a good fit," as she puts it, "to see if it's the kind of place Miss Joanna might like to stay."

The room is just lovely, like the advertisement of a Vermont bed and breakfast brochure. There's a wooden rocking chair with a tasseled pillow, a small desk set up with office supplies, and a single bed covered with a patchwork quilt so delicately beautiful, so Laura Ingalls Wilder couture, that I'm sure that with no connections in the textile market whatsoever, I could sell it this weekend for $1,500.

"Look at this!" I say. "Oh my goodness!" Then I add to Aliya, "This is just beautiful. Wow. What a stunning place." I expect Aliya to . . . well, if not melt at my praise, then at least like it, but she shows no interest in my feedback, and her attention remains entirely on Joanna.

Shit, I think. She sees through my act like a pane of glass. She recognizes my Hollywood flattery for what it is, a hustle, one she's seen many times before. Aliya knows exactly what I am.

Joanna, oblivious to my insecurities, stalks around the room suspiciously, inspecting every item. She sees a basket wrapped in crinkled sparkly-purple cellophane on top of a chest of drawers and exclaims, "An Easter basket?"

"It's a *welcome* basket. No Easter bunnies involved," Aliya says with an understanding laugh. "The young lady who decorated this room left it for you. I'm not sure what's inside, but it's awfully pretty, isn't it?"

Joanna eyes the basket greedily, but then looks up at Aliya as if she might be the kindly seeming witch luring her with sweets down the path to a walk-in oven.

"Alright," Aliya says brightly. "Miss Joanna, would you like to meet Sister Louise?"

"Oh, I—" Joanna lifts her hands and begins flattening her hair over her ears.

"Sister Louise would like to meet *you*."

"A nun? Sister Louise is a nun?"

"That's right." Aliya says, "You know what's going on."

In a plain room with a small conference table, we find a petite woman in a full nun's habit seated next to Jim, who gives us a little salute. When Joanna sees Jim, she appears to be utterly transported. "Jim!" she gasps in the voice of a newly rescued Disney princess, "Oh Jim, I can barely believe my eyes."

"Hello, Miss Joanna." The pint-sized nun pops up from her seat, shoots over to Joanna, and offers her hand. "I am Sister Louise."

Joanna's arms remain loose, dangling at her side. Sister Louise reaches down and wraps her fingers around Joanna's right hand, then pumps the limp appendage firmly up and down several times. "It is wonderful to meet you." She turns to me and reaches out to give my extended hand one firm shake.

"Please sit down," she says to us both, pulling out a chair for Joanna before returning to her seat. "What do you think about Good Shepherd so far, Miss Joanna?"

"It's alright." Joanna grips the edge of her chair with both hands and looks quickly from Aliya to Sister Louise, then down at the table in front of her seat.

Interlacing her fingers on top of the table and leaning forward, Sister Louise takes Joanna in quietly and then asks, "Do you know why you're here today?"

"Yeah."

Sister Louise waits for a moment before asking again, "Why are you here today, Miss Joanna?"

"Because Jim won't let me live at his house," Joanna answers matter-of-factly. "Because I'm not family."

"I should probably explain," I say with a nervous laugh. "Jim and I would love to have Joanna stay with us. It's just that we don't—"

"I see," says Sister Louise, quieting me. She is polite but clearly does not find my input relevant. "And so, Miss Joanna, you are looking for a place to live? Is that right?"

"I can't live on Van Ness anymore."

"Van Ness is where you have been living?"

"With my mother."

"But your mother is no longer with us, is that right?"

Joanna is silent, but the sadness in her eyes answers yes.

"When did your mother pass, Joanna?"

"Five months she hasn't been here."

"And you need to find another place to stay?"

Joanna nods shyly, her eyes straying to her hands.

"We understand, Miss Joanna. Isn't that right, Aliya?"

"That's right," Aliya answers, and I see that these two have walked frightened women through this process many times before.

"And so," Sister Louise continues, "based on what you've seen, do you think Good Shepherd might be a good fit for you?"

Joanna's eyebrows bunch together.

"I'm sorry, Miss Joanna. Let me ask that another way. Do you think you'd like to live here?"

Yes, yes! I will Joanna to answer, balling both my hands into fists under the table. Say *Thank you! Thank you so much.* Say *Oh my goodness.* Say *This place is amazing for me!*

But Joanna says nothing.

"It's a big decision," Aliya offers. "We understand that."

"Yeah, yeah," mumbles Joanna, beginning to rock back and forth.

"Change can be very scary."

"Yeah."

"Being scared can be very scary."

How true, I think, as Joanna's movement grows into overt rocking and she starts roughly rubbing her hands over her face as if trying to scrub something away. "Yeah, yeah," she repeats, "yeah, yeah."

"Take your time," Aliya says.

I have to hold my breath to keep quiet as Joanna gives no sign of coming to a conclusion. If this were a scene in a movie, the hands of the clock would be whirling around. Aliya and Sister Louise sit quietly, with even breaths, focusing interested but not overly prying eyes on Joanna's face. Eventually, the women's calm, well-intentioned presence seems to reach through to Joanna. Her scrubbing gesture softens, and the rocking becomes less urgent. When her movement has come almost to rest, Sister Louise looks over at Aliya and nods.

Aliya picks up a blue folder and hands it to Sister Louise. "This is an agreement, Miss Joanna," Sister Louise says. "It says you understand the rules of living at Good Shepherd. I'm going to tell you what all the words in this agreement mean so you know exactly what you're signing. Does that sound alright to you?"

Joanna nods.

"Okay, then. The first rule, right here at the top, says that there are no drugs or alcohol allowed at Good Shepherd, not at any time or for any reason."

"But, but, but," Joanna sputters, suddenly animated with excitement, "I've never done a drug in my whole life! Not in my whole life!"

She's smiling and shaking her head in astonishment, as if she's just found out she passed a test she is unaware of having taken with flying colors. "I've never even had a beer!" she rejoices. Then, turning to Jim: "Isn't that right, Jim? Tell them! Tell them, Jim! Tell them I've never done a drug in my whole life, not even a beer."

"That is right," Jim says, turning to Sister Louise and Aliya and holding up his hand like a Boy Scout. "Joanna Hergert is, I can attest, a 100 percent drug-free zone. She has never even had a beer . . . or even coffee . . . or gum." Jim delivers just about everything he says in the rhythm of a joke and people tend to laugh whether they want to or not, but Aliya and the Sister remain focused on Joanna without cracking a smile.

Jimmy turns to me with his "tough room" face.

"Or even gum," Joanna repeats, laughing. My husband's number one fan comes through.

Then Jim starts laughing too, a laugh he's perfected on sitcom sets, a laugh that lets everyone else know it's time to join in. I dutifully follow my husband's lead, thinking we're demonstrating to the Good Shepherd ladies the mirth of our merry ol' crew.

Sister Louise's cleared throat, however, lets us know our quite obvious attempts to ingratiate ourselves can be put to rest. We settle down immediately and listen with exaggerated focus as she continues. "Two. Good Shepherd has zero tolerance for racism."

"Oh," Joanna says brightly, in a second rush of self-confidence, ready to ace another test. "You don't have to worry about that with me either. I think Black people are just like you and me. My mother and I have always thought that. Jim will agree with us because he . . . he . . . he wrote on *My Wife and Kids* with Damon Wayans. Damon Wayans is Black and . . ."

Oh dear God.

"Right, Jim? Right?"

"I . . ." Jim looks over at me helplessly before offering a shrug of shame to Aliya and Sister Louise. But surprisingly, Aliya is nodding, and her warm smile remains unchanged.

"Good, Joanna," Sister Louise says in a voice as even as Aliya's countenance. "It sounds like number two will not be a problem for you, then."

Joanna nods, pleased. A wave of relief washes through me.

"Three. All residents must return to the center by 11:00 p.m. and sign in. If you choose to stay out overnight, you will be asked to leave Good Shepherd. No exceptions."

I can't imagine Joanna leaving to go anywhere once she settles into her quarters and gets used to the TV room, and I begin to lose focus as Sister Louise reviews a few more basic rules. "Respectful," I hear, clean and tidy, weekly meeting, and something about "courteous manner of address," but the majority of my attention turns to the paper in front of Aliya, the pen she holds in her right hand, and my silent urging that she pass it to Joanna. *Let her sign it*, I think. *This place is perfect for her. Let her sign it now.*

"By signing the document, Miss Joanna," Sister Louise finally concludes, nodding to Aliya, who slides the paper across the table, "you will be saying you agree to these rules."

We are so close to finding a solution to the Hergert Housing Crisis. I look over at Jim and know he and I must be thinking exactly the same thing: *Just pick up that pen, Joanna. Just pick up that pen and sign that paper. Just do it, Joanna. Just do it,* now. Joanna, however, doesn't move. She remains still, both hands pressed flat on the table on either side of the paper.

"Would you like to do that, Joanna?" Sister Louise asks gently. "Would you like to agree to these rules?"

Joanna stares at the piece of paper, then swiftly retracts her hands and stashes them out of sight below the table, as if in their absence nothing could be required of them.

"Do you have any questions?"

Joanna shakes her head, then gnaws at her lip. She begins again to rock.

After ten seconds or so, I can bear the tension no longer and hear myself blurt with excessive brightness, "So then. You can just go ahead and sign it, can't you, Joanna? You can just go ahead and sign it right now." I nod vigorously and smile in that way that raises your eyebrows and crinkles your forehead and makes you look like an idiot.

Jimmy almost immediately cracks as well. "Joanna, c'mon," he says, nodding along with me like a perfect moron. "These nice ladies have work to do."

"We're fine," Aliya snaps with an edge to her voice that Jim fails to pick up on.

"C'mon, Joanna," he repeats, adopting for some reason a spaghetti-western-posse leader's growl, "Let's git 'er done. Let's get 'er done 'n go get some grub at one a' them IHOPs they got round here."

The bit clearly hits Joanna wrong, because she squeezes her eyes shut, bunches her lips into a pout, and draws in the deep and ragged breath of a child about to cry.

"But I don't wa-*a-a-anna*!" she wails. "And you can't—you can't—you can't m-*a-a-ake* me! You can't make me s*i-i-i-ign* it."

Joanna raises her wrists to her shoulders and flaps her hands like she's trying to shake off a stinging liquid. "What if—what if—what if—" she rushes, casting her eyes about the room, "what if I have a rich relative who wants to take me in?"

"A what?" Jim asks, impatience disrupting his cowboy act. "What are you talking about?"

"I don't know. I don't know. *I don't know.* What if . . . what if . . . what I have a rich relative and I . . . *don't know it?*"

"C'mon, Joanna."

"I might! I might have a long-lost rich relative and not know it. A long-lost rich relative who—who—who wants to take me in because I'm family."

"Joanna." I put a hand on her shoulder, but she pulls away and looks directly at Jimmy. "I know I can't live with you, Jim, because I'm not family. But—but—but . . . a rich relative might find me like on *The Golden Girls*, like Blanche and Uncle Nunzio. Remember Uncle Nunzio, Jim? Uncle Nunzio—"

Jim snaps flatly, "This isn't *The Golden Girls*."

"Uncle *Nunzio*!" Joanna insists, working through the thought as her words race ahead.

"Uncle Nunzio is a made-up character!" Jimmy snaps. "There is no Uncle Nunzio. There's no Sophia or Dorothy or any of it. It's a *story*, Joanna."

"I'm not signing it. No. I'm not. You can't make me. It's my choice."

"Joanna!" Jim shouts, bringing the flat of one palm down on his thigh. "There is no decision to make. If you don't sign this, you will be homeless. Do you understand that? There will be no apartment. There will be no place to sleep. You will be living on the *streets*! Is that what you want? Is that what you *want*, Joanna, to live on the *streets*?"

Sister Louise shoots to her feet. "May we please speak outside?"

Jim looks up at her, suddenly aware of himself. His shoulders collapse.

Sister Louise nods once and heads for the door, indicating with an articulate eyebrow that Jim should follow her. Jim trails behind, obedient, throwing a backward "Sorry I fucked up" look toward me.

I watch the door close and then turn to Joanna, whose eyes are fixed on her lap.

Aliya, still seated at the table, appears at ease, chin lifted, fingers interlaced, hands resting lightly on her lap while I anxiously twirl my rings with my thumbs.

After several minutes, Sister Louise returns *sans* Jimmy and, taking her seat, addresses Joanna directly without explanation or reference to me. "Miss Joanna," she says, "of course no one can make you sign anything. You are absolutely right. It's your choice, and your choice alone, and there's no hurry here. You can take your time."

What did she say to Jim? Did she send him home? Was he escorted out? Did she summon security?

"You know, Miss Joanna," Sister Louise continues, "many of the women here have been in relationships with men where they didn't feel they could make their own choices, where they felt pressure to do things they didn't want to do. That will not happen here. You are safe here."

I find myself ruffled by the implication that my husband isn't safe for Joanna after all his generosity toward her and her mother. I want to say something in his defense, but when I think about it, *You will be homeless if you don't sign this contract now!* does come off as more than a little bit pushy and, I have to admit, too coercive for comfort.

"If you find a rich relative you can live with," Sister Louise says, as if this were a perfectly reasonable possibility, "we won't keep you here."

"But I'll have to pay," Joanna protests. "I'll have to pay anyway."

"What will you have to pay?"

"The four hundred dollars. And if my rich relative lets me live with them because I'm family, I won't have the four hundred dollars anymore."

"Joanna," I offer evenly, taking my cue from Sister Louise, "how about I promise that if you *do* find a rich relative like Uncle Nunzio on *The Golden Girls*, I will reimburse you the four hundred dollars?"

"Reimburse?"

"Give back. How about if I promise to give you back the four hundred dollars if a rich relative shows up to take you in?"

Joanna's eyes liven up and she starts tapping her fingers one at a time with her thumb. "So let me get this straight, Maggie," she says, calculating. "If a rich relative asks me to stay with them because I'm family—a rich relative like Uncle Nunzio—you will give me four hundred dollars?"

"That's right," I say, with as little inflection as possible, "but it's your choice."

And for some reason, this little indemnification balances the scale for Joanna and she nods.

I think she's probably happy with the deal because she got the opportunity to negotiate. She got to object to a point, make a demand, and have that demand addressed.

The following morning, I step into Sunny and Joanna's apartment for the first time ever. Both women had been adamant through the years about meeting them in front of their building and not coming up the stairs to their unit, and we had never had any reason to press.

With each step, the air, thick and pungent, morphs through ever changing notes of sweet and sour. Chest-high stacks of newspapers and yellowing storage boxes stand between piles of outright trash, clothes strewn on the floor, and collections of animatronic animals. In the small kitchen crammed tight with a sink, dishwasher, stove, and refrigerator, there sits a smaller Fisher-Price sink, dishwasher, stove, and refrigerator.

In the apartment's single bedroom, a dark imprint streaks down the middle of a bare mattress, the soiled depression where Joanna's body has clearly lain for many, many years. To its left is a second, equally worn mattress, where Sunny must have slept, folded up against the wall. Between the two, a nightlight shaped like a turtle shoots multicolored lights out to the ceiling and walls from pinpricks in its shell.

If where a person lives reveals the nature of their mind, Joanna's mind is one that can let go of nothing. Every inch of floor space in the apartment is covered, every corner crammed. Stacks and stacks of stuffed and mechanical and plastic light-up animals tower to the ceiling. I imagine the animals were gifts from Sunny to Joanna to celebrate birthdays and Christmases, but probably also used as bribes to coax obedience and quell tantrums. But why did Sunny never require her daughter to get rid of any them? How had she let her home be overrun by possessions, infested with the discardable materials of everyday living? Why had she balanced egg cartons into a towering monolith or stuffed the insoles of gym shoes into a flowerpot?

Because, I think as I pull on latex gloves, *life gave Sunny, like millions of other people, more than she could handle.*

"Okay," I tell my assembled crew—Joanna, our friend Janet, who Joanna has long resented for being able to stay overnight at our home for several weeks, and Jim—"here's the plan. We're going to make two piles. First pile is trash. Second pile is for storage."

Jim reaches into his bag and pulls out the masks he bought at Home Depot. Janet and I take ours, immediately pressing the white paper domes over our mouths and pulling the thin elastic behind our ears. But Joanna refuses to take her mask, arguing that she has lived in this apartment for eighteen years without wearing one, so why start now? It's a hard argument to counter.

We begin sorting through newspapers and broken dishes and moldy empty cans of pork and beans. We go through milk cartons and apple cores and ant traps matted with Elizabeth Taylor–black hair. The most astounding thing is that Joanna has been able to tolerate the odor for all these years. Even with the mask, it's as if I'm breathing sewage into my lungs. I suppose the odor did not appear overnight, and Joanna would have had time to have grown accustomed to it.

I've anticipated the sorting process will be arduous, but I also hope it might be freeing for Joanna to get rid of all the detritus she has accumulated over the years. However, she can find nothing expendable, nothing she can envision a life without. I understand wanting to hold on to all of her memorabilia and pictures, her clothing and shoes, her dishes, her crayons and markers and paper and glitter and glue, her Cabbage Patch dolls and the Halloween costumes for the Cabbage Patch dolls. But one hundred stuffed animals?

We go through them all. All the animals. Like two rivalrous sisters with opposing agendas: we bargain, we fight, we scowl, we pout, we settle with resentment. Then we regroup, each determined to win the next round. As we continue the heated cycle into the afternoon, everything I touch begins to feel increasingly furry. I start to sense the bacteria creeping under my nails and crawling into the corner of my eyes. I imagine parasites drilling into my ears, boring into my brain, and then a shock tears through my body. Suddenly my right hand is ripping the mask off my face and I am barking, "Joanna, I can't take this anymore. *Enough.* You have to get rid of some stuff, okay? You can't keep everything. The storage unit is not to store garbage."

"It's not garbage. It's . . . it's . . . it's my life, Maggie. *It's my whole life.* The pictures of my mother and all the papers from Barbizon modeling school . . . and . . . and . . . all my animals that Anna Michaela loved when I did my show for her. Anna Michaela loved my animals." Joanna presses her hair into her ears with her palms and eyes me savagely. "It's easy for you to say. It's easy for you. *You* don't have to throw away your whole life, Maggie."

That silences me.

Until I hold up a McDonald's fry container with a collection of fuzzy black peach pits. "Can we at least lose this? *Please.*"

We continue our sifting and bargaining and resentment throughout the day, then at 3:00 p.m. we pack two suitcases of essentials. The plan is for me to take Joanna shopping for groceries and toiletries before driving her to Good Shepherd, leaving Jimmy and Barbara the unenviable task of taking the garbage to the dumpster and putting the rest in a storage pod. Joanna and I are about to head out when Jimmy stops us. "Oh, wait, Joanna. Give me your key. I need to turn it in to the landlord."

Joanna digs through what I've come to think of as her classic distended-organ purse and pulls out a stainless steel key attached to a

Spider-Man keychain. She stares at it, looks up at Jim, and then back down at the key.

"C'mon, Joanna," Jim says. "It's time."

"Oh, okay, Jim," Joanna says, but she doesn't make a move except to grab a fistful of hair, pull it beneath her nose, and inhale. I recognize the strategy. I've employed it myself. When you're disoriented and terrified and everything else fails, smell your hair. It's familiar and warm and scented with focus-group-tested shampoo and conditioner fragrance.

Fifteen minutes later, Joanna hands over the key.

After stops at Pavilions and Rite Aid, Joanna and I arrive at Good Shepherd loaded down with suitcases, three bags of groceries, and a crate of toiletries. Aliya greets us warmly at the metal gate and we follow her down the path past the scattered wood chips, past the morning glories, past the madonnas, and into a courtyard where she directs us to leave our bags for inspection.

"Inspection?" Joanna panics. "Are they going to take everything I own?"

"No, no, Miss Joanna. It's just protocol."

"Yes. Just protocol." I echo, arranging the suitcases, groceries, and sundry essentials on a folding table by the door. "That makes sense."

Aliya invites us in and offers us seats at a table before floor-to-ceiling windows that overlook the courtyard. "Tomorrow," Aliya says to Joanna, "you have your first appointment with our life-skills coach, Monique. Monique will help you think about the goals you're going to work toward during your stay here."

Through the window, I watch a ponytailed young woman with blue rubber gloves approach the table with Joanna's bags. She unzips one of the suitcases and flops its lid open. *What is she looking for?* I wonder.

"The rules for kitchen use are simple," Aliya informs us.

As Aliya reviews signing up for stove time, the use of communal pots and pans, and cleanup and storage, I watch the bag inspector reach her gloved hands into the suitcase and attentively turn over and pat down the contents. She works steadily, systematically. She zips the first suitcase closed, sets it to the side, opens the second, and continues her attentive inspection.

But then she leans down to get a closer look at something she's found in the bag. Now she's holding it up. I crane my neck to catch a glimpse of what must be confused for contraband, but the lid of the suitcase blocks my view. She returns the item to where she found it, straightens her spine, and looks through the window at us. She waves an arm to get Aliya's attention. When Aliya looks up, she beckons her over by flicking her fingers toward her palms.

"Excuse me," Aliya says, standing up, politely nodding first to Joanna and then to me before walking briskly out to the courtyard.

Something in the woman's gesture and the slight shake of her head and Aliya's swift response triggers a stab of anxiety. *Oh no. What is happening?*

Could Joanna have packed a knife in with her underwear? Could there be a health consideration? Something to do with cleanliness? Something contagious? *Bedbugs? Oh my god*, I think, *I should have washed her clothes. Why didn't I think to wash her clothes?*

A blue glove points to something in the suitcase. Aliya leans forward and peers in, then nods before turning and walking briskly back inside. "May I speak with you?" she says in a clipped tone, indicating with a lift of her chin that she means me.

"Of course," I say, shooting to my feet as she breezes past.

Once we are out of view of Joanna, Aliya abruptly stops and pivots to face me. "This," she says, extending a plastic baggie of green powder toward my nose, "was found in Miss Joanna's suitcase."

I look at the baggie, genuinely befuddled as I read a white printed label: .05 OZ KEEF.

"Keef?" I ask. "What is that?"

"I believe," says Aliya calmly but not lightly, "keef is a form of marijuana."

Right. I remember it has something to do with the resin, or crystals of resin, or something. But how could *any* form of marijuana get into Joanna's suitcase? Could it be Jimmy's? No, Jimmy is committed to his standard fare. It can't be his, but under Aliya's austere gaze, I suddenly exclaim, "It must be my husband's!"

Aliya raises an eyebrow.

"He's got a prescription from his doctor," I say. "For his epilepsy. My husband has seizures," I pile on. "But the THC or the CBD or the combination helps. Seizures are so scary."

Aliya observes me, neither stopping me nor encouraging my desperate, solicitous display.

"This is not Joanna's fault. It has nothing to do with her. That," I say, "is not hers. Joanna doesn't do drugs. That, I can promise."

I watch Aliya's face and believe I can detect a fluttering of thought beneath the calm surface. She does not know yet what she is going to do. She is deciding right now. Right this moment. It's like I can see the whole decision process play out in the slight little twitches in her lips and eyebrows. Aliya, I read beneath her mask, believes me that the pot is not Joanna's. Even from that short meeting, she can tell Joanna does not do drugs. But still, there are rules. It strikes me that I am observing Aliya's eyes as I might a slot machine, watching cherries and sevens whizz by and waiting to find out where they will land. If we will win the jackpot or go bust.

Then her eyes fix, and I know a decision has been made. "Would you like to take this," she asks, lifting the bag between pinched fingers, "to the dumpster outside and dispose of it?"

·

"She's in!" I say, twirling around the marble island in our kitchen. "We did it! Operation Joanna successful! The Hergert Housing Crisis has come to an end."

"I can't believe it," Jim says, contentedly sipping his final cup of coffee for the night.

"I can't either," I say, grabbing his free hand and diving under his arm, forcing him to spin me around. As I spin, the picture of Aliya holding up the baggie flashes in my mind and I stop twirling and start laughing. "Oh, Jimmy, but the whole thing almost got blown. It was so crazy. They found keef in Joanna's suitcase."

"But how did keef get in Joanna's suitcase?

"I have no idea!"

"That's insane!"

"I *know*!"

"Where did it come from?"

"I don't know."

"I mean, it wasn't Joanna's, right?" Jim asks.

"Obviously."

"That's impossible."

"Completely."

"Do you think . . . I mean, could it be from the Other One?"

"But *keef*?" I ask. "That's pretty fancy, isn't it?"

We volley theories back and forth but keep coming up empty.

I pause for a moment. "Wait," I say. "Where did you find that suitcase you gave Joanna?"

"In the front closet. It's Janet's. She left it when she stayed here."

Then Jim Vallely and I laugh one of those laughs that it's worth staying married twenty years in order to laugh. The keef hadn't belonged to Joanna's drug-addled *brother*. It belonged to *our* drug-addled *friend*.

After our grand laugh, we brush our teeth and wash our faces, and

I take my many, many pills—like a true expert, tossing back no more than a swallow of water with my wee fistful of psychotropics. Then my husband and I scooch under our comforting comforter, curling around each other as naturally, as easily, as instinctively as the paramecia I once saw under a grade school microscope.

I sigh deeply into the back of his neck, a mighty "Whew!" escaping my mouth. Joanna is finally settled in not just a facility or a house, but ensconced in a home, with women committed to her best interests and to helping her forge a new path through what I know must feel to Joanna like the scary forest of life.

I become drowsy in a way that is sweet and syrupy and heavy and soon find myself on a ship with an enormous hull, rocking back and forth on rolling, chuckling waves. I try to figure out how I've gotten here. I look forward and aft but recognize nothing on this unfamiliar ship. I do feel as if I've seen the hull from the outside before, a snapshot somewhere, or observed directly from a wharf. But what wharf? Where?

I lean over the bow, which is high, and see a swirling ocean below made not of water but of light.

An ocean of light?

I catch a hazy glimpse of a memory. I'd seen the ship before on a stage, a play that was part of a summer theater festival in downtown Chicago I attended with my mother. I remember having been impressed by a large, looming ship lit on the stage, as if it were actually out at sea, rising and falling on top of pools and swells of blue light. The illusion was so penetrating I could feel the wind on my skin.

My body jerks involuntarily and I open my eyes. The linens on my side of the bed are, as they have been for the last six months, heavy with sweat. I peel the top sheet off my thighs, but this time the act for some reason seems refreshing, like removing a spa body-wrap instead of a shroud. *Maybe it's because I get to see Eleanor today,* I think, swinging my legs off the bed more freely than usual and padding to the kitchen to make tea.

It's not that I think Eleanor can save me. I am no longer pinned by hope, an exposed target, ready for reality to puncture. Still, I have some sort of faith in Eleanor. For one thing, she speaks in the Buddhist language I love, talking about *bodhicitta*, the *awakened heart of loving-kindness* that *blooms like a lotus in the mud of existence*, that is like *the open sky, undiminished by temporary, obscuring clouds*, that is like *finding a jewel in a heap of dust*.

Kalene makes similar points, but with all the poetry of my Toyota Camry owner's manual. I want to find a jewel in a heap of dust. If life's a journey, then *that's* the journey I want to be on. Even if certain passages are harrowing along the way, at least the jewel-in-a-heap-of-dust journey has some nobility to it, some dignity.

It's sort of poetry, I suppose, a literary tradition, but it's more than that. It's also a practice, a method for managing those harrowing passages where everything is dark and muddy and obscured by heaps and clouds of dust. It's many little procedures for equanimity and insight that have been handled and polished and handed down from one generation to the next over thousands of years.

Kalene instructs me to accept unpleasant thoughts.

But how?

No answer.

Dial that number a dozen times, and you just get the old busy signal all day long.

Eleanor, on the other hand, suggests I will learn to accept unpleasant thoughts through a disciplined practice of daily meditation and mind training.

Which I've done a bit of before, but in the manner of, well, a dilettante. This time, I commit myself wholeheartedly to the practice and apprentice myself to the tradition.

I begin like a beginner.

I do the steps each morning.

First, this.

Then, this.

Arrange myself on the cushion.

Cultivate a vast, open mind. A sky mind.

Let the looping appear like cloud formations, dense and sticky, but incapable of defiling the sky.

Contemplate a lotus heart that blossoms amid the fears and petty slights and envies, and all the shabbiness inside.

And all this confusion.

Confusion that, as I remember from the heart sutra, *will dawn as wisdom.*

I pick up the phone on the first ring when I see the caller ID: GOOD SHEPHERD WOMEN'S CENTER.

It's Aliya, who informs me with a voice so measured and official I think it's a recording, "Joanna Hergert left the Good Shepherd facility. She signed out at 6:03 last night and has not returned since."

"What?"

"She broke curfew."

"But . . . where did she go?"

"I afraid I don't know. I'm sorry, but it appears Good Shepherd is not a good fit for Joanna Hergert at this time."

"Oh, Aliya, no! Please don't kick her out. Don't do that."

"Nobody is kicking anybody out," Aliya replies, her voice sharpened by an institutional edge. "Miss Hergert was not able to meet the rules of the agreement."

"But she might have gotten lost," I cry. "It was dark. She doesn't know downtown. She can't even take a bus by herself. Only her mother could take a bus."

"Do you know where Miss Hergert is now?"

"No, but please. Please *please please*," I plead, almost keening into the receiver, thinking how seldom as adults we ever nakedly beg for something. "I'm sure I can find her. I'll go out and I'll find her right now. I'll bring her back right now. I promise."

There is a long pause, but Aliya doesn't hang up. As with the keef, I feel as if I'm catching her in a moment of working out a decision.

"Well," Aliya sighs heavily through the receiver. "Considering Miss Joanna's needs, I believe we can—I am willing to make an exception for this occasion. However, she has a meeting with her life coach at 3:00 p.m., and I want to be clear, if Miss Joanna has not signed back in at the center by 3:00 p.m., I'm going to reassign her room to another of our many applicants."

"Got it. Thank you so much, Aliya. She'll be there."

"Three p.m., on the dot."

I hang up the phone and stare blankly out the window for a brief moment. Joanna's favorite pink swan floatie is covered with leaves and pushed up against the side of the pool with one wing deflated.

"She flew the coop!" I scream. "Joanna flew the fucking *coop!*"

"Maggie?" Jim calls back from the bedroom.

I whirl through the doorway and fling my arms in the air. "Joanna left Good Shepherd. She's in the wind."

"Shit," Jim says, jutting out his jaw.

"I just got off the phone with Aliya. We have to find her." I pound the digits of Joanna's phone number into the touch screen of my phone. "If we can't get her back to the center by 3:00 p.m., they're kicking her out."

"The person you have dialed is not available to take your call," an impersonal, oblivious voice informs me.

"AAaaagh!" I scream in retaliation at our bedroom walls before turning my rage on Jimmy. "Joanna's not answering her phone and I have my appointment with Eleanor, which is really important to me because I *finally* feel it's something *helpful* I can do instead of just sticking money into a cross-cut paper shredder in order to feel increasingly hopeless. But *no-o-ow* I won't get to *see* her because Copernicus was *wrong*. The whole *solar system* actually rotates around *Joanna fucking Hergert*."

"Go to your appointment."

"I'll skip it. It's fine."

"It's *not* fine," Jim says, his hands springing up to stop my objection. "Stop saying things are fine when they're not fine."

"IT'S FIIIINE!" I bellow, "It's FUCKING FINE, OKAY?"

I cancel the appointment with Eleanor and within less than a minute, we are in Jimmy's car. "Pick up your phone; pick up your phone!" I command the hands-free phone system.

"She can't hear you, Maggie."

"I know."

"You're just yelling at the dashboard and it's done nothing wrong."

"Oh cool. Sarcasm always helps. That's great."

"I'm just—"

"Pick up your fucking *phone*, Joanna!" Pure liquid frustration shoots through my body.

Jim jams the bumper against a salvia bush. "I can't back up while you're yelling," he yells.

"Fine," I yell back.

He jerks forward and tries again, while huffing, "Where should we go first?"

"I don't know."

"Her apartment?"

"I don't know."

Now he's run off the edge of the bricks on the other side of the driveway.

"Her apartment?" he asks again.

"You locked the door after you cleaned everything out, right?"

"Yeah."

"You returned the key."

"Of course. Handed them to Mr. Zhukolavski himself."

"Go to Larchmont. Let's try Koo Koo Roo." I check the clock on the dashboard. "We've got three hours."

Jim tears down the street to Rosewood, runs the stop sign at Cahuenga, and pushes a yellow light to cross Rossmoor, only to get stuck behind a city water crew stuffing a big yellow hose down the manhole at North Lucerne.

"Shit," he says.

There's nothing we can do. We just have to wait.

"Where do think she slept last night?" I ask, becoming increasingly agitated by the roadblock. "Did she just park herself on a bench?"

"Maybe she found a rich relative."

Finally the crew waves us past and Jim races down Larchmont, by which I mean—as anyone who has ever been on Larchmont on a weekday will know—he carefully navigates past phone-gazing pedestrians crossing the street and phone-gazing drivers pulling in and out of parking spaces and the meter-maid giving everyone tickets.

"Go," I instruct, uselessly.

"Don't panic."

"I'm not panicking."

"We're almost there."

"I know that."

"Where is Koo Koo Roo?" I say, scanning the intersection.

"It used to be right there," Jim says, his focus pulled from the road.

"Fuck! Koo Koo Roos's a Chipotle now? When did that happen?"

Then I look to my left and see SALT & STRAW hand drawn on a slab of weathered wood and remember Joanna saying she loved Salt & Straw's mint chocolate chip, that it was even better than the mint chocolate chip at Rite Aid.

"Stop. I'm getting out," I snap. I fling open the door, dash across the street, and dart through a group of Larchmont mothers with strollers. "Please be here, please be here, please be here." The distressed, painted-wood, farm-style door swings inward and the shop-keeper's bell goes ding-a-ling.

I scan the room, but no. There is no Joanna.

Outside, Jim is double parked in the middle of the block. I jump back into the car.

We try Burger Lounge.

No Joanna.

'Lette Macarons? Wine and Cheese? Bricks & Scones? Teeny cakes?

No, no, no, and no. Still no Joanna.

"Should we try the Grove?" Jim asks.

"Yes. Go. Hurry, we only have two hours and twenty minutes."

While Jim zooms down Beverly, I give Joanna another hopeless dial.

Ring. Ring. Ring.

"Hello?"

Jim and I freeze, afraid to blow the moment.

Jim points to the phone, and I nod silently to put the call on speakerphone. Jim mouths, "Okay."

"Where are you, Joanna?" I say directly at the number displayed on the screen.

"I'm . . . I'm . . ."

"Where are you, Joanna? Tell me where you *are!*"

Then, like a river of thought diverted suddenly to an entirely new bed, her words come in a rolling flood. "Board and care takes your whole paycheck. They take your whole paycheck. You can't go see movies when they take your whole paycheck. You can't go see the movies on the billboards."

"What?"

"The new movies. The new movies on the billboards."

"What are you talking about? *Where are you?*"

Jim puts his hand on my shoulder.

"We don't want you to feel like you can't make your own choices, Joanna," he says in a much gentler tone.

"Oh, hi, Jim," Joanna says nicely, as if he'd caught her watching an episode of *Andy Griffith*, sipping a glass of sweet tea, "I'm pleasantly surprised."

"We want you to feel safe," he continues, channeling Aliya and Sister Louise. "If you tell us where you are, then we can help you. But it's your choice. You don't have to tell us."

"I don't—I don't—"

"We want to help you, but it's up to you."

"Um . . . um . . . I know I can't live with you because I'm not family. I know that. Because I'm not family, I can't live with you, Jim, at your house."

"Still, though, we're going to do everything we can," Jim says soothingly, "everything. You can count on us."

I, however, don't have Sister Jim's patience.

"*Where. The. Fuck. ARE. YOU?*" I explode.

Jim throws up his hands in exasperation and shakes his head.

"There's lots of billboards in Hollywood!" Joanna screams back at me. "There's lots of billboards for movies. Billboards show you what movies are playing in Los Angeles."

I get it. Joanna's mind is bearing her down a channel beyond her will, and I know what that feels like. I've been that bit of flotsam and jetsam rather than the ferry cutting across the current. I've been thrown under and rolled by the waves, borne toward disaster, knowing there's nothing I can do but hold my breath and wait for the crash. But the truth is in two hours, if Joanna does not tell me where she is, she is going to be without a home.

"I've lived my whole life in Hollywood. My whole life. I live on Van Ness Avenue. That's where I live. I've never even been out of Los Angeles or even California because I live in Hollywood. I'm a Hollywood girl. That's what my mother says. A Hollywood girl on Van Ness

Avenue in Hollywood, California. That's where I live. That's where I live. I live on Van Ness."

I grab Jimmy's thigh and I mouth, "Go to the apartment."

He doesn't understand.

"Va-a-an Ne-e-ess," I silently enunciate.

He nods and whips a sudden, illegal U-turn across two lanes of traffic. We shoot past Pavilions, the tattoo parlor, Iglesias Pentecostes, whoosh, turn left on Van Ness, and then, maddeningly, lurch to a crawl as we make our way past inordinately long stoplights at Melrose and Lemon Grove and Santa Monica.

Finally, we reach the familiar Van Ness building with the chain-link fence and the oak tree roots lifting up the sidewalk.

Jim slows as we approach the address, and I do a visual search of the premises.

Where would she find shelter?

It's pretty bare. Behind the fence across the front of the building are scraggly shrubs, insufficient to hide an adult. There's a covered parking area. *She could be in there behind a car*, I think, so I peer in but can see nothing. There's a hedge that with the oak tree obscures a corner where she might have camped.

I look up to the apartment landing. That would be like being on stage, I think, completely exposed, and . . .

. . . the door swings open . . . and Joanna emerges.

She turns to close the door and lock it behind her.

"There," I say, pointing.

Jim eases to a stop.

"We've got you cornered, Hergert!" I want to shout through a bullhorn. I want to leap out of the car. I want to command her to surrender, to come down with her hands raised, to let us help her before it's too late. But of course, I can't do that. I can't just . . . *nab* her.

"Pull forward," I instruct Jim, pointing to the curb directly in front of the gate. And then, "Okay, stop."

Joanna starts down the stairs, placing her phone in her bag and then her keys—

"*Keys?*" I hiss to Jim. "Where the hell did she get keys?"

I roll down my window, reach to the back door, and push it open so that if Joanna comes out the gate and keeps going, she'll walk straight into our car.

Jim and I are still and silent, drawing barely perceptible breaths, as if even the slightest fidget or cough could somehow give us away.

She'll look up, see the car, and step right in, right?

Of course she will.

Then, as she closes the gate behind her and steps forward, my calm explodes. "Get in the car!" I scream, my head shooting out the window like the barrel of a gun. "Get in the car, Joanna!"

Joanna reels like I've slapped her face, or rather like I've materialized from a different dimension and then slapped her face, because the main thing I notice is she that looks astounded. Her eyes dart every which way. "I don't—I don't—" She's shaking her head and pushing at the air with her right hand like she's warding off a ghost. "I don't—"

"Get in the car, Joanna!" And then, with a deep roar that shocks even Jimmy, I command, "*NOW!*"

Joanna becomes completely immobile. Then, suddenly a docile child, her body simply relaxes and she gets in. Just like that. As if Jim and I were picking her up from school.

I reach back and yank the door closed. Then I punch the door-lock button, not once or even twice, but three times: *bang, bang, bang.*

"Okay," I spit out, giving it one more whack. "Drive, Jim."

He obeys, screeching the car out into the street like an under-the-gun action hero. We've got an hour and a half.

I whip back around toward Joanna. "How did you get in there?"

Joanna fixes her stare on the seat back in front of her.

"How. Did. You. Get. *In there?*"

Joanna involuntarily glances at her right hand, which I see is curled into a fist with a bright orange rubber band sticking out one side and a set of keys sticking out the other. Some of the keys are colored and plastic, of the Fisher-Price jewelry box variety, I suppose, and one looks like an infant's teething chew, but there's another that looks perfectly suitable to an ordinary front door lock: a notched stainless-steel shaft with a red rubber ring around the grip.

"Did you keep a spare key?"

Joanna sneaks her fist under her thigh while looking at me blankly. Jim glances over at me as he cuts in and out of traffic.

"You never were going to stay at Good Shepherd, were you?"

Joanna says nothing.

"You *want* them to kick you out, don't you? You want them to kick you out so you'll have nowhere to go and we'll be forced to let you stay with us! That's been your plan all along, hasn't it?"

Still nothing.

"*Hasn't it?*"

I'm shouting, and it's getting me nowhere. Joanna just grips the keys more tightly, her fingernails cutting into her palm. But noticing doesn't slow me down.

"Well, you can't stay with us! Got it?"

I feel reckless, mean, and I don't quite recognize myself.

"Never ever, Joanna! Ever, ever, *ever!*"

Jim stops at a light and I become conscious that I haven't closed my window and the people in the next car must be hearing everything I say, must think I'm a maniac, but I don't care what they think. I'm not lining up witnesses in the case for or against me right now.

"And you can never go back there, either, okay? It's not your property. You're not allowed. You're breaking and entering, and they can put you in jail for that, okay? How'd you like to *live in jail?*"

Joanna's face is impassive, defiant; my meltdown is only strengthening her resolve.

"Do you know they can arrest you? It's a crime. It's trespassing, Joanna! You were *trespassing*!"

"Okay, Maggie," Jimmy is saying, "calm down. Enough. Jesus," but his voice seems so small, like a pestering little gnat that I could wave away with one hand if I needed to bother.

"Give me the key, Joanna, right now. Give it to me."

Joanna looks at me and digs her nails deeper into her palm.

"GIVE IT TO ME!"

Now Jim is yelling. "Stop it, Maggie. Stop it! Cut it out!"

But I'm yelling louder. "Give me that fucking key!"

Then everything around me goes gray and shadowed and all I can see is Joanna's fist, and the orange rubber band, and the stainless steel front door key. Even the other keys, the bright plastic toys, turn gray and seem to disappear. Only the key to the apartment glints up from Joanna's grip.

Wham! Without a conscious choice, both of my arms shoot forward and I latch onto the orange rubber band with one hand and pry at Joanna's fingers with the other.

She's surprisingly strong, and fierce. "It's mine!" she screams. "Let go! Stop it!"

But I am equally ferocious and absolutely determined. "No, it's not!" I roar, surprising myself with the depth of a vocal apparatus I didn't know I had. "I won't let go! I won't stop it!"

The inside of the car becomes pixelated. Everything I can perceive or clearly think dissolves into sparkles of pure frustration, and I am angry, shockingly angry. Angry at Joanna for leaving Good Shepherd and lying about the keys. For showing no gratitude. For taking the place of the cute, adorable baby Josie Rose or little Babette I want so badly it sometimes feels like I'm being stabbed by a precisely, intuitively placed knife. I'm angry at Sunny for sticking me with her dysfunctional daughter, with stinky old ungrateful Joanna who doesn't even like me, who actively wishes I were dead so she could marry my husband and take my place on Easy Street. I'm angry that Dr. Saraf told me three months ago that I was angry and that even though he was a fool with fool's gold chandeliers, he was not foolish about my anger. He was right, in ways I didn't yet realize. I am fucking pissed.

Even more than that, I'm angry that my mind has turned against me. I'm angry at the horrifying rot that's been bubbling forth from its cauldron of terrors for months and months now and seems like it will never, ever be released. I'm angry that nobody can help me, that I'm alone, that my demons tower like monsters in a child's dream. I'm angry that I'm trapped, and I'm enraged at my entrapment. And under all of that, I also recognize, I'm scared. I'm terrified, like a cornered animal, that someday someone may come to take me—just like they took my grandmother—away to a lovely wide lawn and rocking chair and irremediable, gibbering senescence.

But none of that really matters now because I'm past the fear and into the roaring fight, and I'm yanking at that orange rubber band and prying at Joanna's powerful fingers, and my heartbeat is punching my chest like a fist, and my blood is hissing in my ears, and there's a strange taste of iron in my mouth.

Then—bang—somehow my arm is over my head, and Joanna's fist has opened into an outstretched palm, and I have won.

I have won.

I have the keys. I *have* them, and . . . whoosh, everything is quiet.

I see Jimmy's face contorting and his mouth making words, but I hear nothing. Then, everything around me starts to slow down. Now *I* am moving slowly; *Joanna* is moving slowly. We are in a car sailing slowly on a rolling, chuckling sea.

I've been on this sea somewhere, sometime before. I look out the open window to trees going past and feel a soft breeze on my face.

I see Joanna's hand reaching forward toward the keys, but it is miles away.

I have plenty of time.

I notice Jimmy is looking at me instead of the road. His eyes are wide, I observe, his eyebrows raised in alarm, like in a cartoon.

Then I see that Joanna's hand has traveled many, many miles and is now quite close to mine.

I feel as if I'm watching our very personal drama from a distance, curious what will happen next. Then my fist whips back behind my ear. My arm slingshots forward in the instinctive arc of our ancient rock-throwing ancestors. My fingers release the orange rubber band and its set of toy keys with the transgressing apartment key into the wind.

Time lurches back to normal as the blur of orange and metal disappears behind us and the car swerves left into oncoming traffic. Jimmy jerks the wheel back by reflex just in time to avoid getting T-boned by a landscaper's truck.

Joanna and I both scream.

We scream and scream. Even after it's clear we're no longer in danger, we still scream. We scream our frustration. We scream our complaint. We scream out, *This is not fair! This is more than we can handle!*

Jim has pulled over. Joanna and I sit slumped, flushed, and limp, like two overwrought toddlers after a tantrum, drawing our breaths roughly.

My jaw hangs loose, my tongue heavy, lips apart.

My jaw is never slack like this. My lips are always pressed neatly together in a thin line, the corners pulling up slightly but firmly into a controlled smile. All through my day, I hold the back of my tongue tight and the nape of my neck taut, as if somehow rooting my intelligence, stabilizing the controller in my head.

But now that tension is not there.

It's strange. Now I feel . . . almost *dumb*, as if loosening the little muscles around my mandible has somehow turned me into some slack-jawed creature for whom thoughts do not come easily.

I'm alert, however. I am aware.

Breath rushes in and out of my body.

My heart beats in my ears. Then the beat in my ears fades and picks up again in my chest.

There is a row of parked cars lined up in front of our Camry under the evenly spaced sycamore trees. A group of girls in school uniforms walks toward me on the sidewalk. One of them has a thermos looped around a finger.

My eyes drift downward to the dashboard clock, which reads 1:25, and I realize that I have not suffered a single loop or even thought about looping since getting that call from Aliya this morning.

"Joanna," I hear Jimmy's voice in my left ear. "Joanna," he repeats, channeling some perfect wise authority he has somehow accessed, "I'm going to say something very clearly and I'd like you to listen to me. We are going to take you to Good Shepherd for your meeting at three o'clock. Then, after that, it'll be up to you what you do. If you want to stay at Good Shepherd, you'll stay at Good Shepherd. If not, you can walk right out that door. No one is going to *make* you do anything. I promise. Do you understand?"

Joanna must have said "yes" or nodded because Jim's voice says, "Well, we have a little time before three. Who wants to go Salt & Straw?"

We sit around a rickety iron table on rickety iron chairs, because Salt & Straw is old-fashioned and discomfort is part of its charm. We wobble together on an uneven sidewalk, the three of us, enjoying the cool sweetness of our well-earned treats, Jim holding his cup of Rocky Road, me my scoop of raspberry swirl, and Joanna licking the top scoop of her double mint chocolate chip.

Not the typical Larchmont family, I think. *The envy of no one.*

I run the pink spoon around the outside of my raspberry swirl, taking care, responsibly scooping up the lost and runny bits before proceeding to the more solid middle.

Of course Joanna went back to her apartment. Of course she was scared to be in a new place. The apartment on Van Ness had been her home for as long as we've known her. It's the only place in the world she ever slept without her mother at her side, the place where she made peace in whatever way she did with her loss. Its stained mattress and soiled pillow, its tiny rooms crammed with junk, its complicated, redolent smell were familiar. Nothing changed unless she changed it. No one came or went except herself.

But how did she get back there? It would have been at least a five-mile walk from Good Shepherd to the apartment, and it would have been dark by the time she walked the first mile and a half.

Did one of the employees of Good Shepherd point her west toward Hollywood?

I think of the dream Hollywood conjures for most people in contrast to what it represents to Joanna. I think of Joanna trying to find her way back to an apartment with a familiar mattress on Van Ness Avenue, twelve blocks from the brass-starred sidewalks of the Walk of Fame.

Did she just walk blindly, hoping for something familiar? Was she confident? Scared?

I picture Joanna as a little girl lost in the city, buildings looming, mute, one indistinguishable from another, unwelcoming, offering no guidance. Would she have asked someone for the way? Someone she passed on the street? Someone *living* on the street, perhaps?

She wouldn't have interacted with a man. But maybe a woman? Would Joanna have asked a woman how to get home? I imagine Joanna approaching a figure slumped on the sidewalk, wrapped in a blanket pulled over her head like a prayer shawl, eating from a Styrofoam container. I picture Joanna slowing her pace as she approached. Did she get a glimpse of what she could become? Did she feel a kinship with the woman? Or did the gulf seem unbridgeable?

I swirl the swirl of my raspberry ice cream with the pink plastic spoon round and round.

I, too, am lost: running, stumbling between looming treatments, caught by the rough branches of strange therapists and experts, taking shelter in unfamiliar waiting rooms, passing among wise and not so wise owls. Joanna may stay at Good Shepherd after we bring her back or she may not. Even if she does, though—God, I hope she does—Good Shepherd won't save her. She's got a rough lot on this "road to nowhere," I think, remembering Dr. Nestor's favorite Talking Heads song.

I watch Joanna lick her scoop and see the pale green mint and flecks of chocolate accumulate around the sides of her mouth. It will take time for her to learn to manage without her mother, I recognize, as I eat my raspberry in very precise bites, with no ice cream lodging at the corners of my mouth or even showing on my lips, just the way my mother, with her slender, precise, mathematical fingers, taught me.

Because she took care of such things.

But Sunny, with hair like sunflowers, did not. Because she didn't know to? Because she didn't know *how* to?

What did she think would happen to her daughter when she died? Were Jim and I her considered plan? Or some kind of instinctive, animal hope?

Hope gets a lot of great press these days. Even anxious hope, desperate hope, hurry-up-and-work-because-I-can't-take-it-anymore hope, hope fueled by impatience, hope that's really a demand, hope that seeks to strong-arm the universe, to wrestle and somehow pin the infinitely superior foe.

The straitjacket of hope, I think, and imagine myself being carried away.

Maybe I'll get better. I'll escape like Houdini. If I do, though, it's not going to be a trick I can perform instantly.

Or maybe it's not a trick I do at all. Maybe it's a trick done to me. Maybe healing will arrive imperceptibly, like a mist. One day I'll just discover myself soaked suddenly through.

The mint and chocolate have spread toward Joanna's nose and chin.

Were Joanna a child, my child, my Josie Rose or Babette, I might lick my thumb and reach over to smudge it off her apple cheek. Instead, I pick up my napkin and hand it to her. Joanna takes it, crumples it in her hands, and drops it on the floor.

"Joanna," I say, pointing to the paper she has discarded, "your napkin."

She looks at me, confused. I gesture to her ice cream-covered lips and cheeks and chin and then back to the napkin.

She nods and looks back at me, unmoving.

I smile.

"Yeah," she says, then leans over to pick up the napkin and wipes her face.

Afterword
(2020)

Joanna stayed at Good Shepherd for eighteen months and was never again absent or late for her nightly sign-in. The sisters taught her how to clean her room, do laundry, shop for groceries, and practice healthy hygiene. She learned to cooperate in a kitchen, cook simple meals, complete daily chores, engage in group discussions, set goals, and manage bus rides along familiar routes. Joanna can now make her way throughout Los Angeles to see movies advertised on the billboards, though not yet anywhere in the city, like her mother. But close.

Good Shepherd shepherded Joanna into a new life. With help from the sisters, Jim and I were able to locate a bachelor apartment with a kind landlord willing to overlook her non-traditional appearance and lack of facility with social niceties, as long as we cosigned the lease. We help Joanna with a couple hundred dollars every month, but mainly she is doing it on her own and working within the means of her disability check. Her new pad is a long walk and short bus ride to our home, so she continues to have easy access to me and Jim. And our pool. And those chocolate-covered frozen Oreo cookies I still take pleasure in whipping out from the freezer as if I both invented and baked them.

As for me.

I find the word *cure* to be the most enticing, alluring word in the English language. When I close my eyes and *feel* the word, I am swept up by celestial whirls of blue and silver, swirling away all care. It is also, however, a word I wish I'd never heard, one that has beguiled me for too long with its shimmering promises, one that if I were queen of the world I would banish for all eternity.

I am assuredly *not* cured. However, I am pleased to say that my emotional and mental well-being has improved considerably in the past year and half. Inexplicable terror still surfaces at times, and my mind continues to be vulnerable to snagging loops, but I am quite a bit better. For this, I am deeply but cautiously grateful.

I would be heedlessly, raucously grateful if I could articulate, for you and for myself, the exact reasons for my recovery. But I cannot.

I have educated guesses, theories with supporting evidence, but no solid, communicable formula to express how I arrived at my recent stability. There have been weekly meetings with my therapist Eleanor, medication cocktail adjustments, EMDR sessions, a disciplined meditation practice, Buddhist studies and application of principles, enlargement of focus beyond the Maggie Rowe project, shifts in brain chemistry as a result of medication and meditation, as well as natural shifts in brain chemistry. And just—I don't like to admit this—time.

I do not like this uncertainty. I want a formula, which, if my mind were to unravel again, would offer reliable, repeatable steps back to this state of wellness.

A formula would be a cure.

I do not have one of these. But I do have one thing.

My meditation practice involves a formula of sorts, a system for working with my mind, a sequence that when followed leads to a predictable outcome. Meditation was not something new to me when Eleanor suggested a daily practice. I had practiced meditation for over three decades, albeit with varying levels of commitment, adopting assorted regimes before moving on to others, promiscuously flirting with a wide range of contemplative traditions. I had approached the spiritual journey like I do most things—with the spirit of a sincere, enthusiastic dilettante.

But not this time. This time I was singular in my focus. I used Eleanor's largely Buddhist, poetic language when I spoke to myself about my own mind. I sat regularly in the same place, as Eleanor suggested, in front of a makeshift altar, once in the morning and once in the evening. At first I would sit for only ten minutes or so, but as I developed an internal tenacity, I increased the time, training my mind like an athlete would train her body.

My main discipline? Rather than attempting to stop the looping, I practiced *expanding the mental space* around the process of looping itself. I sat there on that cushion though tempests of anxiety until the often long-awaited bell from the meditation app sounded. I sat there on that cushion attempting to connect to an interior vastness, despite storms of panic and looping tornados tearing through the plains of my private terrain. I sat there through the months in that same spot, morning and evening, until the intellectual concept of "creating space" developed into an inner agility, a sense of how to take refuge from the mental twisters by becoming larger than them. Creating space became not just something I could conceive of, but something I could do.

Yesterday, for instance. I'd been meditating for about twenty minutes in a comfortable lotus position and was beginning to feel settled. My feet were folded snugly into my hipbones, my back was lifted upward, and the bones of my skull and jaw balanced without effort at the top of my spine.

Big-sky mind is what Eleanor calls the mental relaxation and inner release that can come after focused, meditative practice, and it does feel like that. The thoughts within my awareness—that busy, entangled chatter—lose sway. Their presence gently fades like dense clouds becoming wispy. They break into insubstantial, diaphanous fluff-thoughts and float like white dandelion tufts, drifting and dancing and eventually dissolving into nothing on the wind.

It's wonderful how *sane* I can feel after less than half an hour of sitting quietly, simply observing my breath, noticing that I have thoughts and sometimes insistent loops, and letting them glide away like clouds.

Then my home phone rang.

The sound clanged through my head like an alarm.

I knew it was Joanna because she is the only one who calls my home phone line.

And she was calling at 7:30 a.m., even though she knows not to call until 10:00 a.m.

I slammed my palms down on the zabuton mat I was sitting on, stood up, kicked the zafu cushion into which my ego had been sweetly melting, and almost knocked over the makeshift altar I have created with an end table and a lotus candle, narrowly avoiding setting my office on fire.

I picked up the phone.

"I know you're not open for business, Maggie. I know you're not open for business, but I was looking at the calendar while I was getting dressed and I thought you might like a minder about the party tonight."

"A what?"

"A minder call."

Well, how could I be mad?

"Minder" calls, I imagine, must be another of the helpful life-skills practices taught her by the sisters at Good Shepherd.

"I had not forgotten about the party tonight, but thank you for reminding me. That was very considerate."

Jim and I were deeply appreciative of Good Shepherd and certainly more than happy to attend their charity gala. For us, it was one of many quasi-obligatory social occasions, but for Joanna, it was another first.

"Do you remember that you have to pick me up?"

"Yes, Joanna. We'll be there at six."

"On the steps?"

"Yes, right on the steps."

"You said there'll be a meal, probably good, probably a good meal, and a band. A meal and a band, Maggie?"

"That's right, a meal and a band."

"Jim's coming, right? That's what you said? Jim's coming, too? Jim will be in the car?"

"Yes, Jim is coming."

"I'm pleasantly surprised, Maggie. I'm pleasantly surprised."

When we arrive, the sisters are greeting guests in the lobby of a historic downtown church that has been dressed up as a banquet hall and looks better than I expected. Aliya's stylish green dress shimmers when she moves; Sister Louise marches tall, lifted on two-inch heels hidden beneath her habit; and a woman I don't recognize has thick, dark brown braids interwoven with brightly colored ribbons that glimmer in the party lighting.

"Hey, there, sister!" the braided woman shouts to Joanna as we enter.

"Hey, Shanice!"

Joanna's eyes shine with recognition.

"Who's that?" I ask.

"It's Shanice," she says, concluding the discussion.

"I never heard you mention Shanice."

"She's a doctor of business, a doctor of business that got into dire straits."

"What's she like?"

"*You* know," Joanna says with the vocal equivalent of an eye roll. "She's . . . Sha*nice.*"

"And she was your friend?" I ask, searching her eyes for some sort of hidden familiarity.

"She lived on the same floor, the room by the bathroom. I saw her on the way to the bathroom."

Good Shepherd supporters and selected alumni are offered a buffet-style meal while guests browse a nicely presented silent auction. Jim and I write down modest bids on a Palm Springs hotel package we expect to go for a much higher price, and a basket of Lego toys we think Anna might like, and then we mosey over to where a large wedding-type band has set up to play.

"Do you want to dance, Joanna?" I ask.

"No." She shakes her head, enjoying a generously buttered dinner roll.

The band starts in with "Crocodile Rock" and I can feel the ions of the air in the hall change as the pleasure and pride of "I know this one" takes hold of the guests. Throughout the song, I stab at cantaloupe balls mixed with honeydew melon in a plastic cup, still on my campaign to learn to like fruit and thereby improve my appreciation of life.

The crowd applauds enthusiastically at the end of the final refrain and then the band starts playing a familiar intro. I'm pretty bad with intros and melodies and rhythms and all those "Name-That-Tune" kind of things, so I'm stumped even though everybody around us seems to recognize the song right away. They're all smiling and clapping.

What is it? What is it? I think. *You* know *this one.*

"Friday night and the lights are l-o-o-w," the singer starts. "Looking out for a place to go-o."

No way! That's crazy! What are the odds this band's gonna play Joanna's favorite-of-all-time song as the second number of their first set?

It does seem crazy to me. I mean, it's probably true, given that

"Dancing Queen" has got to be one of the most popular party-dance songs of all time, the odds are actually something around 17 percent, but in that moment 17 percent seems uncanny.

Joanna feels the magic, too.

"'Dancing Queen!'" she yelps, dropping what's left of her roll to her plate.

"The night is young and the music's hi-i-igh."

The singer beckons to the crowd with her mic at the end of each phrase.

"C'mon" I say. "It's 'Dancing Queen.' C'mon."

Joanna stares at me, frozen, her face losing color.

"C'mon," I repeat. "We've got to dance to 'Dancing Queen'!"

I grab her buttery hand, feeling like a junior high student pulling my slippery girlfriend onto the dance floor.

"What about Jim?" she says, craning her neck and torso back to the table. "Hey, Jim, will you dance?"

Jim stands and shoots us one his devasting grins.

"Joanna," he says. "Don't you know I was born to dance?"

The three of us hit the floor.

Joanna reclines comfortably in the backseat on the drive home, tired and happy, her jacket pulled tight around her shoulders and up to her ears. She looks like a little girl back there—seven years old, maybe eight, ten at the most. *In another world,* I think, *this would be* my *little girl bundled up back there. With a blanket kept on the seat just for her.*

I quickly shake the thought, rubbing my palms together and staring out to the empty stretch of road in front of us. It's hard to make out everything Joanna says, mumbled words about how wonderful the "ball" was, and how handsome Jim was, and how great Jim looks in a suit, and how no one has ever looked as generally handsome as Jim.

Then she stops. I turn back to see if she's fallen asleep.

She hasn't. Instead, she's sitting up at attention while digging around in her purse.

"Where is it? Where is it?" she says. "I almost forgot. I almost forgot."

Finally, she takes hold of the bag with both hands and opens it wide.

"Here it is!"

She pulls out a small book and hands it to me.

"You need to give this to Anna. You need to give this to Anna, okay?" she tells me. "It's from Landis' toy store, on Larchmont. It's a coloring book."

She grabs it back from me for a moment and taps the front cover with an index finger.

"I bought it with my own money and Anna Michaela told me she likes princesses. She likes skunks. I remember that from my animal show. She said she wants to live in Florida because Florida is the only state you can legally own a skunk, she said, so she likes skunks, and this coloring book has princesses *and* it has skunks, princesses *and* skunks."

"Thank you," I say, taking the book from her. "We'll give this to Anna the next time we see her."

This is one of Joanna's new things, finding presents for Anna, now ten years old, and I love it. Joanna has found another ship in Anna Michaela, a grace-bearing vessel not her own, a bit of heart outside her body.

"I was a princess once. I was a beautiful mermaid princess," Joanna suddenly says, leaning forward against her seat belt and pushing her head between Jim's and mine in the dark. "Do you remember? It was the first year I came trick-or-treating to your house, Jim. On Halloween. Do you remember? Do you remember the first year I came trick-or-treating to your house?"

The memory seeps back to me slowly.

"Remember how we laughed about the camera? The camera and that Maggie didn't know people in the world speak Spanish?"

"Si! Si! No habla español," Jim needles me, grinning.

Joanna yowls in glee.

"Well, I am aware," I say over her laughter. "I am aware that people in the world speak Spanish. You do know that I've always known about Spanish-speaking people."

I'm correcting her, but I'm also smiling.

"I hope Anna Michaela likes my present," Joanna says, her laughter and happiness suddenly mixing with insecurity. "Do you think she'll like it? Do you?"

Then with an emphatic nod, she answers herself, "Yes, I think Anna Michaela will like my present a lot."

This conclusion seems to release her from all resistance to the world, and she relaxes as the seat belt pulls her into the darkness of the Camry backseat.

She clutches her purse against her chest and leans back against the headrest.

"I was pleasantly surprised when I saw the coloring book," she murmurs. "I was pleasantly surprised . . . pleasantly . . . pleasantly . . ."

Then she seems to drift off, her words and thoughts carried away, like dandelions, maybe, on a soft wind.

Acknowledgments

Thank you to David Chrisman who assisted in writing this manuscript to an obscene degree. I am extravagantly grateful.

To Dan Smetanka (aka Stan Pretanka). I loved all of your notes, including ones I hated, like, "I have a thought. How 'bout throwing away the first chapter and writing a new one?"

Thanks to Dan López, who I enjoy calling #1 Dan. Don't tell Stan Pretanka.

To Stacy Testa, for your belief in this project and the ideas that elevated it from a notion to a book. Thanks for picking me. How lucky I be.

To Jane, for the *metta* you have shown both this book and me.

Thank you, readers of early drafts: Jane, Ilyse, Joy, Joe, C. Brian, Rodney, Sarah, Rebecca and to my wee intrepid writers' group: Chris, Ilyse, Gabe, Etta.

To Mike and Pam for use of Jim's Deck as a writer's retreat and for renaming the space Maggie's Nook.

To Mitch, thank you for championing me through the years, especially your support of the "Buster as Quasimodo" pitch in the writers' room.

To Joe Ringwood, for the use of "must be nice." Clown Construction, Athens GA. 2004

To Lisa and Sarah, for being securely and reliably in tow for the plot twists and turns of my life.

To Eleanor, for pointing to how "confusion can dawn as wisdom" and gently establishing yourself as the kind voice in my head.

To Mom and Dad, for those Worlds of Wisdom and Wonder writing classes and for your lavish love throughout my life that has blessed me with resilience.

To Handsome Jim. Thank you for enthusiastic support of early drafts, including the one both Stacy and Dan responded to with "Uh, Maggie, I think you're a little rough on Jim here."

To Joanna, for allowing me to share details of her life, for driving me crazy enough that I stopped being so crazy myself, and for remaining my lifelong snapping partner. *Wanna snap?*

To Good Shepherd Women's Center. My goodness, you did right by Joanna. And so many others. https://catholiccharitiesla.org/gss-how-you-can-help/

© Bradford Rogne

MAGGIE ROWE has written for television shows including *Arrested Development* and *Flaked*. She penned the screenplay, with Andersen Gabrych, *Bright Day: An Exposé of Hollywood's Fastest Growing New Religion*. Rowe is the author of *Sin Bravely: A Memoir of Spiritual Disobedience*, an NPR Best Book of the Year. Find out more at maggieroweauthor.com.